KIND OF COPING

an illustrated look at life with anxiety

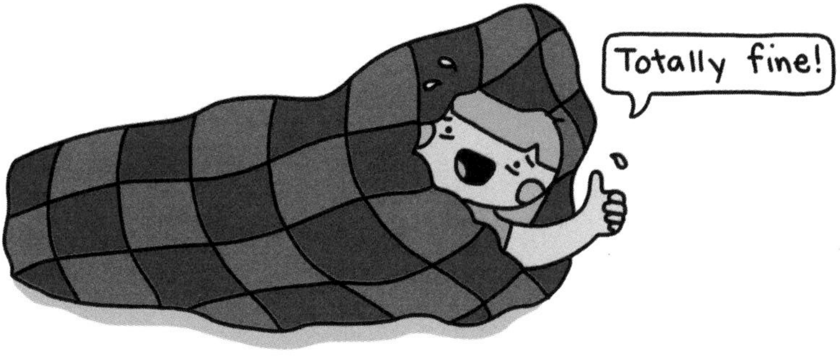
Totally fine!

by Maureen "Marzi" Wilson

ADAMS MEDIA
NEW YORK LONDON TORONTO SYDNEY NEW DELHI

Adams Media
An Imprint of Simon & Schuster, Inc.
57 Littlefield Street
Avon, Massachusetts 02322

First Adams Media hardcover edition January 2019

ADAMS MEDIA and colophon are trademarks of Simon & Schuster.

For information about special discounts for bulk purchases, please contact Simon & Schuster Special Sales at 1-866-506-1949 or business@simonandschuster.com.

The Simon & Schuster Speakers Bureau can bring authors to your live event. For more information or to book an event contact the Simon & Schuster Speakers Bureau at 1-866-248-3049 or visit our website at www.simonspeakers.com.

Interior design by Sylvia McArdle
Interior illustrations by Maureen Wilson

Manufactured in the United States of America

10 9 8 7 6 5 4 3 2

ISBN 978-1-5072-0918-9
ISBN 978-1-5072-0919-6 (ebook)

◦◦ TABLE OF CONTENTS ◦◦

INTRODUCTION

FYI: THIS BOOK WILL NOT "CURE" YOU. It isn't a psychology text, a medical tome, or a self-help book. It doesn't even contain a recipe for an anti-anxiety smoothie. But I do believe that if you're living with anxiety, this book will make you feel less alone. Because I'm right there with you, and I get it. I've been (kind of) coping with anxiety since I was a teen. At times, it's been debilitating. Other times, I feel like it's well managed. But no matter what, it's always present to some degree.

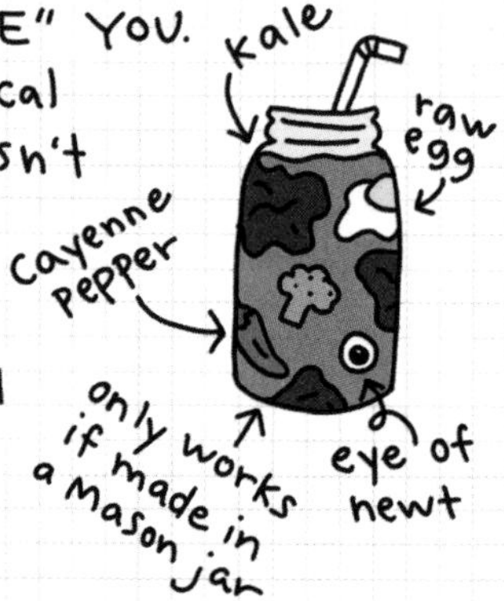
kale
raw egg
cayenne pepper
only works if made in a Mason jar
eye of newt

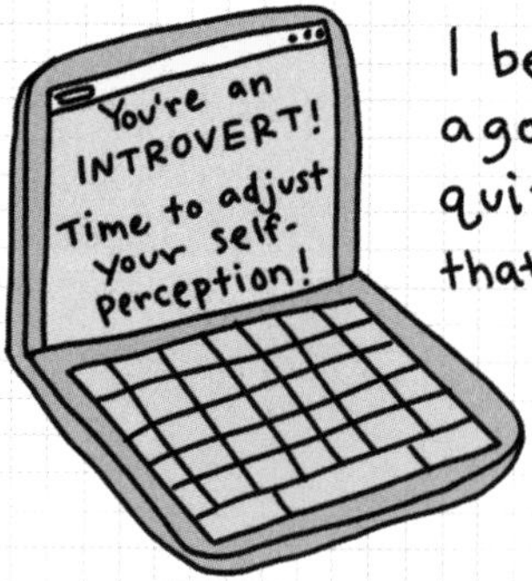
You're an INTROVERT! Time to adjust your self-perception!

I began these doodles several years ago, after taking a personality quiz online. That was the first time that I realized I'm an introvert. I'd always presumed that my limited social circle and my preference for solitude were due solely to anxiety.

But it turns out I'm an introvert who has anxiety. And I became committed to understanding what that means.

Which of my behaviors are motivated by introversion, and which are symptoms of anxiety? Which habits should I embrace as being perfectly acceptable, and which should I work on changing?

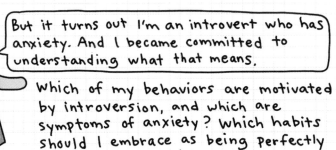

Introversion — Keeping to myself at a party.

Anxiety — Ducking under the table at a party.

Along the way, I've doodled my thoughts and experiences, and come closer to understanding—and accepting—myself. I hope you'll find validation in these doodles too.

XOXO, Marzi

PS: Be sure to check out the final section of this book for positivity & pep talks!

ALL THE
FEELS
-but mostly panic-

Anxiety is an unwelcome houseguest. It takes up residence in the pit of my stomach, my chest, my mind.

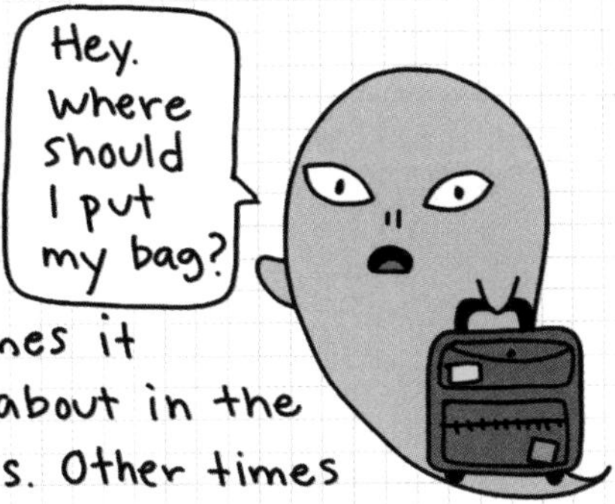
Hey. Where should I put my bag?

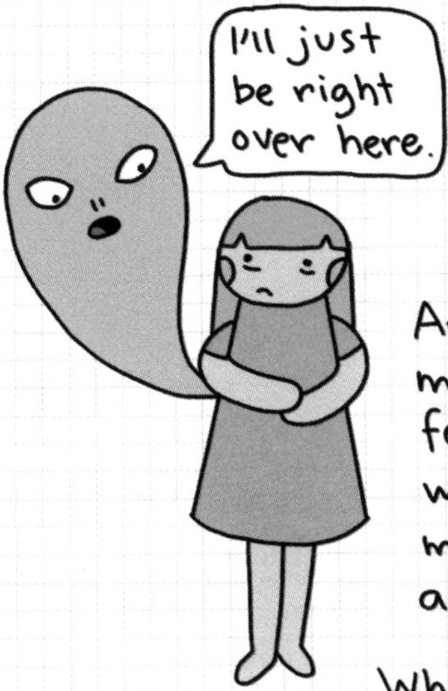
I'll just be right over here.

Sometimes it creeps about in the shadows. Other times it takes up all the space.

Anxiety is emotional—a muddled mess of worry, dread, and fear. But it's also physical—with symptoms like nausea, muscle tension, increased heart rate, and difficulty breathing.

When people tell me, "It's all in your head," I want to tell them that it may start there, but it doesn't just stay there. It's everywhere. I can't help but think, "If they only knew, they would be kinder." I want the world to see: this is what it's like...

WHAT'S IT LIKE TO LIVE WITH ANXIETY?

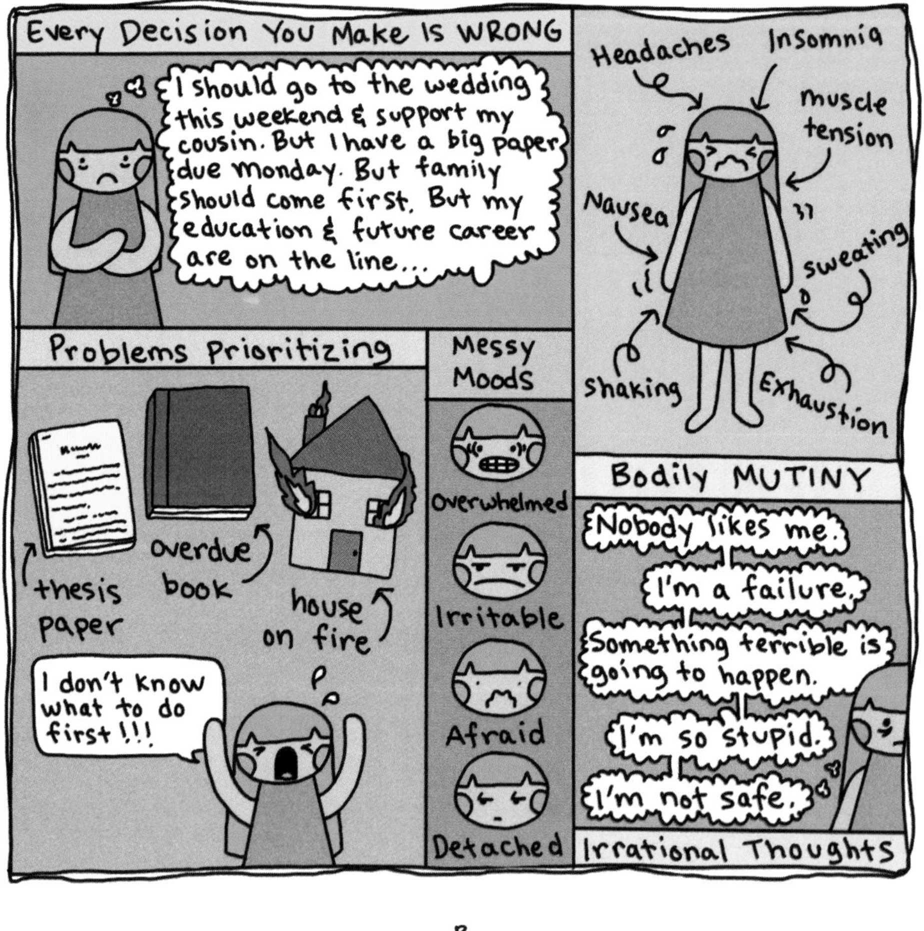

Every Decision You Make Is WRONG
I should go to the wedding this weekend & support my cousin. But I have a big paper due Monday. But family should come first. But my education & future career are on the line...
Headaches
Insomnia
muscle tension
Nausea
sweating
Shaking
Exhaustion
Bodily MUTINY
Problems Prioritizing
thesis paper
overdue book
house on fire
I don't know what to do first!!!
Messy Moods
Overwhelmed
Irritable
Afraid
Detached
Nobody likes me.
I'm a failure.
Something terrible is going to happen.
I'm so stupid.
I'm not safe.
Irrational Thoughts

HOW ANXIOUS ARE YOU TODAY?

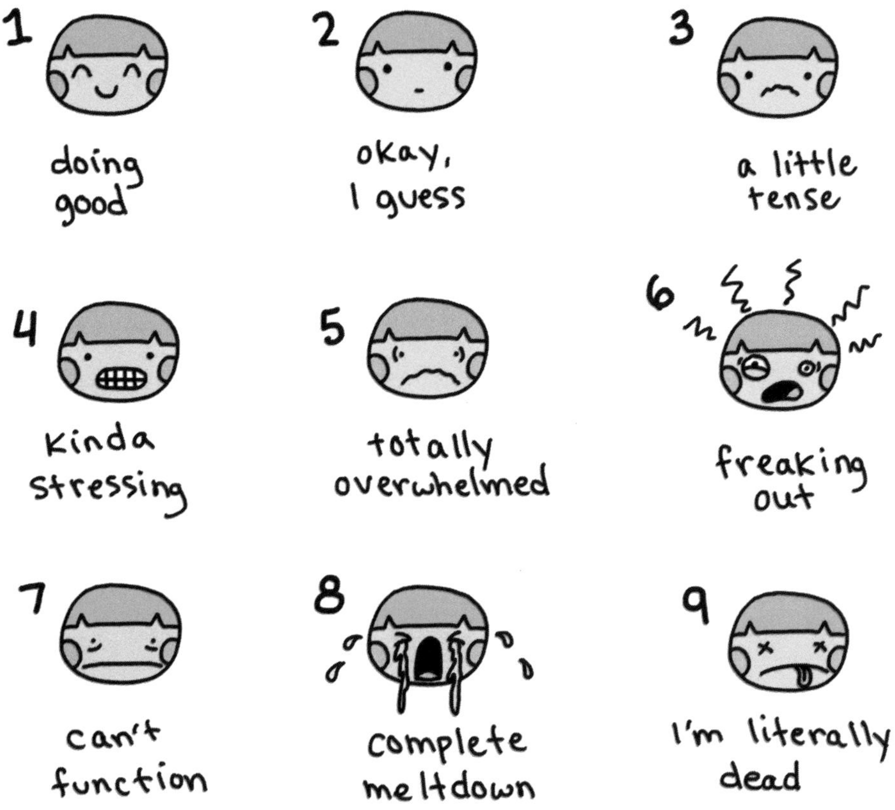
1
doing good
2
okay, I guess
3
a little tense
4
kinda stressing
5
totally overwhelmed
6
freaking out
7
can't function
8
complete meltdown
9
I'm literally dead

MY BEDTIME ROUTINE

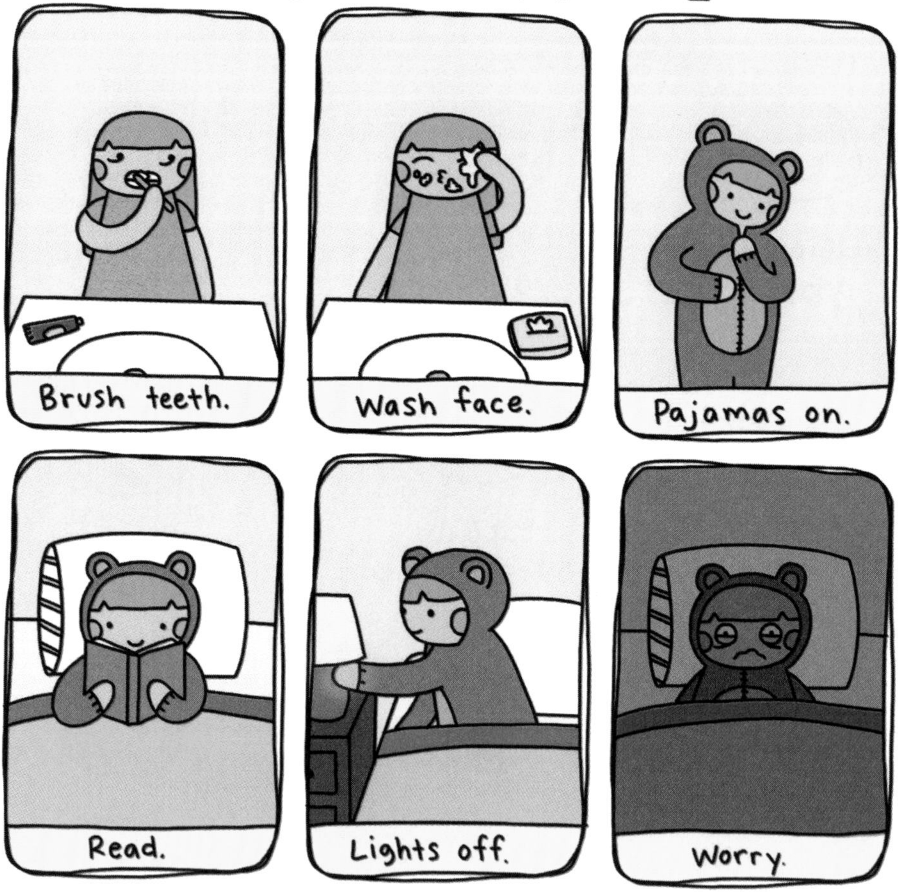

Brush teeth.
Wash face.
Pajamas on.
Read.
Lights off.
Worry.

THE MOST FRUSTRATING ASPECTS OF ANXIETY

your body doing weird things

the exhaustion of endlessly reasoning with yourself

trying to explain yourself to people who just don't get it

the fear that it will never get better

not being able to tackle your to-do list, so it just keeps getting longer

11

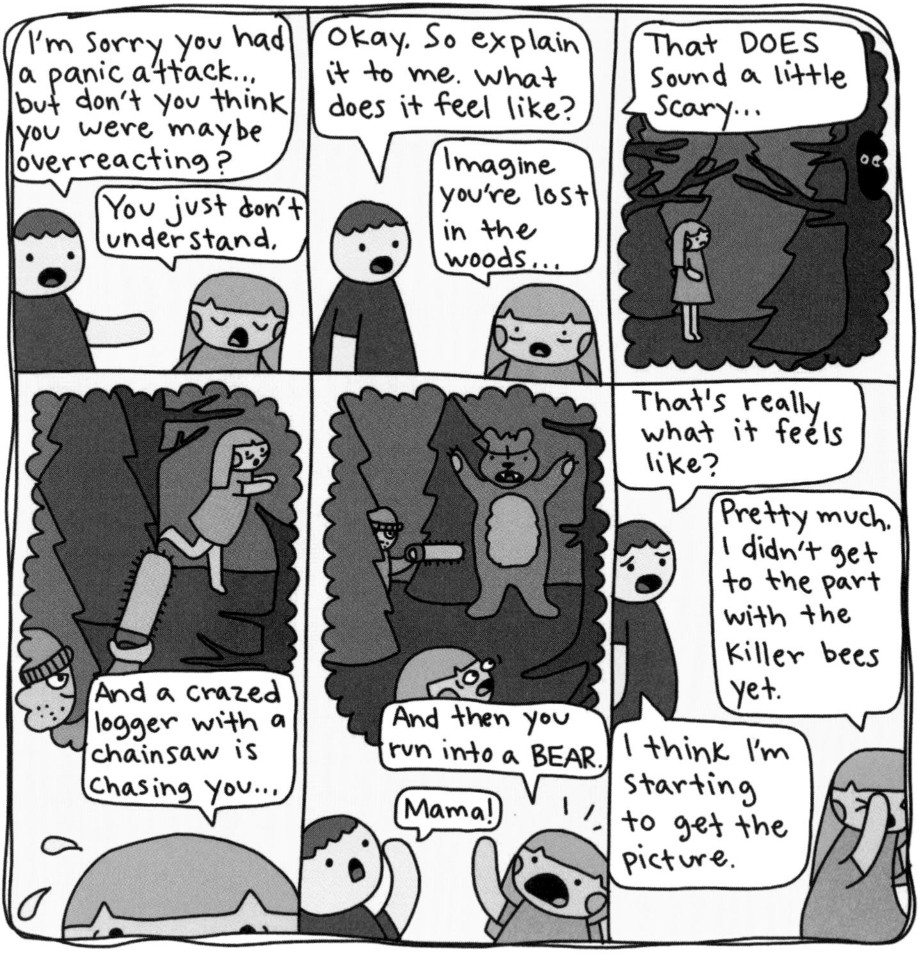
I'm sorry you had a panic attack... but don't you think you were maybe overreacting?
You just don't understand.
Okay. So explain it to me. What does it feel like?
Imagine you're lost in the woods...
That DOES sound a little scary...
And a crazed logger with a chainsaw is chasing you...
And then you run into a BEAR.
Mama!
That's really what it feels like?
Pretty much. I didn't get to the part with the killer bees yet.
I think I'm starting to get the picture.

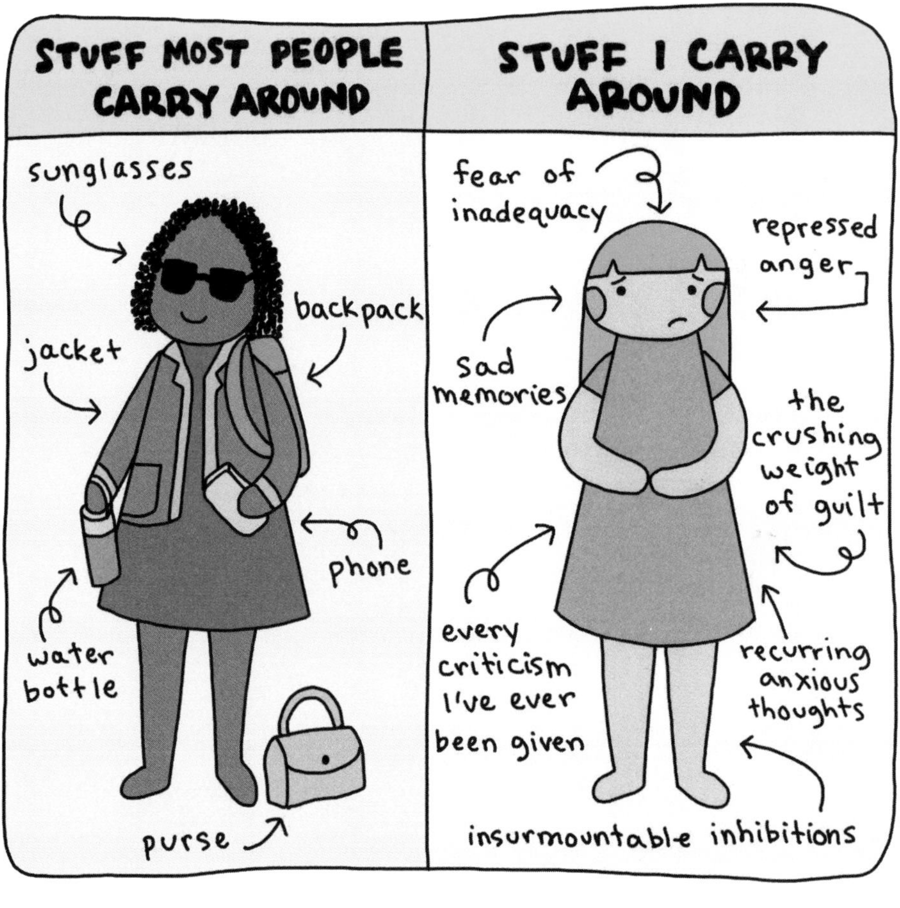
STUFF MOST PEOPLE CARRY AROUND
STUFF I CARRY AROUND
sunglasses
backpack
jacket
phone
water bottle
purse
fear of inadequacy
repressed anger
sad memories
the crushing weight of guilt
every criticism I've ever been given
recurring anxious thoughts
insurmountable inhibitions

WHEN MY ANXIETY POPS UP

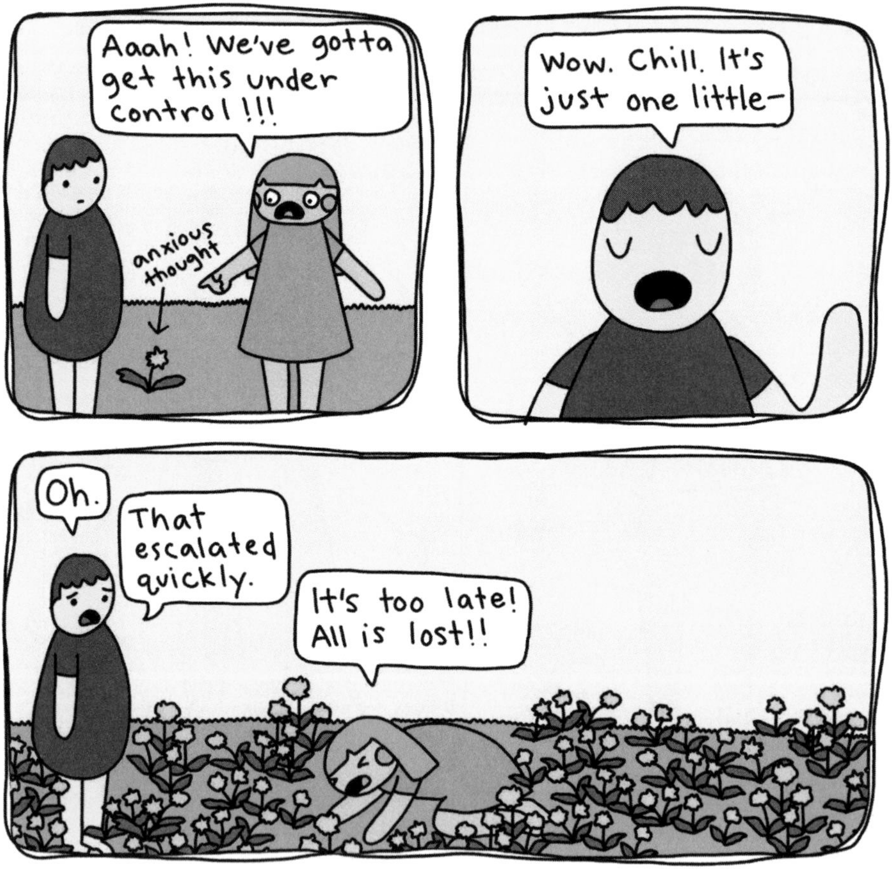
Aaah! We've gotta get this under control!!!
anxious thought
Wow. Chill. It's just one little-
Oh.
That escalated quickly.
It's too late! All is lost!!

ANXIETY BINGO Mark off all your symptoms!

Shivering like a chihuahua	Desperate for oxygen	Irrational	Exhausted but sleepless	Saying "no" when you wish you could say "yes"
Urge to hide	phobias worries concerns fears doubts hang-ups	Stampeding heart	Can't sit still -or- can't move	Awkward St-st-st-stuttering
Even when nothing is wrong, everything is wrong	Blushing	Never feeling FREE	Rumbly tummy sounds like a birthing whale	Eating too much (or too little)
Self-critical	muscles in knots	Sweaty palms (gross)	Sweaty pits (grosser)	Disturbed by little things, like the fact that this box is smaller than the first one
Over-thinking	Under-achieving	Panic attacks	Failing at the words when the thoughts are to be verbalized	Cannot adult today

15

HOW HE FEELS

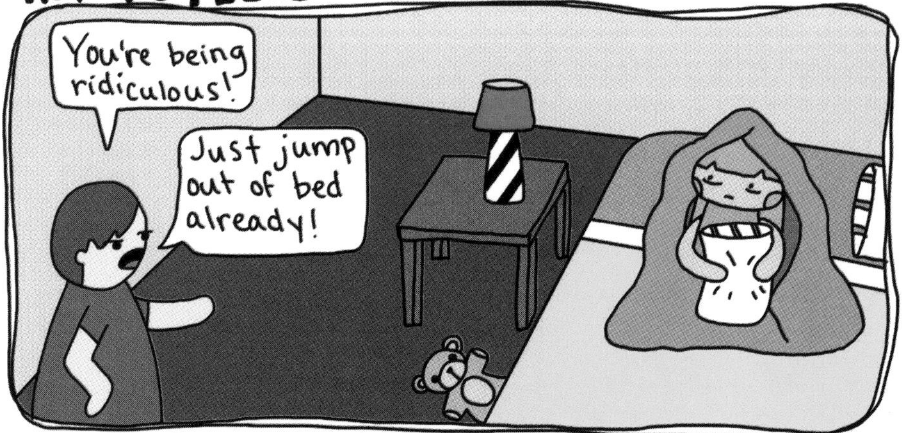
You're being ridiculous!
Just jump out of bed already!

HOW ANXIETY FEELS

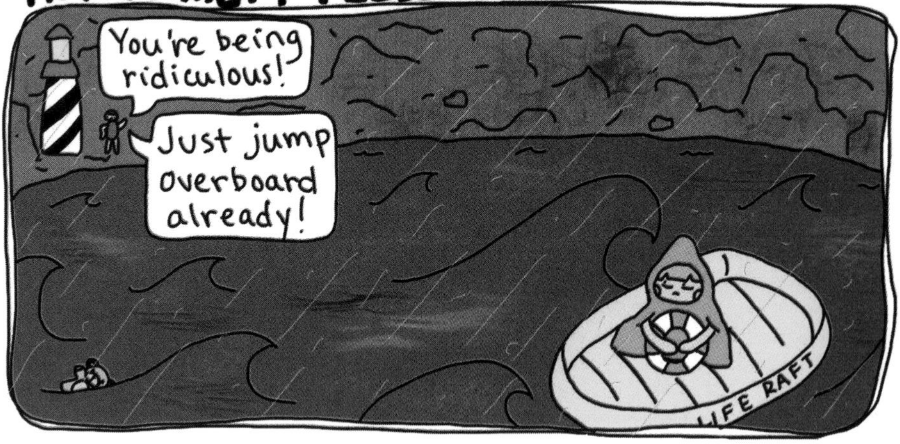
You're being ridiculous!
Just jump overboard already!
LIFE RAFT

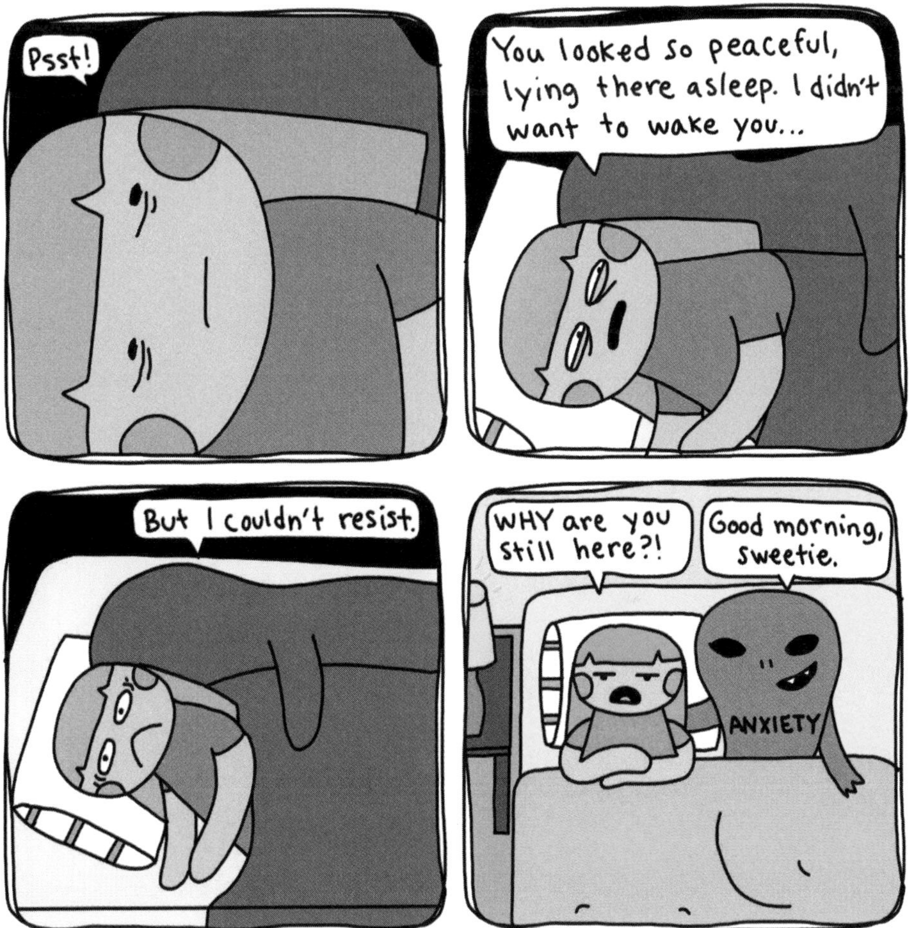
Psst!
You looked so peaceful, lying there asleep. I didn't want to wake you...
But I couldn't resist.
WHY are you still here?!
Good morning, sweetie.
ANXIETY

IRRATIONAL FEARS THAT ARE ACTUALLY VALID

Being afraid to leave the pool because my swimsuit is wedgie-inducing.

worrying that the DVR might not be recording while I'm out.

The fear that I'll mispronounce a word while reading aloud.

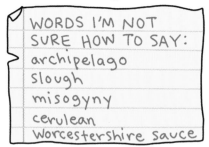

WORDS I'M NOT SURE HOW TO SAY:
archipelago
slough
misogyny
cerulean
Worcestershire sauce

When the card reader is slow, so I internally panic that my bank account was hacked and my life savings stolen.

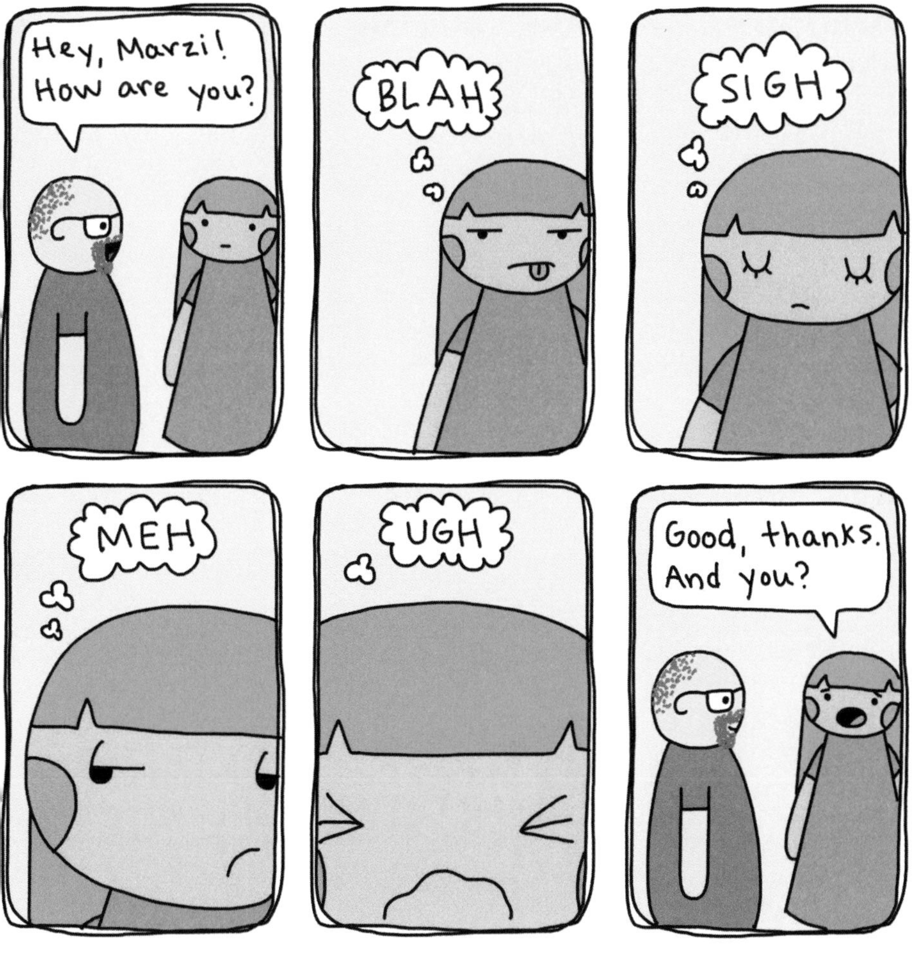
Hey, Marzi! How are you?
BLAH
SIGH
MEH
UGH
Good, thanks. And you?

THOUGHTS I HAVE DURING A PANIC ATTACK
Uh-uh. I see it coming, and it ain't gonna happen this time.
Shh. Be quiet, heart. We are just fine.
Uh-oh. Nope. Not fine. Not fine at all! Extremely NOT FINE!
This room is much too big. Or too small. It's both.
Somebody is talking to me, but I don't understand. It sounds like they're underwater.
I can't feel my hands.
What happened to the air? WHERE IS ALL THE OXYGEN?
I am most definitely having a heart attack.
This is it. I'm dying. Goodbye, cruel world.

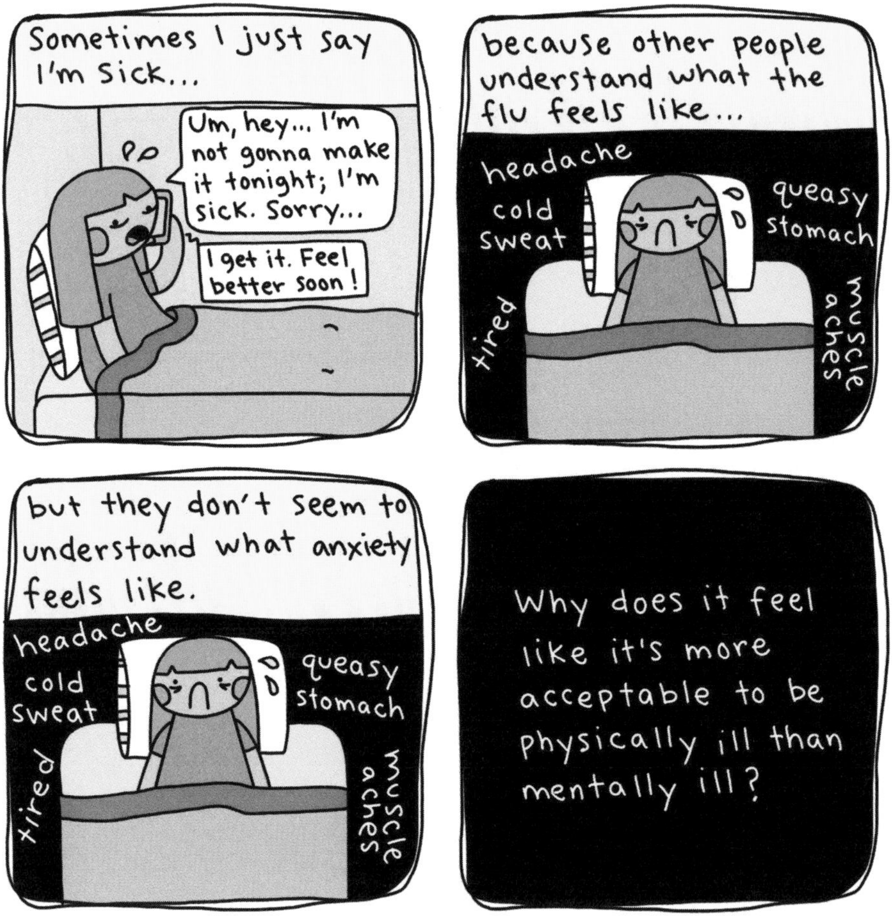
Sometimes I just say I'm sick...
Um, hey... I'm not gonna make it tonight; I'm sick. Sorry...
I get it. Feel better soon!
because other people understand what the flu feels like...
headache
cold sweat
queasy stomach
tired
muscle aches
but they don't seem to understand what anxiety feels like.
headache
cold sweat
queasy stomach
tired
muscle aches
Why does it feel like it's more acceptable to be physically ill than mentally ill?

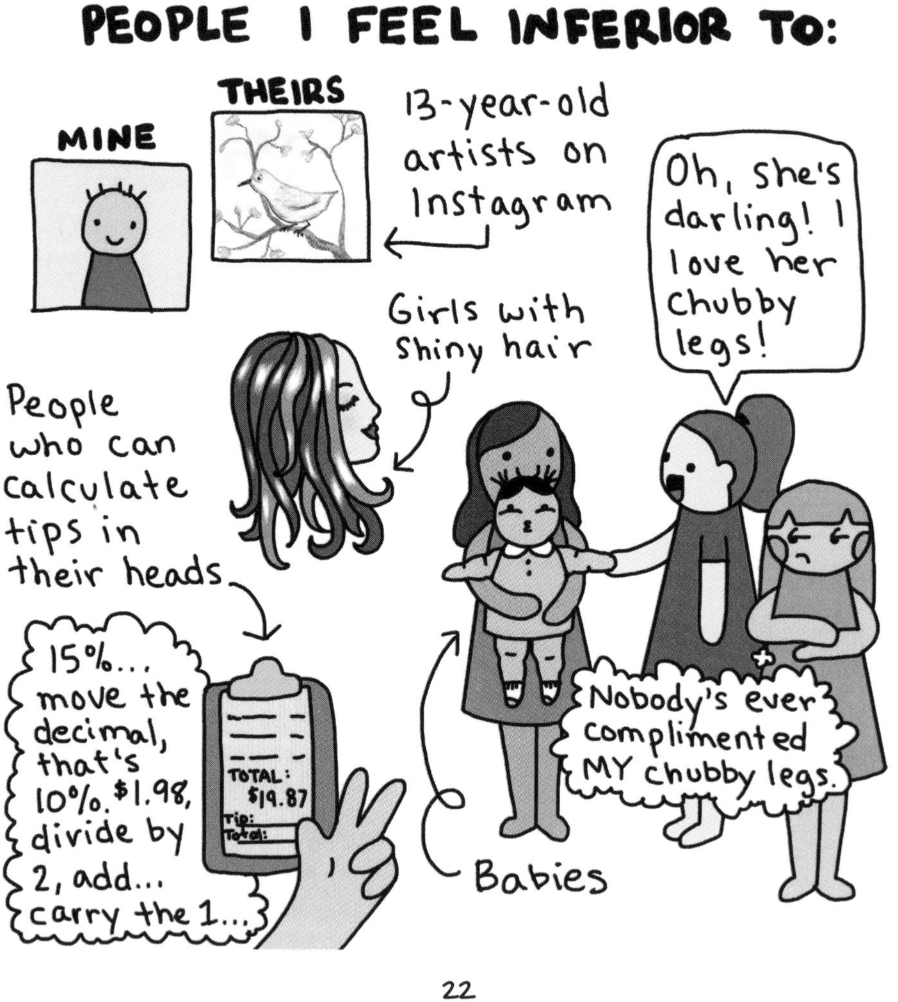
PEOPLE I FEEL INFERIOR TO:
MINE
THEIRS
13-year-old artists on Instagram
Girls with shiny hair
Oh, she's darling! I love her chubby legs!
People who can calculate tips in their heads
15%... move the decimal, that's 10%. $1.98, divide by 2, add... carry the 1...
TOTAL: $19.87
Tip:
Total:
Nobody's ever complimented MY chubby legs.
Babies

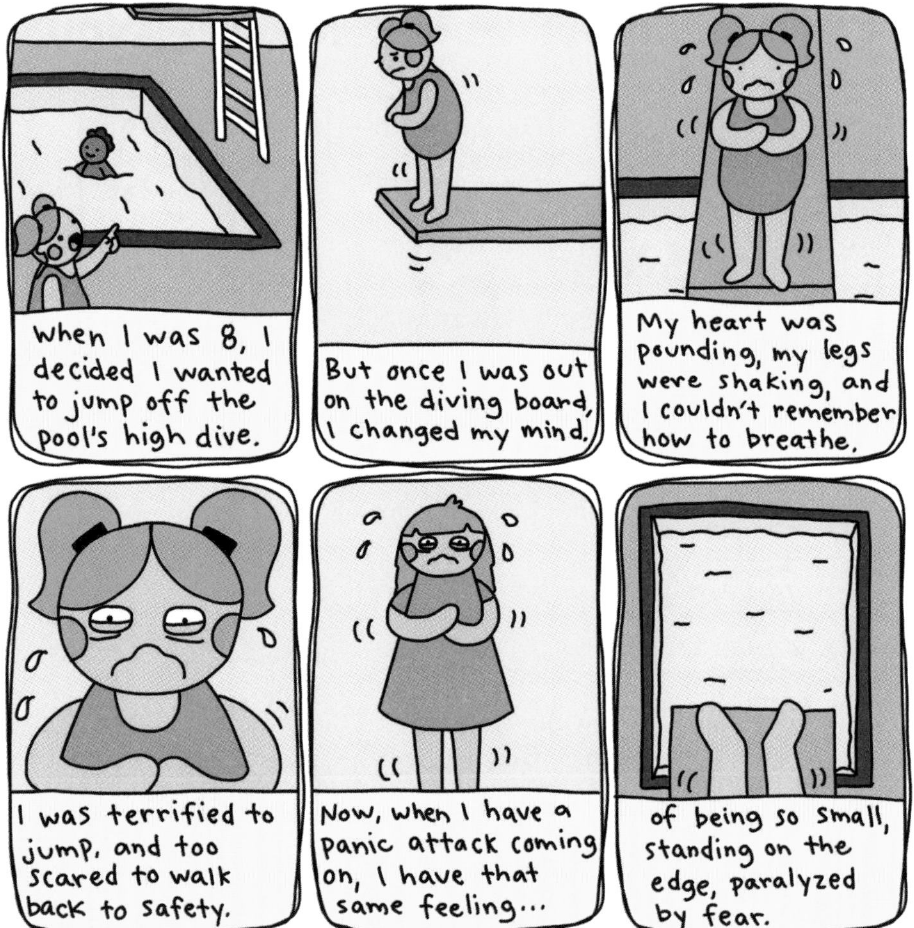
When I was 8, I decided I wanted to jump off the pool's high dive.
But once I was out on the diving board, I changed my mind.
My heart was pounding, my legs were shaking, and I couldn't remember how to breathe.
I was terrified to jump, and too scared to walk back to safety.
Now, when I have a panic attack coming on, I have that same feeling...
of being so small, standing on the edge, paralyzed by fear.

THINGS THAT MAKE ME NERVOUS

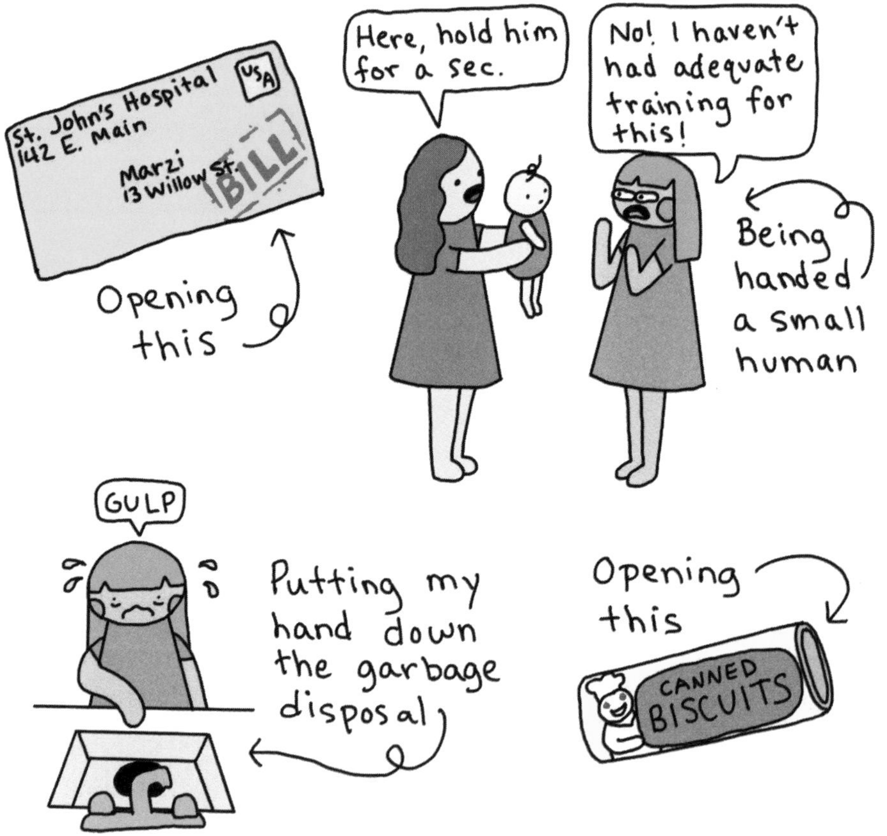

St. John's Hospital
142 E. Main
Marzi
13 Willow St.
USA
BILL
Opening this
Here, hold him for a sec.
No! I haven't had adequate training for this!
Being handed a small human
GULP
Putting my hand down the garbage disposal
Opening this
CANNED BISCUITS

WHAT ANXIETY FEELS LIKE

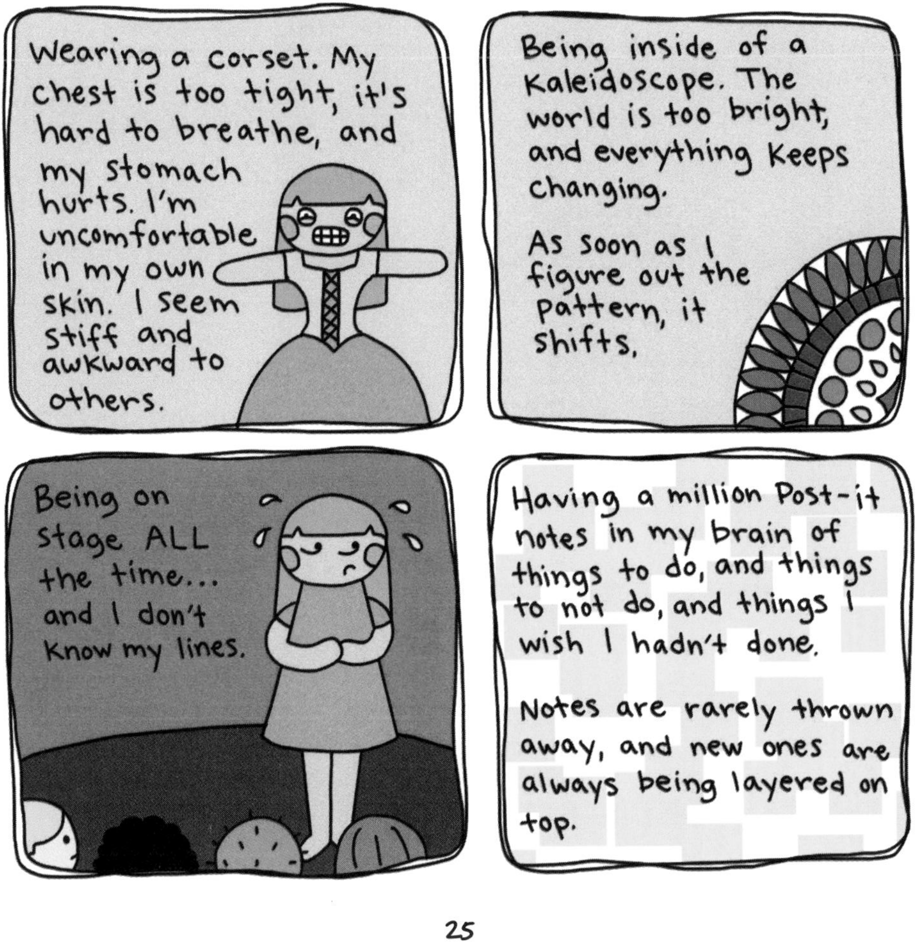
Wearing a corset. My chest is too tight, it's hard to breathe, and my stomach hurts. I'm uncomfortable in my own skin. I seem stiff and awkward to others.
Being inside of a Kaleidoscope. The world is too bright, and everything Keeps changing.
As soon as I figure out the pattern, it shifts.
Being on stage ALL the time... and I don't know my lines.
Having a million Post-it notes in my brain of things to do, and things to not do, and things I wish I hadn't done.
Notes are rarely thrown away, and new ones are always being layered on top.

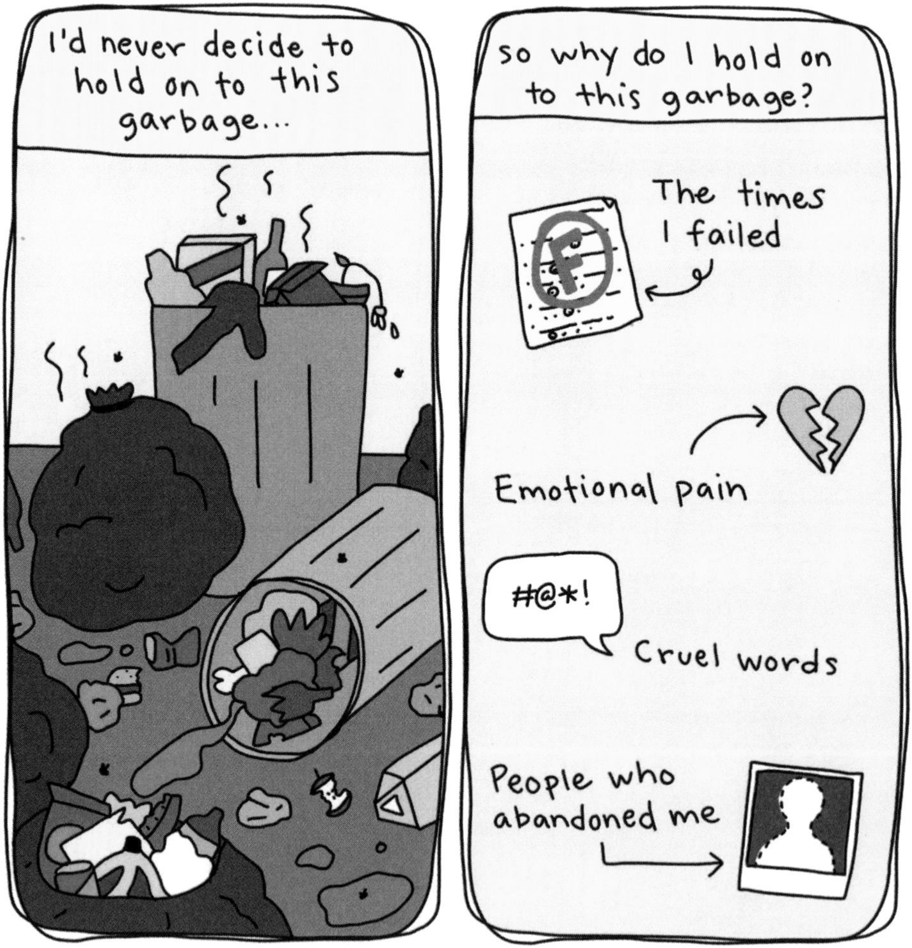
I'd never decide to hold on to this garbage...
so why do I hold on to this garbage?
The times I failed
F
Emotional pain
#@*!
Cruel words
People who abandoned me

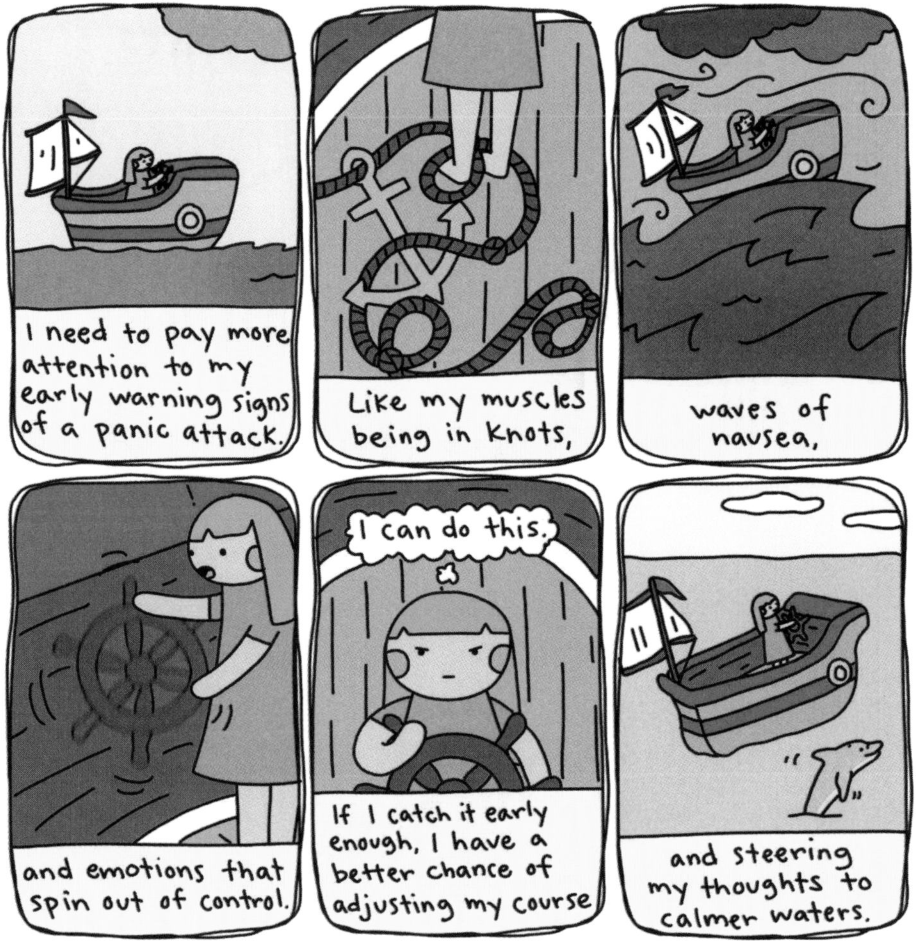
I need to pay more attention to my early warning signs of a panic attack.
Like my muscles being in knots,
waves of nausea,
and emotions that spin out of control.
I can do this.
If I catch it early enough, I have a better chance of adjusting my course
and steering my thoughts to calmer waters.

MY MOST FREQUENT THOUGHTS

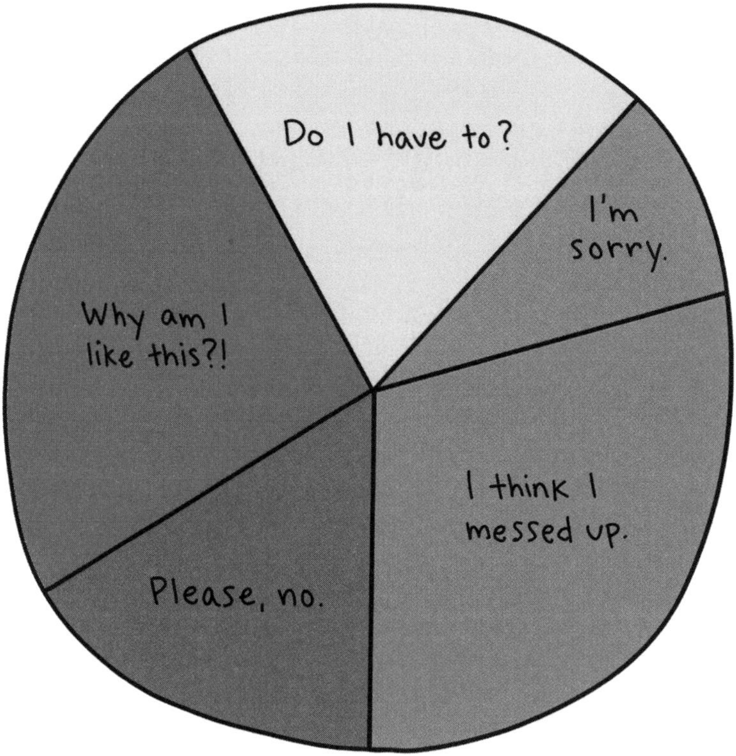

Do I have to?
I'm sorry.
I think I messed up.
Please, no.
Why am I like this?!

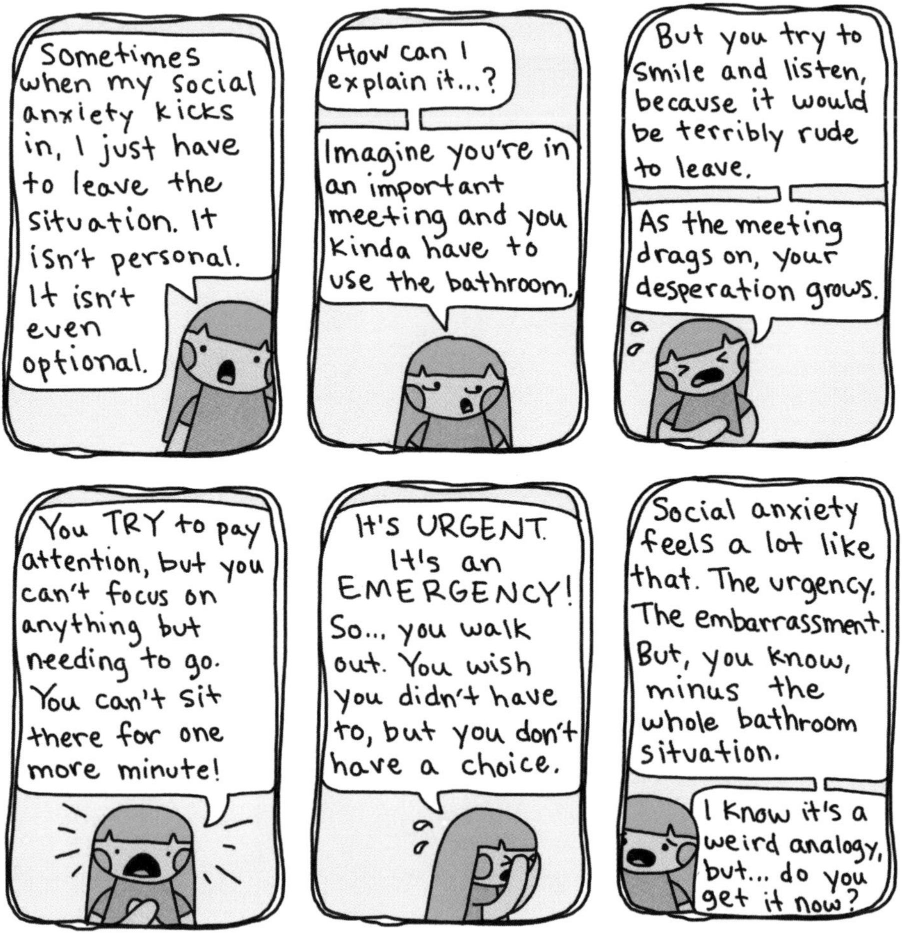
Sometimes when my social anxiety kicks in, I just have to leave the situation. It isn't personal.
It isn't even optional.
How can I explain it...?
Imagine you're in an important meeting and you kinda have to use the bathroom.
But you try to smile and listen, because it would be terribly rude to leave.
As the meeting drags on, your desperation grows.
You TRY to pay attention, but you can't focus on anything but needing to go. You can't sit there for one more minute!
It's URGENT. It's an EMERGENCY!
So... you walk out. You wish you didn't have to, but you don't have a choice.
Social anxiety feels a lot like that. The urgency. The embarrassment. But, you know, minus the whole bathroom situation.
I know it's a weird analogy, but... do you get it now?

THINGS THAT MAKE ME FEEL MELANCHOLY

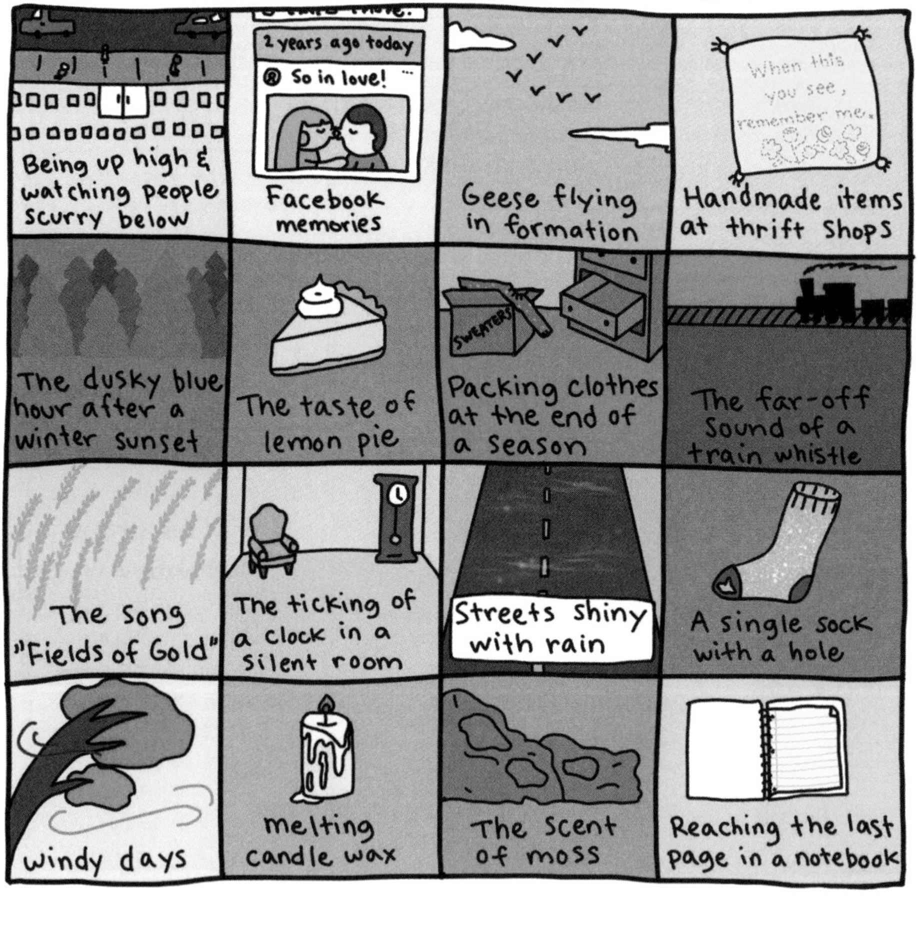
Being up high & watching people scurry below
2 years ago today
So in love!
Facebook memories
Geese flying in formation
When this you see, remember me.
Handmade items at thrift shops
The dusky blue hour after a winter sunset
The taste of lemon pie
SWEATERS
Packing clothes at the end of a season
The far-off sound of a train whistle
The song "Fields of Gold"
The ticking of a clock in a silent room
Streets shiny with rain
A single sock with a hole
windy days
melting candle wax
The scent of moss
Reaching the last page in a notebook

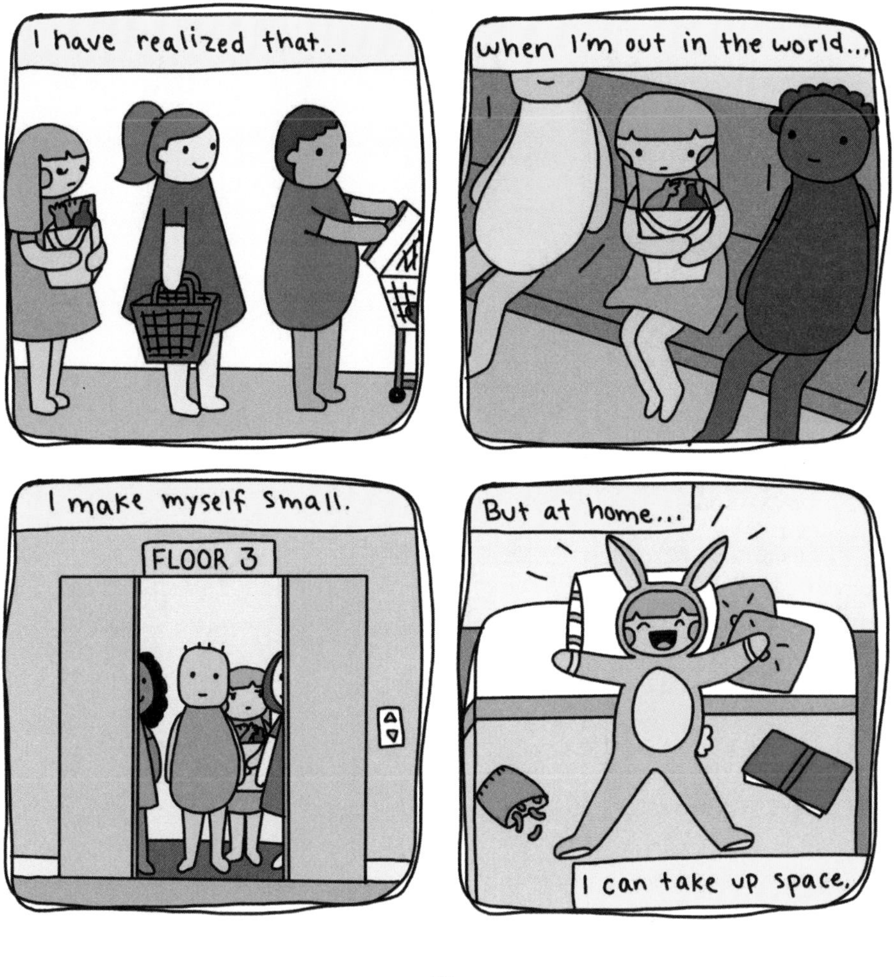
I have realized that...
when I'm out in the world...
I make myself small.
FLOOR 3
But at home...
I can take up space.

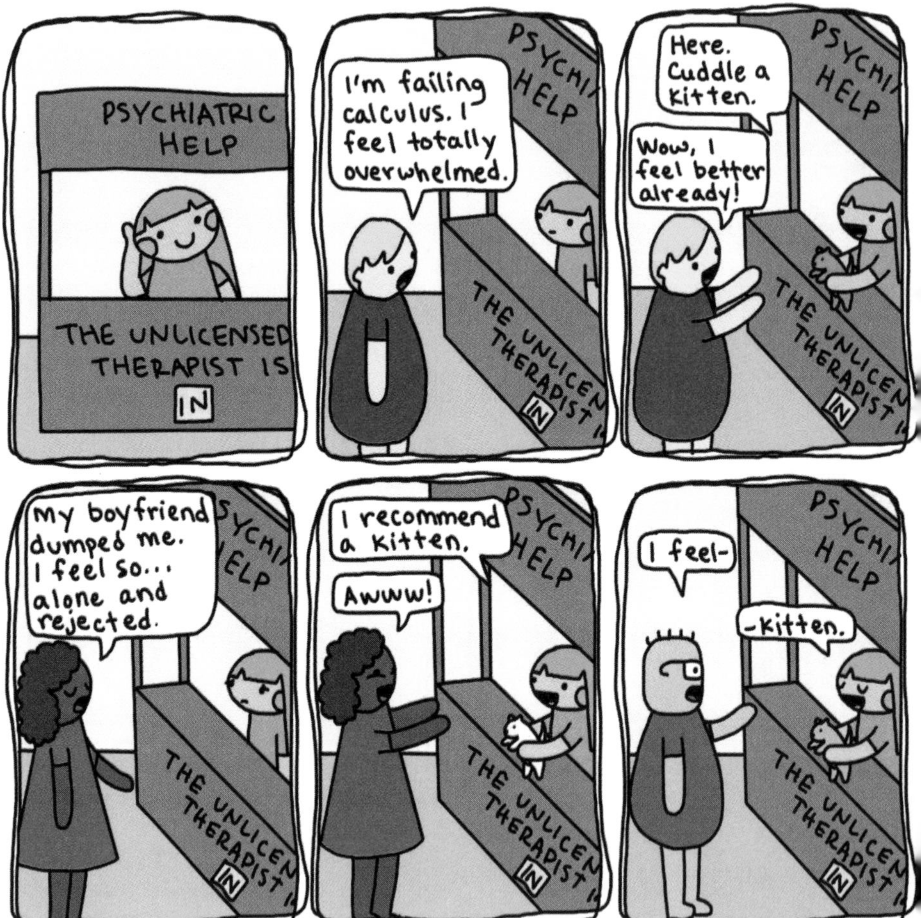
PSYCHIATRIC HELP
THE UNLICENSED THERAPIST IS
IN
I'm failing calculus. I feel totally overwhelmed.
Here. Cuddle a kitten.
Wow, I feel better already!
My boyfriend dumped me. I feel so... alone and rejected.
I recommend a kitten.
Awww!
I feel-
-kitten.
inspired by Charles M. Schulz

IDEAS FOR FEELING BETTER WHEN ANXIETY GETS ME DOWN

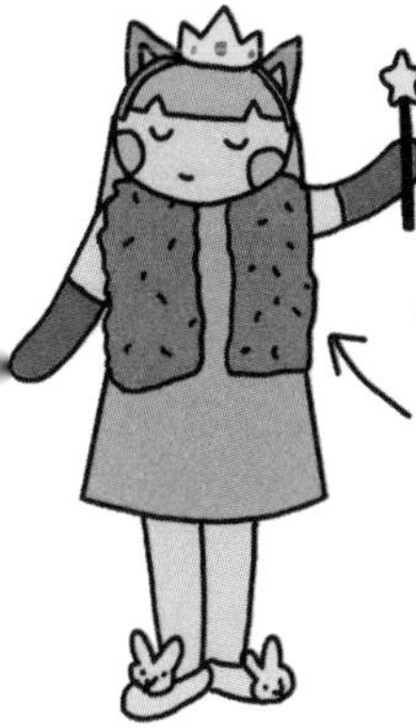

Dress up. Or down. Or undress. Whatever makes you feel good.

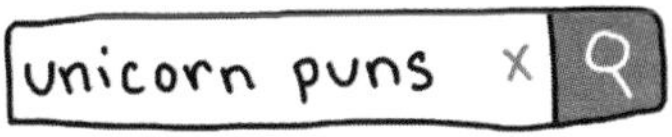

unicorn puns

Read something silly.

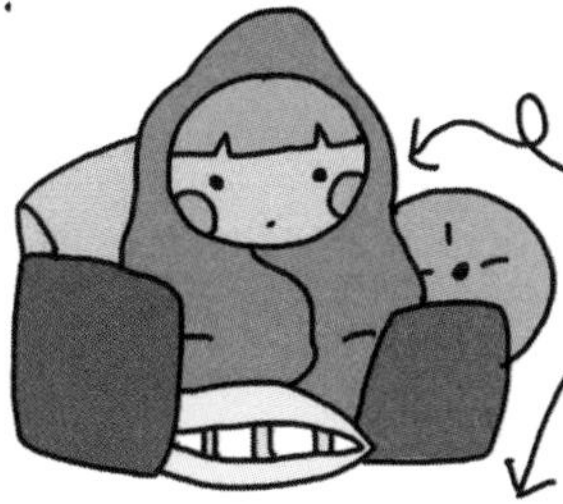

Make a nest.

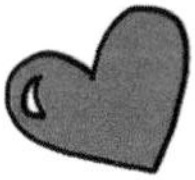

Remember that you are lovable. Say it out loud.

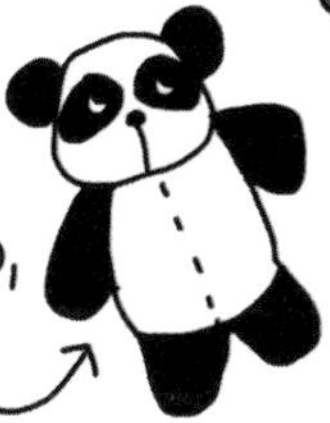

Cuddle a stuffed animal. (No, you aren't too old.)

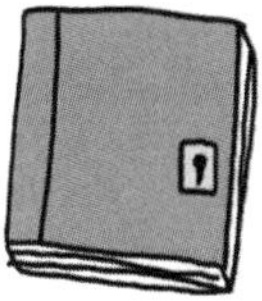

Tell your diary all about it.

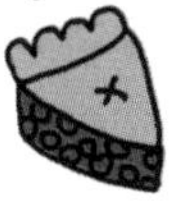

Eat that one thing that sounds better than all the other things. Eat it s-l-o-w-l-y.

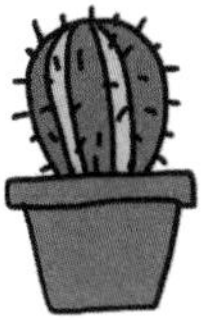

Admire something lovely.

THIS IS AWKWARD

-life with social anxiety-

In addition to generalized anxiety disorder (GAD), I also have social anxiety. This adds an extra level of complexity to my overall worried state. I'm not only concerned about potential catastrophes, I'm also fretting over what people think of me and how I'm presenting myself. Human interactions—from socializing to business transactions—are rife with stress and self-doubt.

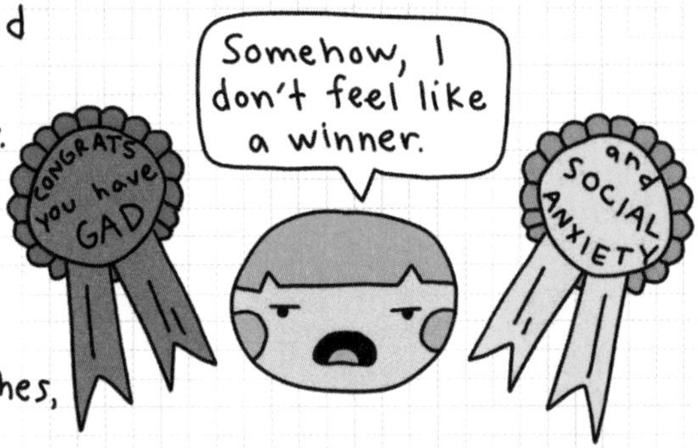
CONGRATS you have GAD
Somehow, I don't feel like a winner.
and SOCIAL ANXIETY

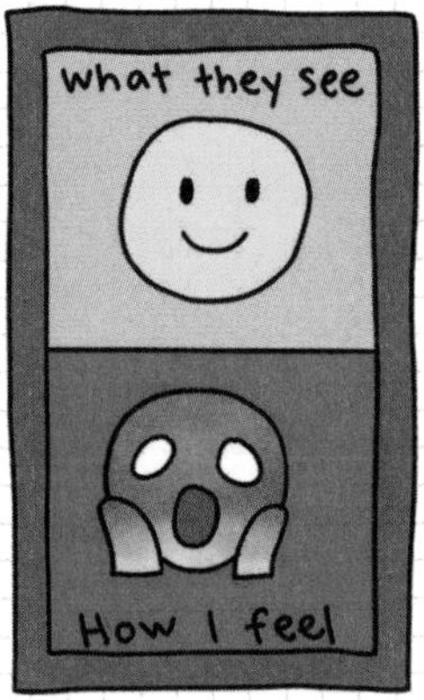
what they see
How I feel

I'm learning how to gradually push myself beyond my comfort zone, but pretending I'm all right when my nerves are jangling is an exhausting endeavor. I've been told I mask it well, and perhaps that's one way I'm kind of coping. But do other people have any idea how difficult these encounters are for me? Maybe I shouldn't expend so much effort trying to hide what I'm feeling. Maybe I should try to show them...

WHAT I'M SAYING

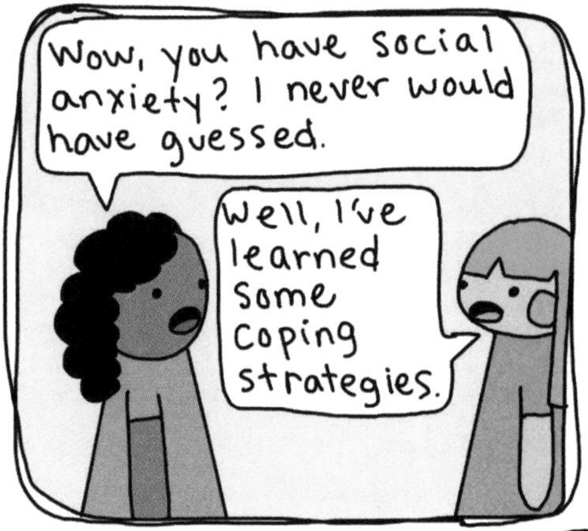
Wow, you have social anxiety? I never would have guessed.
Well, I've learned some coping strategies.

WHAT I'M THINKING

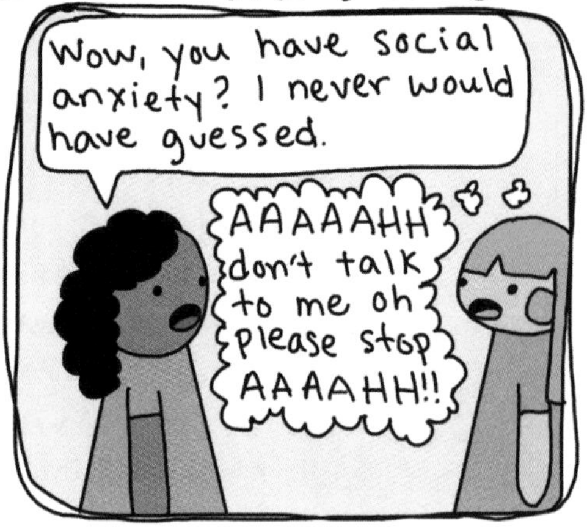
Wow, you have social anxiety? I never would have guessed.
AAAAAHH don't talk to me oh please stop AAAAHH!!

HOW I PARTY

KNOCK KNOCK
Pizza's here!

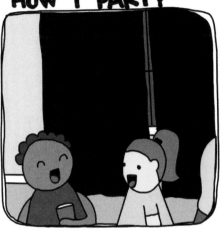

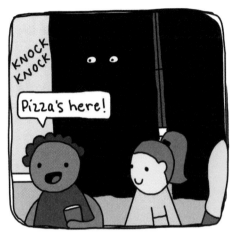

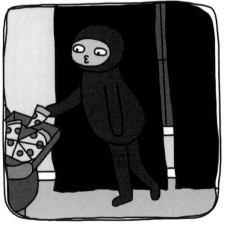

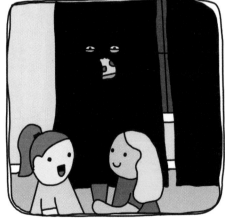

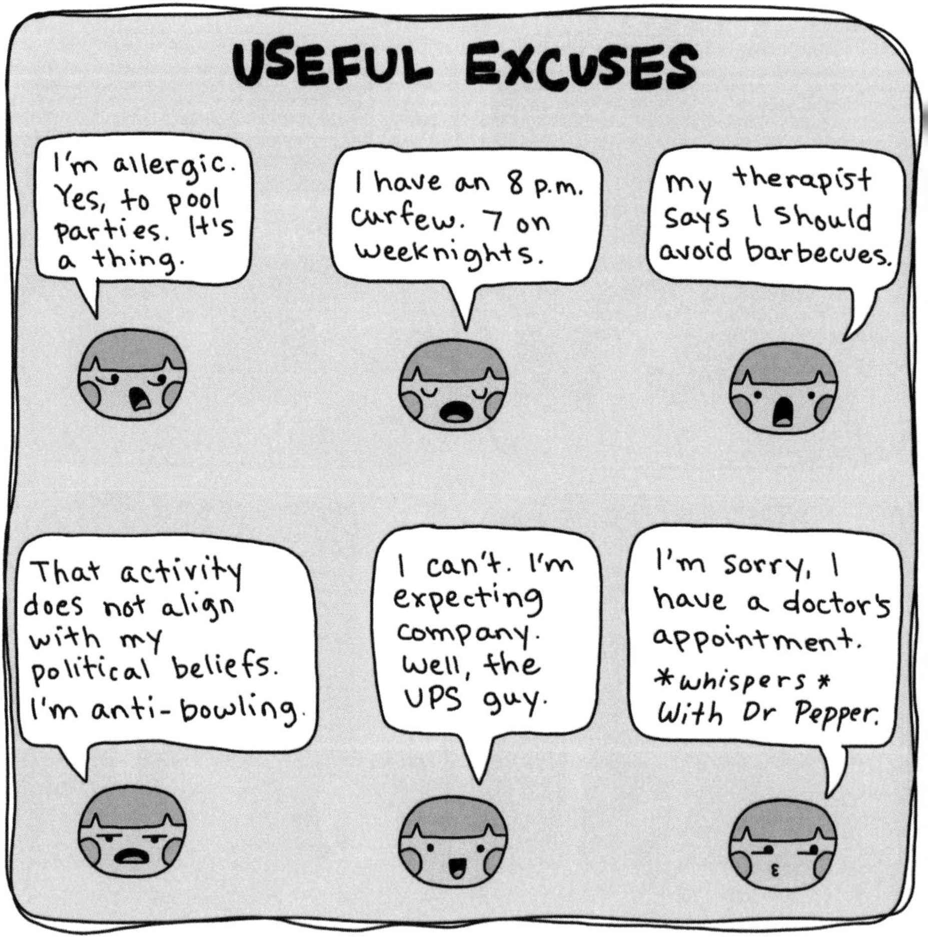
USEFUL EXCUSES
I'm allergic. Yes, to pool parties. It's a thing.
I have an 8 p.m. curfew. 7 on weeknights.
My therapist says I should avoid barbecues.
That activity does not align with my political beliefs. I'm anti-bowling.
I can't. I'm expecting company. Well, the UPS guy.
I'm sorry, I have a doctor's appointment. *whispers* With Dr Pepper.

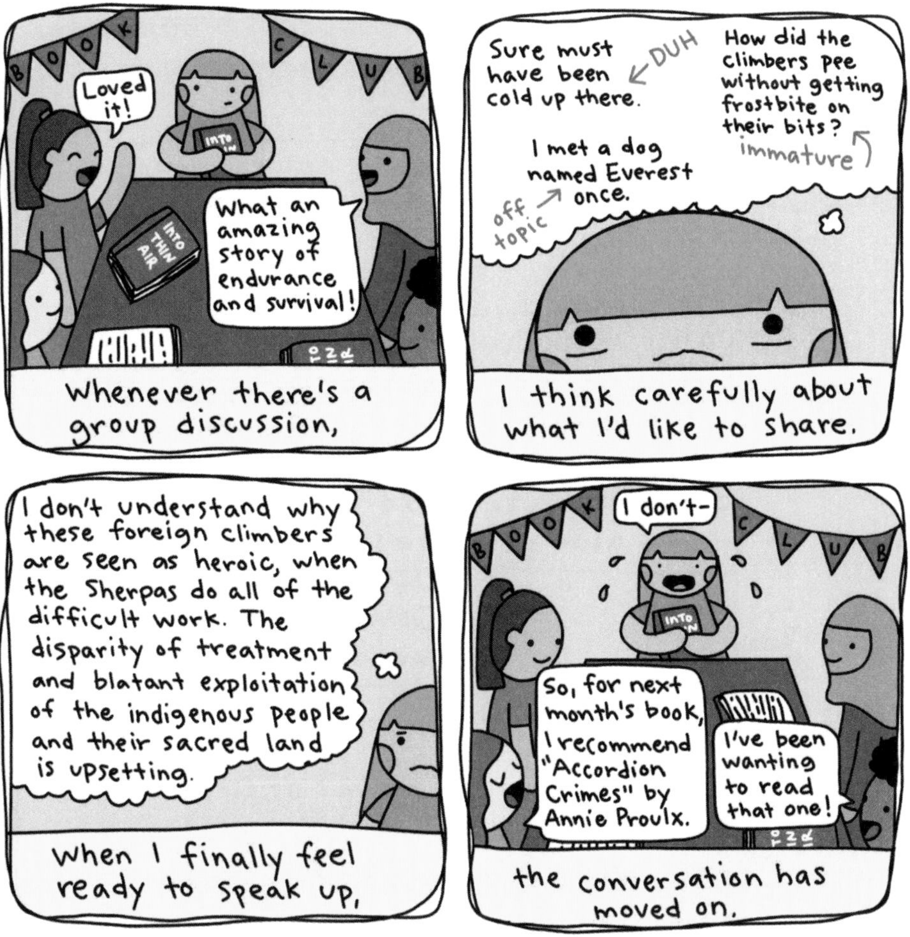
BOOK CLUB
Loved it!
What an amazing story of endurance and survival!
INTO THIN AIR
Whenever there's a group discussion,
Sure must have been cold up there.
DUH
How did the climbers pee without getting frostbite on their bits?
immature
I met a dog named Everest once.
off topic
I think carefully about what I'd like to share.
I don't understand why these foreign climbers are seen as heroic, when the Sherpas do all of the difficult work. The disparity of treatment and blatant exploitation of the indigenous people and their sacred land is upsetting.
when I finally feel ready to speak up,
BOOK CLUB
I don't-
So, for next month's book, I recommend "Accordion Crimes" by Annie Proulx.
I've been wanting to read that one!
the conversation has moved on.

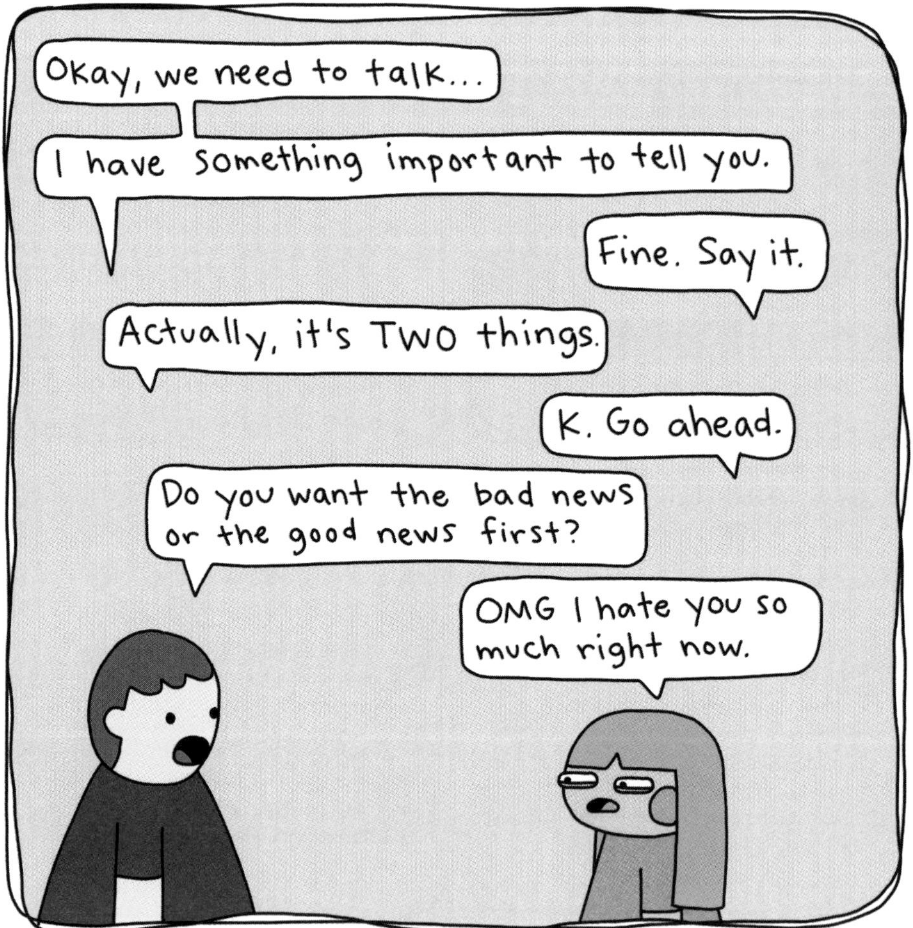
Okay, we need to talk...
I have something important to tell you.
Fine. Say it.
Actually, it's TWO things.
K. Go ahead.
Do you want the bad news or the good news first?
OMG I hate you so much right now.

WHEN YOUR ♥ SAYS YES BUT ANXIETY SAYS NO

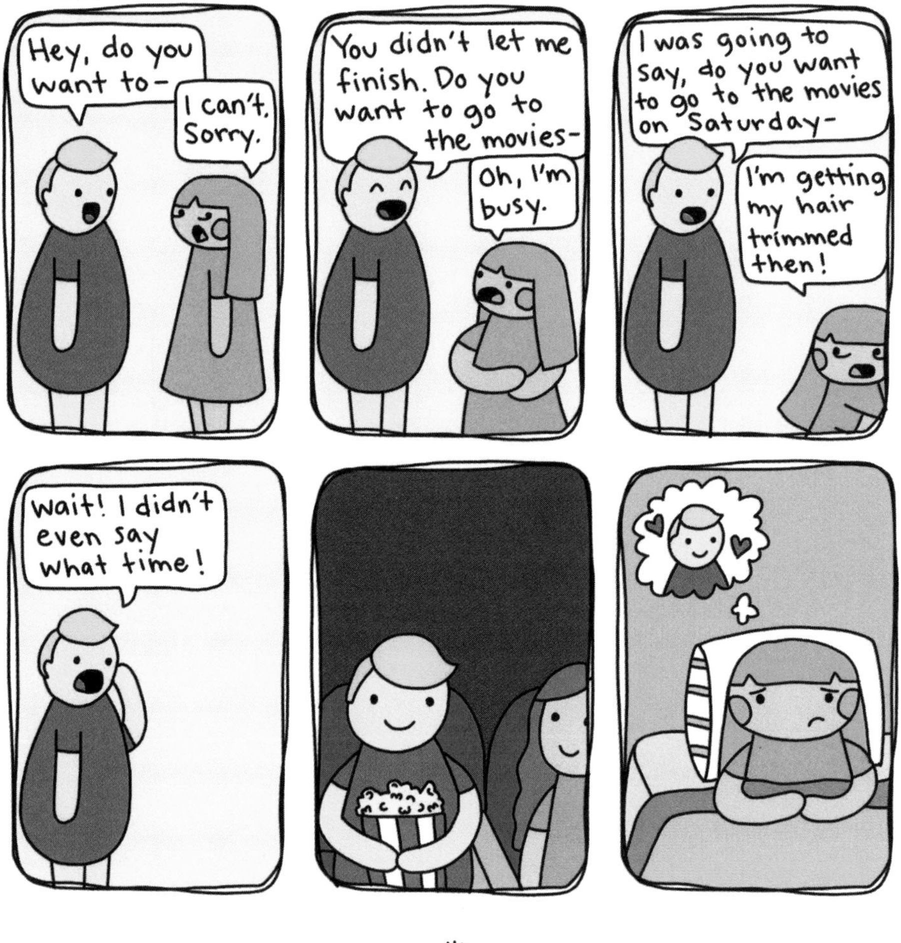
Hey, do you want to-
I can't. Sorry.
You didn't let me finish. Do you want to go to the movies-
Oh, I'm busy.
I was going to say, do you want to go to the movies on Saturday-
I'm getting my hair trimmed then!
Wait! I didn't even say what time!

REASONS I LIE

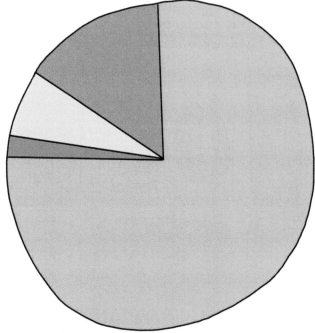

- 🟦 for personal gain
- ⬜ to make someone feel good
- 🟦 to avoid confrontation
- 🟦 to escape social engagements

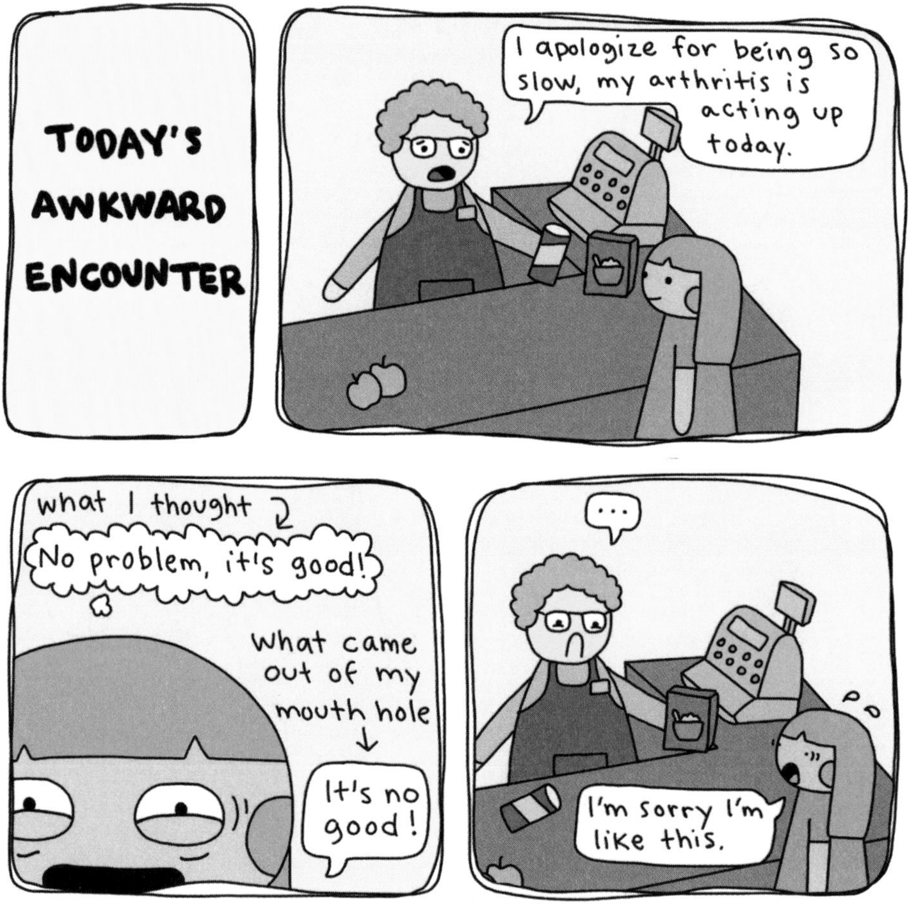
TODAY'S AWKWARD ENCOUNTER
I apologize for being so slow, my arthritis is acting up today.
what I thought
No problem, it's good!
what came out of my mouth hole
It's no good!
...
I'm sorry I'm like this.

HOW TO ENSURE YOU'RE LEFT ALONE

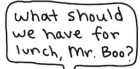

what should we have for lunch, Mr. Boo?

Always wear a hand puppet. Whisper to it often.

Start every conversation with...

On my home Planet...

Create a wardrobe of flesh-tone onesies.

GUM

Chew garlic instead of gum.

WHEN ANXIETY SHOWS UP AT THE PARTY

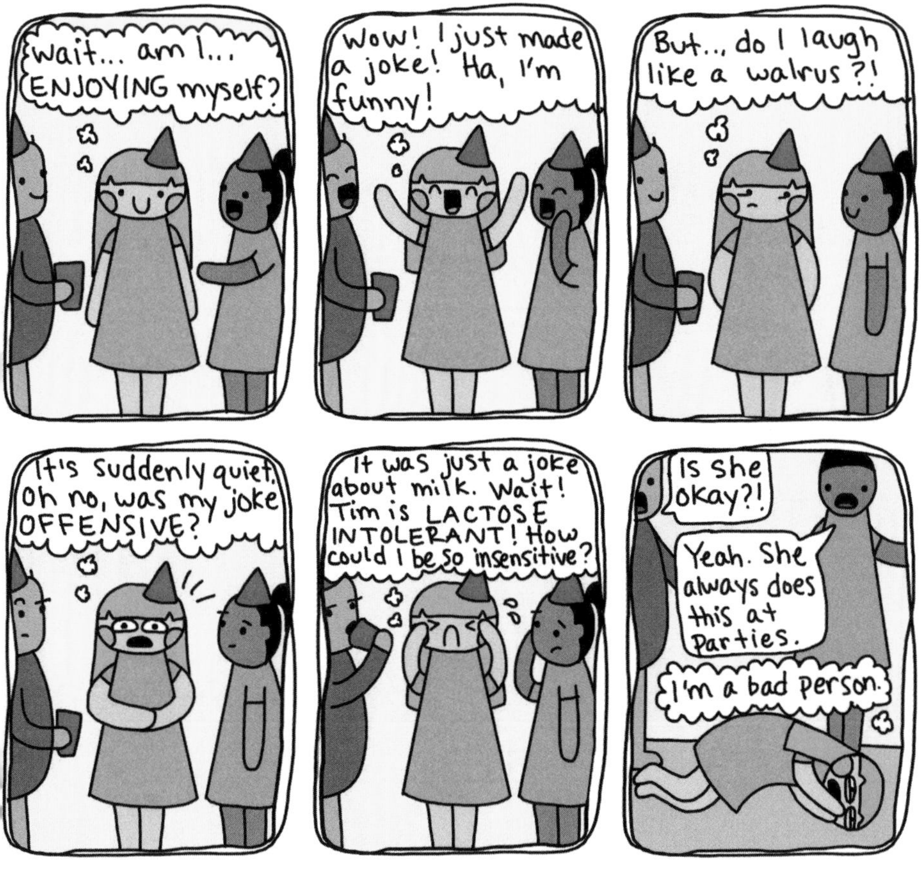
Wait... am I... ENJOYING myself?
Wow! I just made a joke! Ha, I'm funny!
But.., do I laugh like a walrus?!
It's suddenly quiet. Oh no, was my joke OFFENSIVE?
It was just a joke about milk. Wait! Tim is LACTOSE INTOLERANT! How could I be so insensitive?
Is she okay?!
Yeah. She always does this at parties.
I'm a bad person.

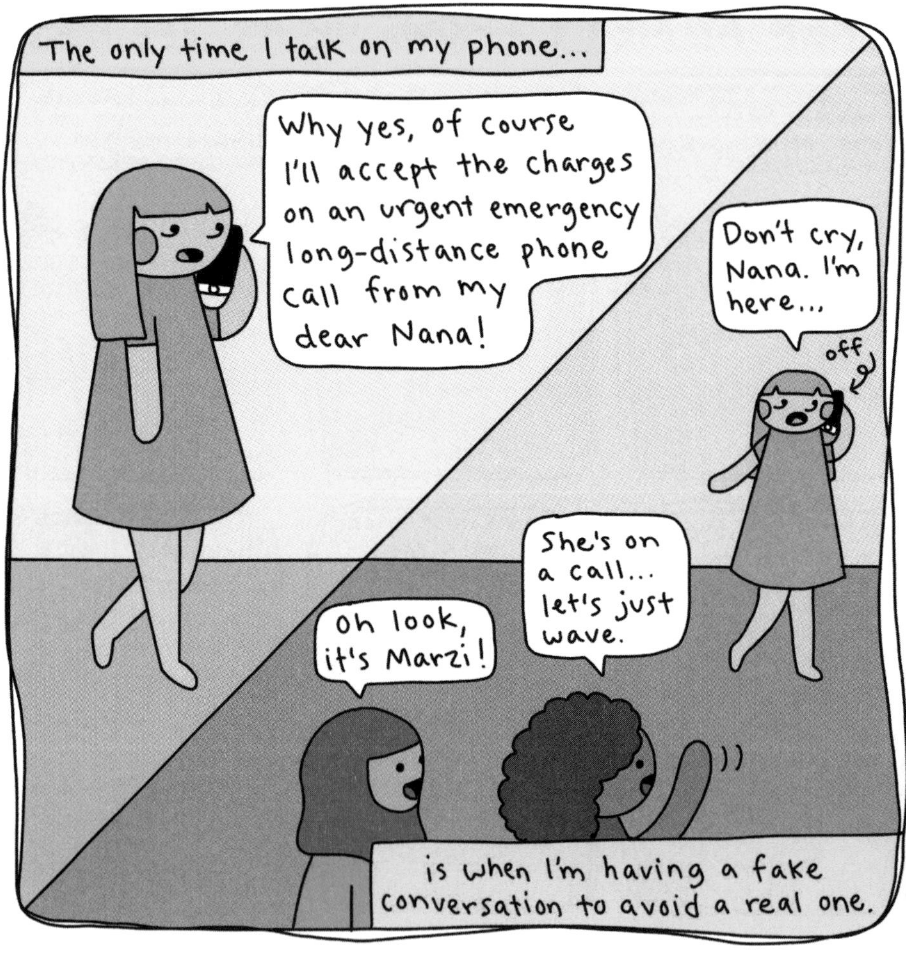
The only time I talk on my phone...
Why yes, of course I'll accept the charges on an urgent emergency long-distance phone call from my dear Nana!
Don't cry, Nana. I'm here...
off
She's on a call... let's just wave.
Oh look, it's Marzi!
is when I'm having a fake conversation to avoid a real one.

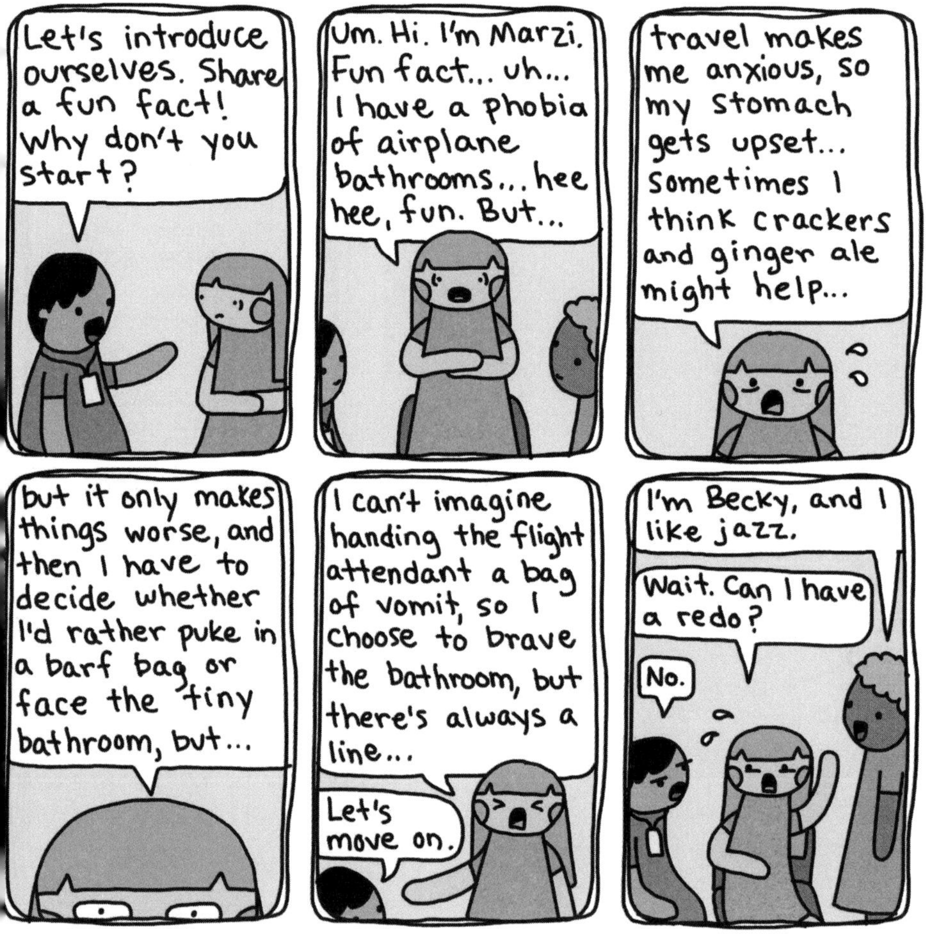
Let's introduce ourselves. Share a fun fact! Why don't you start?
Um. Hi. I'm Marzi. Fun fact... uh... I have a phobia of airplane bathrooms... hee hee, fun. But...
travel makes me anxious, so my stomach gets upset... Sometimes I think crackers and ginger ale might help...
but it only makes things worse, and then I have to decide whether I'd rather puke in a barf bag or face the tiny bathroom, but...
I can't imagine handing the flight attendant a bag of vomit, so I choose to brave the bathroom, but there's always a line...
Let's move on.
I'm Becky, and I like jazz.
Wait. Can I have a redo?
No.

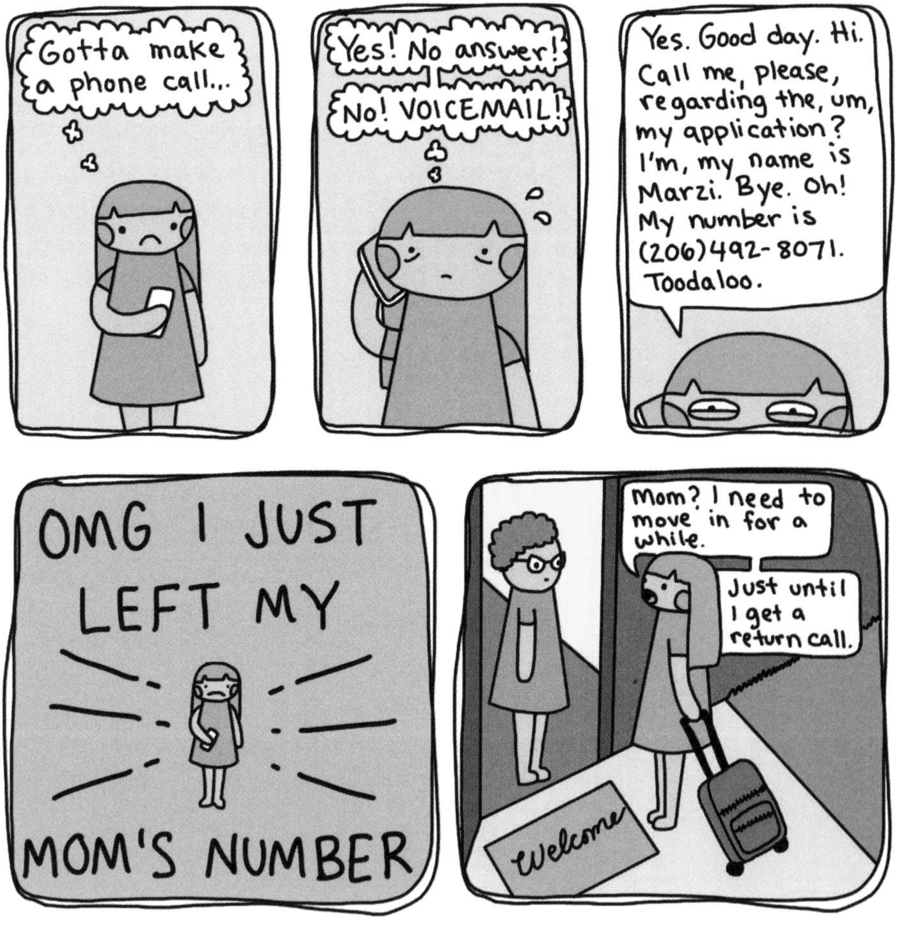

Gotta make a phone call...
Yes! No answer!
No! VOICEMAIL!
Yes. Good day. Hi. Call me, please, regarding the, um, my application? I'm, my name is Marzi. Bye. Oh! My number is (206)492-8071. Toodaloo.
OMG I JUST LEFT MY MOM'S NUMBER
Mom? I need to move in for a while.
Just until I get a return call.
Welcome

SIGNATURE AVOIDANCE TACTICS

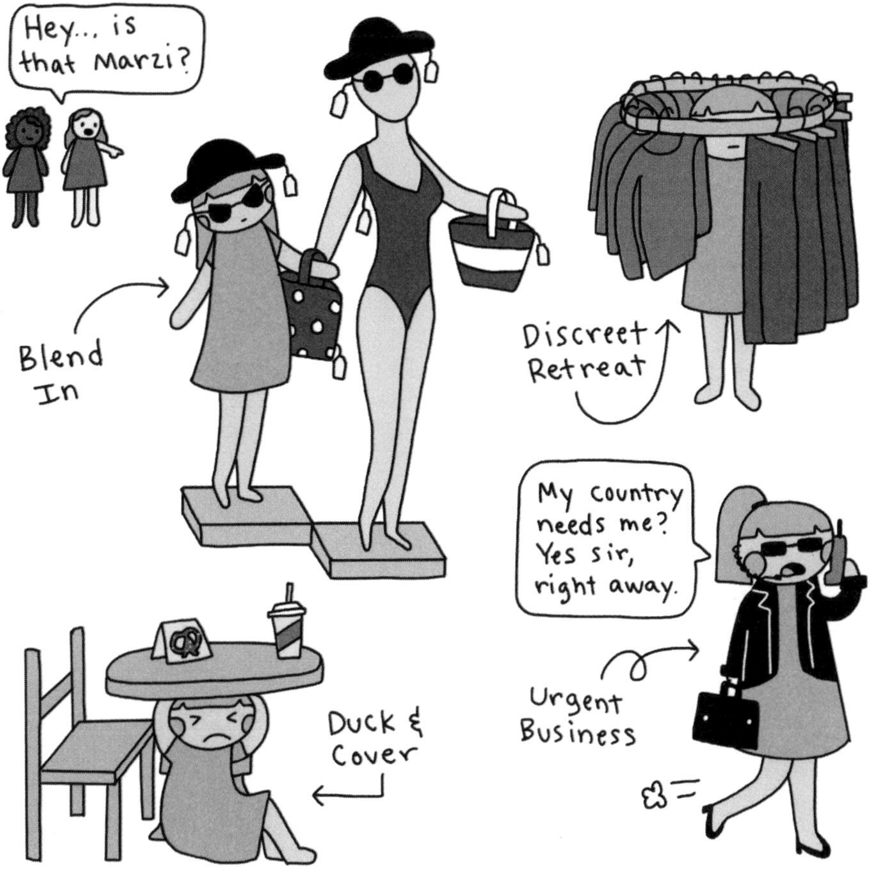
Hey..., is that Marzi?
Blend In
Discreet Retreat
My country needs me? Yes sir, right away.
Urgent Business
Duck & Cover

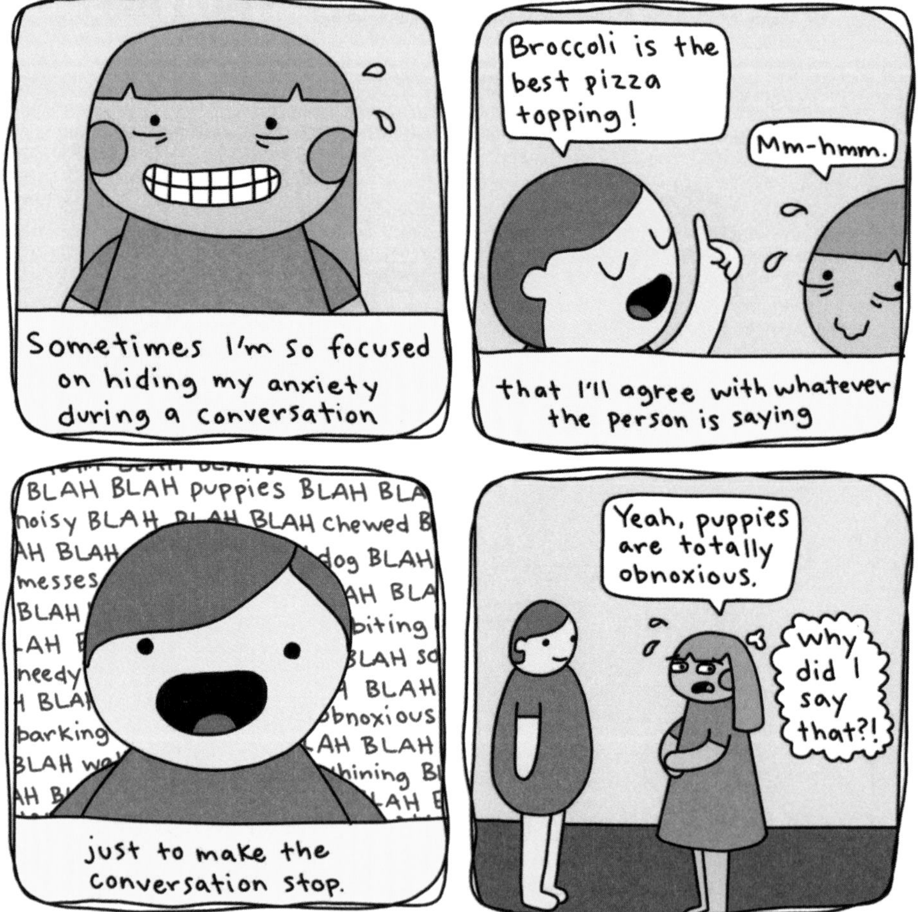

Sometimes I'm so focused on hiding my anxiety during a conversation
Broccoli is the best pizza topping!
Mm-hmm.
that I'll agree with whatever the person is saying
BLAH BLAH puppies BLAH
just to make the conversation stop.
Yeah, puppies are totally obnoxious.
why did I say that?!

FIRST (AND LAST) TALENT SHOW

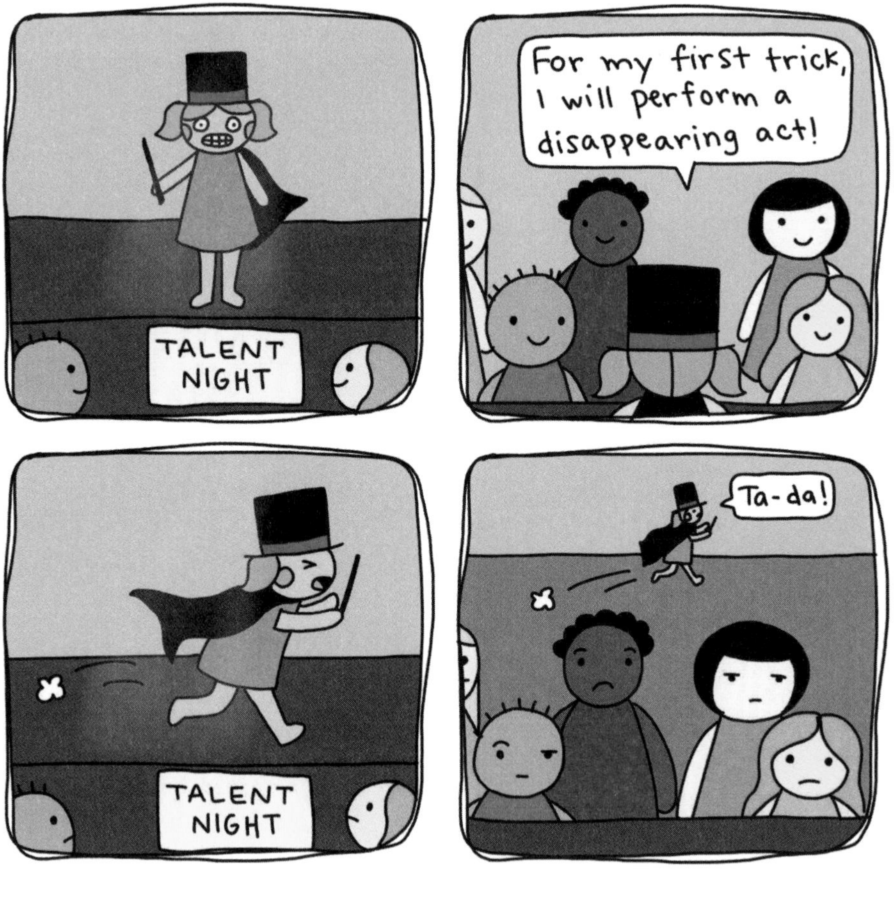
TALENT NIGHT
For my first trick, I will perform a disappearing act!
TALENT NIGHT
Ta-da!

GREAT CHASMS OF THE WORLD

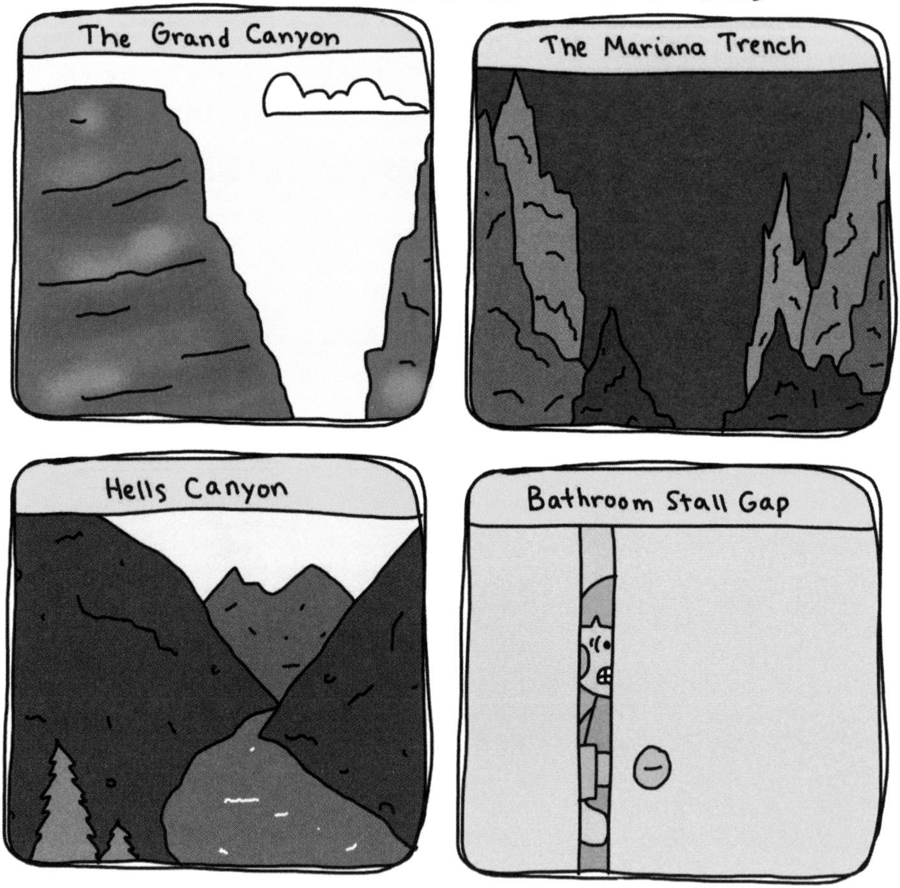
The Grand Canyon
The Mariana Trench
Hells Canyon
Bathroom Stall Gap

SENTENCES THAT MAKE ME NERVOUS

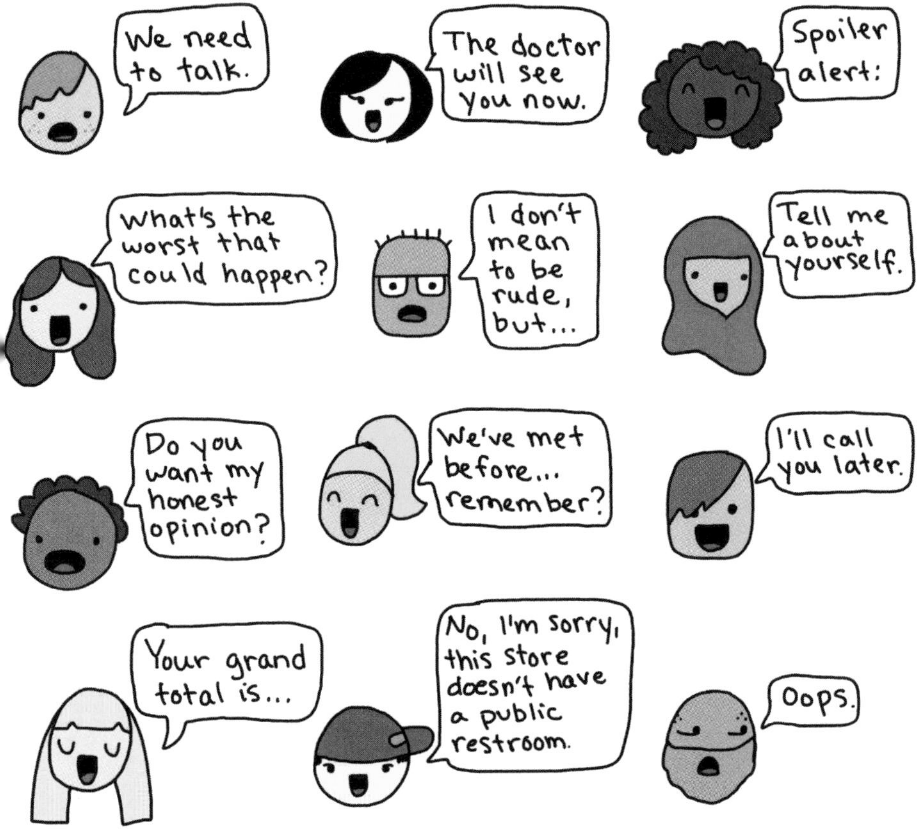
We need to talk.
The doctor will see you now.
Spoiler alert:
What's the worst that could happen?
I don't mean to be rude, but...
Tell me about yourself.
Do you want my honest opinion?
We've met before... remember?
I'll call you later.
Your grand total is...
No, I'm sorry, this store doesn't have a public restroom.
Oops.

WHEN YOU'RE SHY YEAR-ROUND

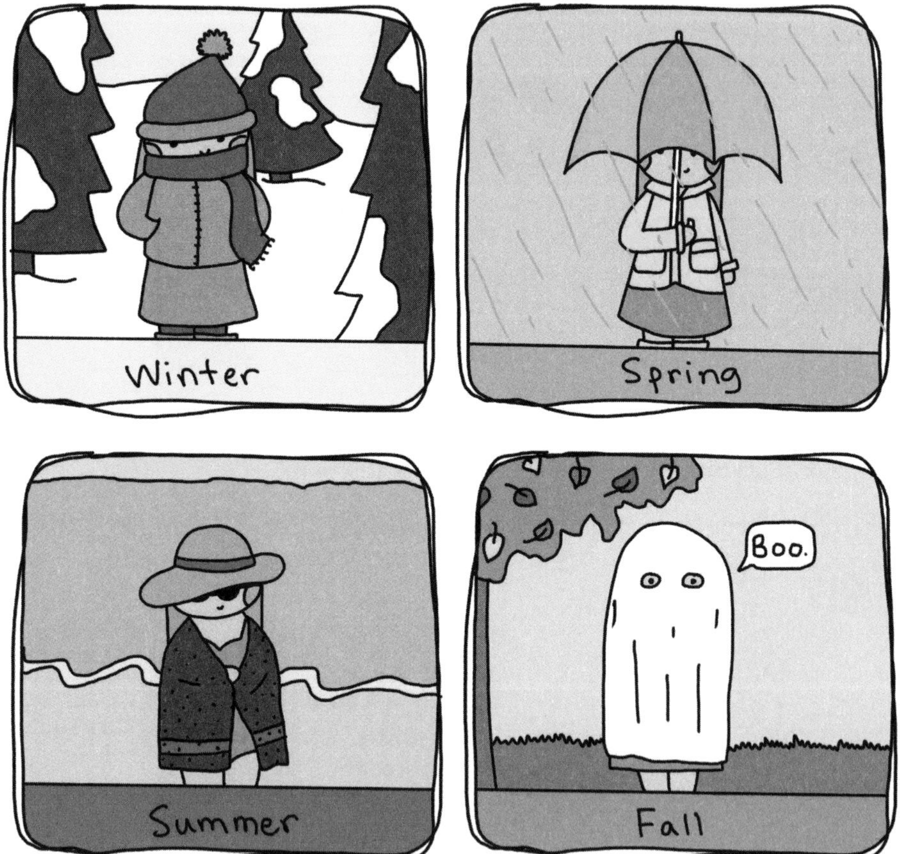
Winter
Spring
Summer
Boo.
Fall

WHY I HATE SWIMMING

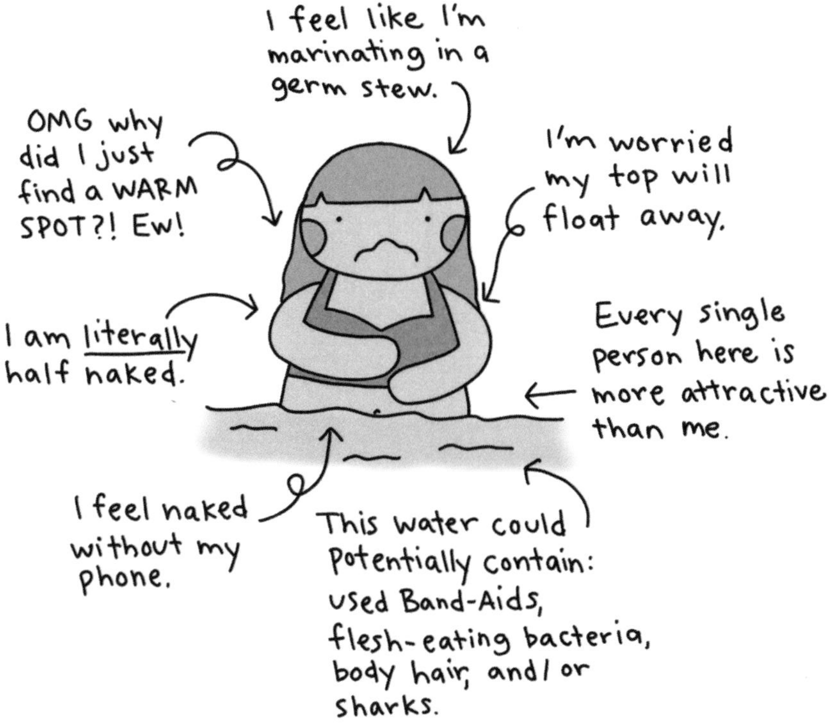

I feel like I'm marinating in a germ stew.
OMG why did I just find a WARM SPOT?! Ew!
I'm worried my top will float away.
I am literally half naked.
Every single person here is more attractive than me.
I feel naked without my phone.
This water could potentially contain: used Band-Aids, flesh-eating bacteria, body hair, and/or sharks.

THE SCARIEST STUFF ABOUT HALLOWEEN

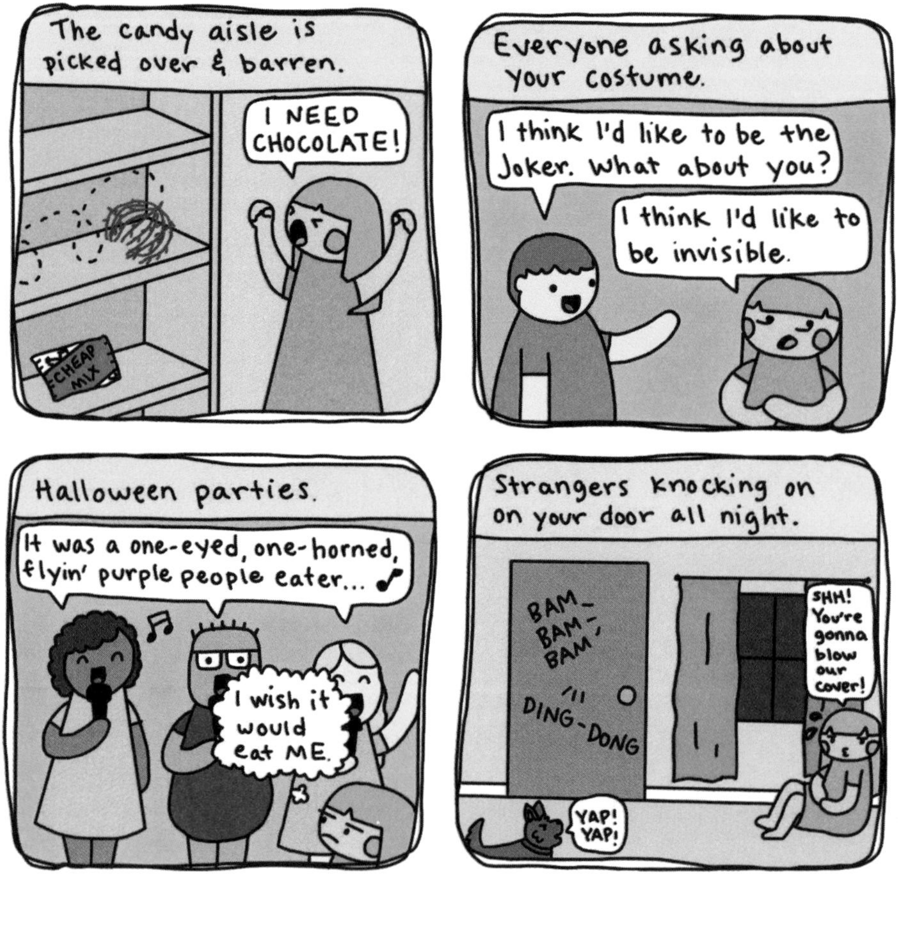
The candy aisle is picked over & barren.
I NEED CHOCOLATE!
CHEAP MIX
Everyone asking about your costume.
I think I'd like to be the Joker. What about you?
I think I'd like to be invisible.
Halloween parties.
It was a one-eyed, one-horned, flyin' purple people eater...
I wish it would eat ME.
Strangers knocking on on your door all night.
BAM-BAM-BAM
DING-DONG
SHH! You're gonna blow our cover!
YAP! YAP!

COPING STRATEGIES FOR SOCIAL ANXIETY

Keep your hands busy.

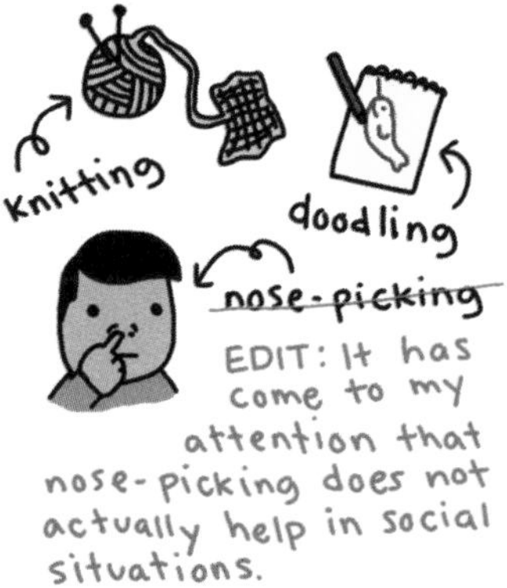
knitting
doodling
~~nose-picking~~
EDIT: It has come to my attention that nose-picking does not actually help in social situations.

Bring along a chatterbox buddy.

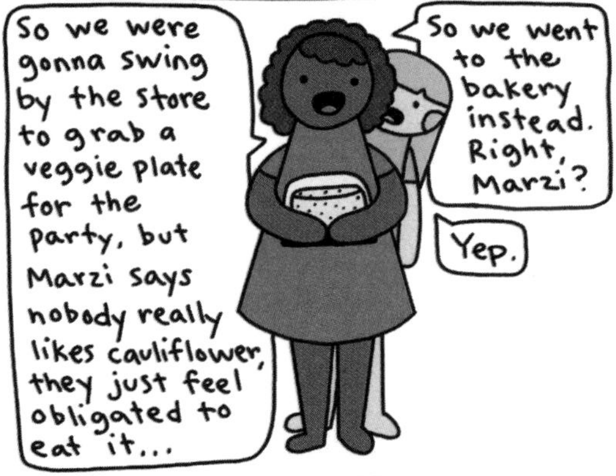
So we were gonna swing by the store to grab a veggie plate for the party, but Marzi says nobody really likes cauliflower, they just feel obligated to eat it...
So we went to the bakery instead. Right, Marzi?
Yep.

Write a list of interesting discussion topics beforehand.

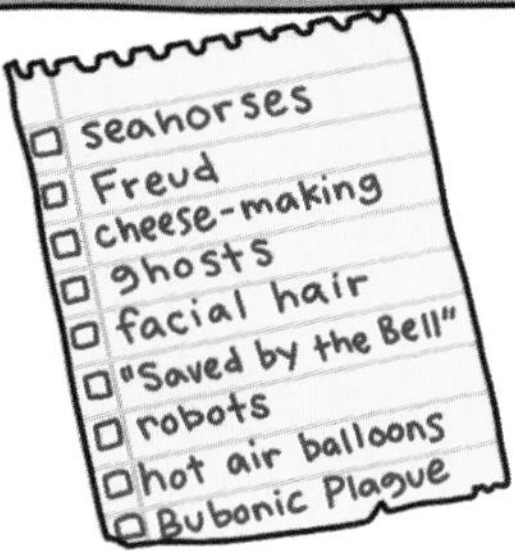
seahorses
Freud
cheese-making
ghosts
facial hair
"Saved by the Bell"
robots
hot air balloons
Bubonic Plague

~~Imagine everyone naked.~~

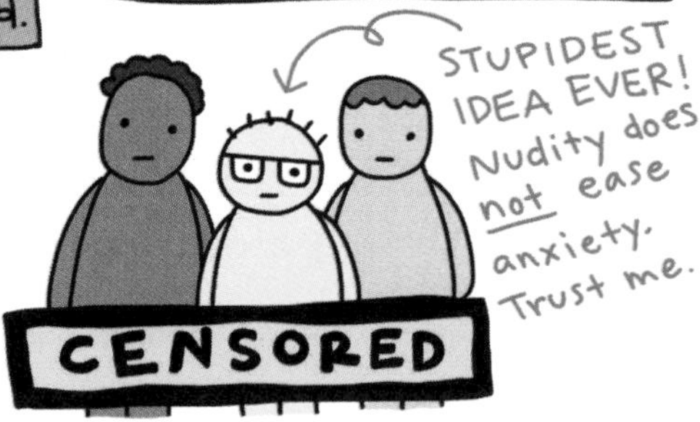
STUPIDEST IDEA EVER! Nudity does not ease anxiety. Trust me.
CENSORED

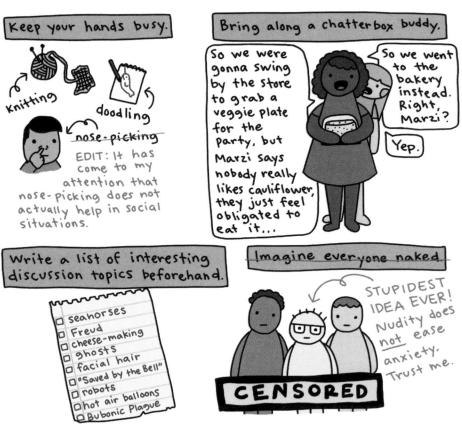

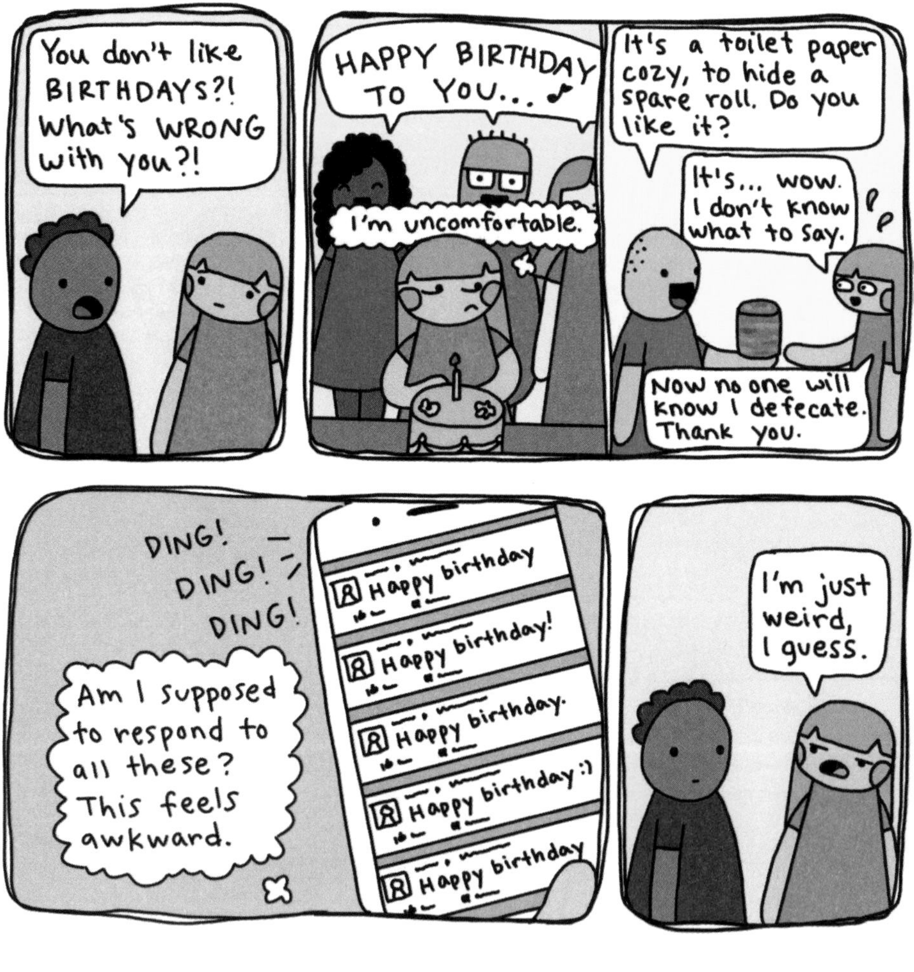
You don't like BIRTHDAYS?! What's WRONG with you?!
HAPPY BIRTHDAY TO YOU...
I'm uncomfortable.
It's a toilet paper cozy, to hide a spare roll. Do you like it?
It's... wow. I don't know what to say.
Now no one will know I defecate. Thank you.
DING!
DING!
DING!
Happy birthday
Happy birthday!
Happy birthday.
Happy birthday :)
Happy birthday
Am I supposed to respond to all these? This feels awkward.
I'm just weird, I guess.

HOW TO ESCAPE A CONVERSATION

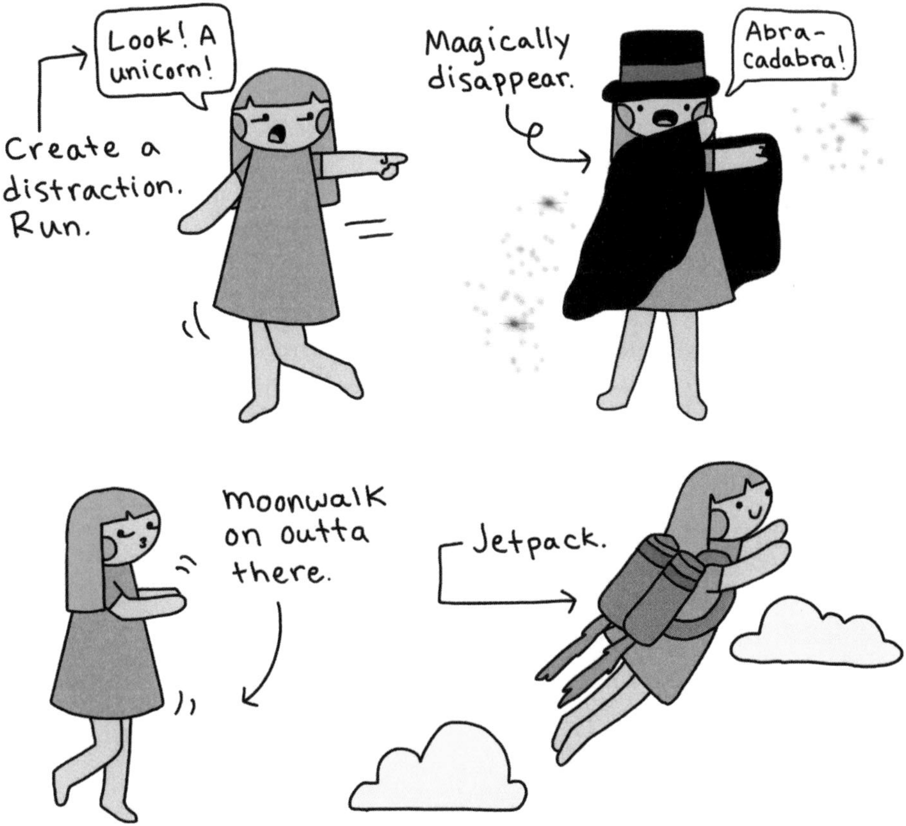
Create a distraction. Run.
Look! A unicorn!
Magically disappear.
Abra-cadabra!
moonwalk on outta there.
Jetpack.

SOUL-CRUSHING THINGS

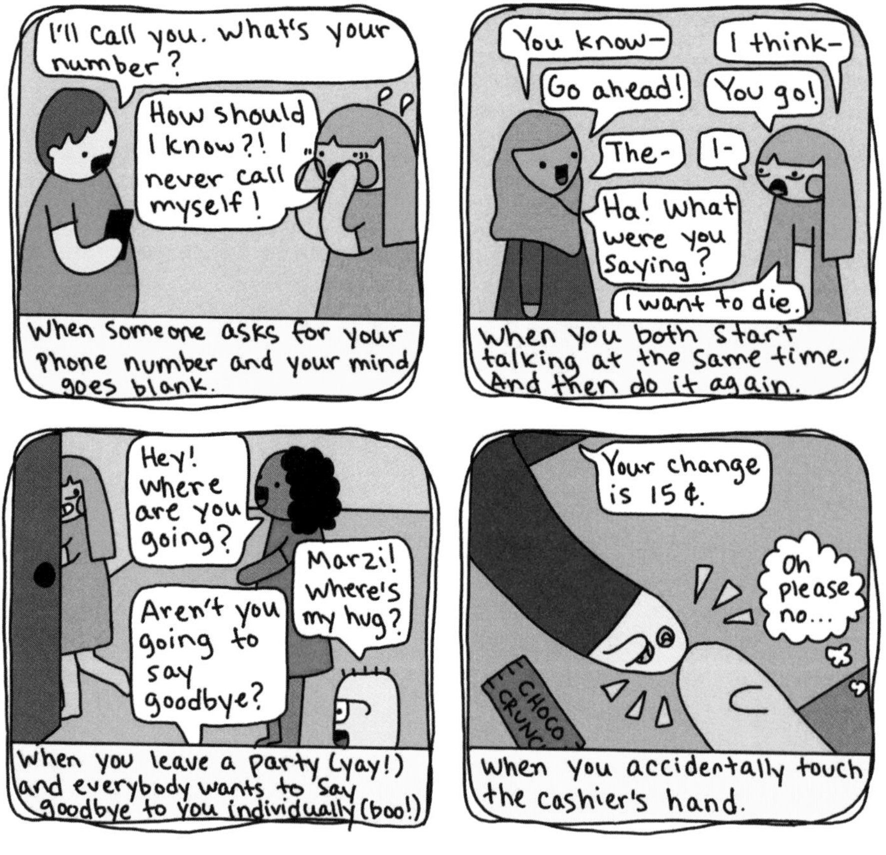
I'll call you. What's your number?
How should I know?! I never call myself!
When someone asks for your phone number and your mind goes blank.
You know—
I think—
Go ahead!
You go!
The-
I-
Ha! What were you saying?
I want to die.
When you both start talking at the same time. And then do it again.
Hey! Where are you going?
Marzi! Where's my hug?
Aren't you going to say goodbye?
When you leave a party (yay!) and everybody wants to say goodbye to you individually (boo!)
Your change is 15¢.
Oh please no...
CHOCO CRUNC
When you accidentally touch the cashier's hand.

THINGS I DO IN SOCIAL SITUATIONS

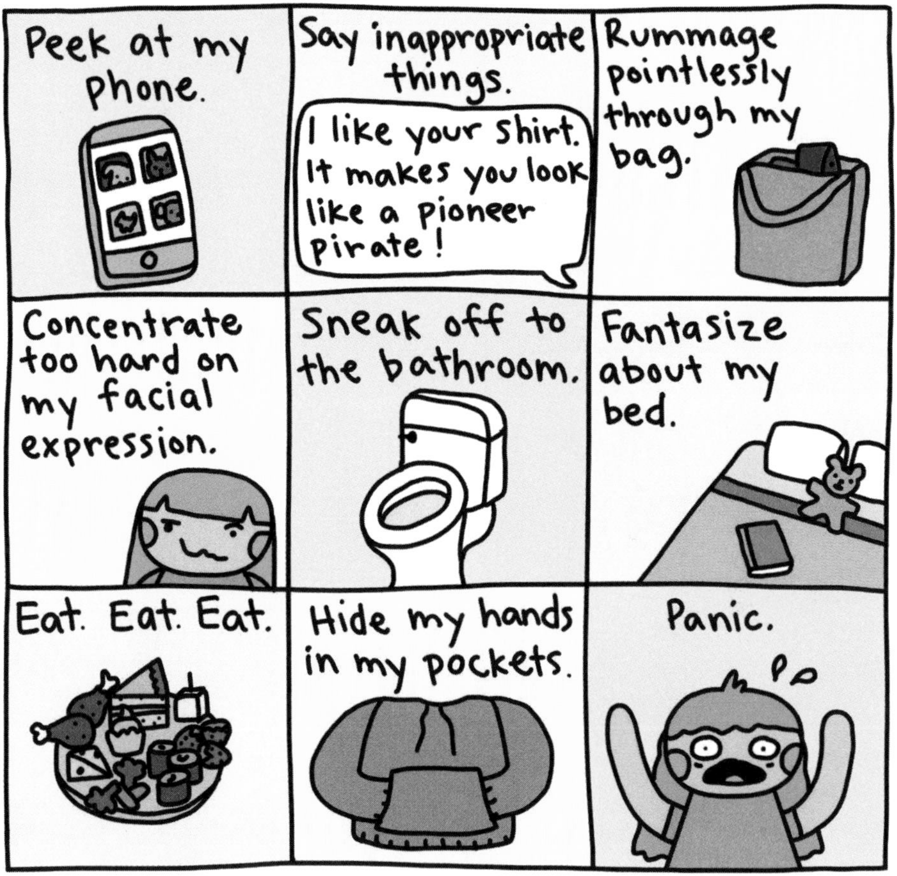
Peek at my phone.
Say inappropriate things.
I like your shirt. It makes you look like a pioneer pirate!
Rummage pointlessly through my bag.
Concentrate too hard on my facial expression.
Sneak off to the bathroom.
Fantasize about my bed.
Eat. Eat. Eat.
Hide my hands in my pockets.
Panic.

WHICH IS WORST?

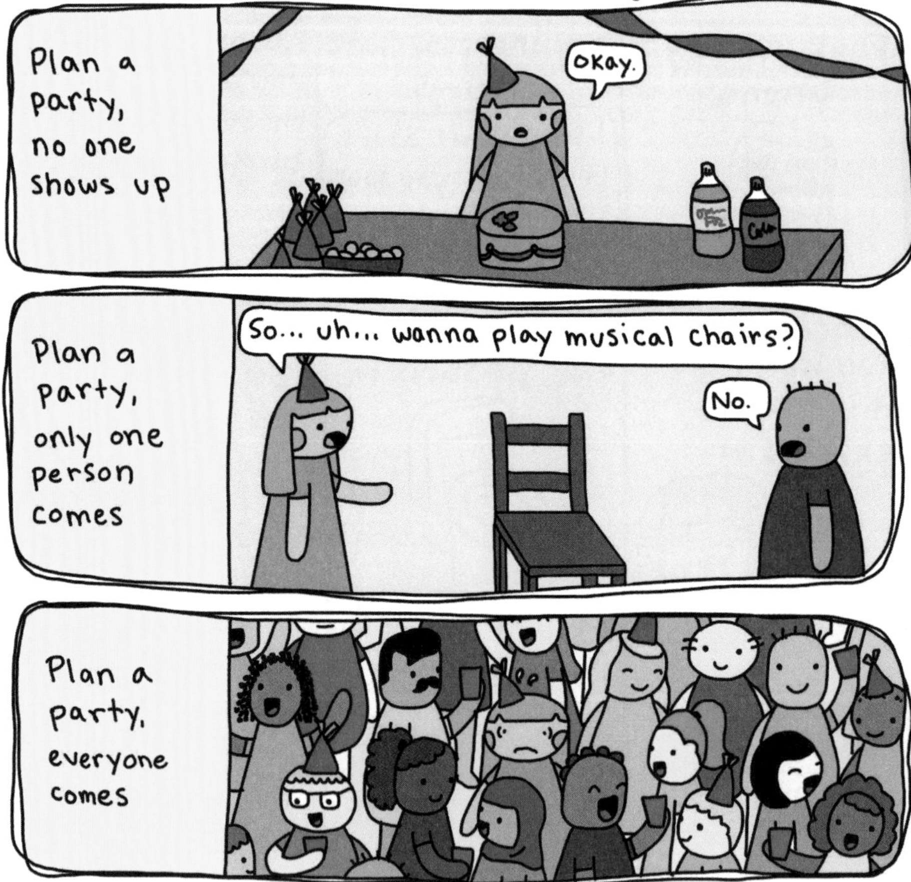
Plan a party, no one shows up
Okay.
Plan a party, only one person comes
So... uh... wanna play musical chairs?
No.
Plan a party, everyone comes

SHOPPING WHILE AWKWARD

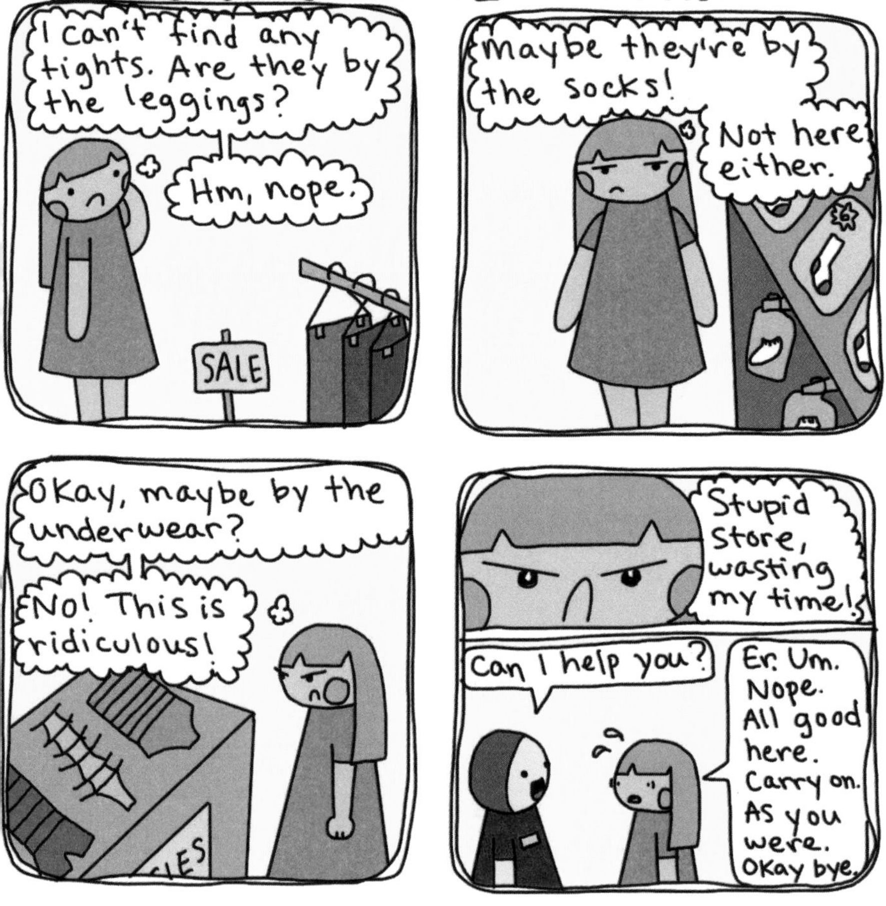
I can't find any tights. Are they by the leggings?
Hm, nope.
SALE
Maybe they're by the socks!
Not here either.
Okay, maybe by the underwear?
No! This is ridiculous!
Stupid store, wasting my time!
Can I help you?
Er. Um. Nope. All good here. Carry on. As you were. Okay bye.

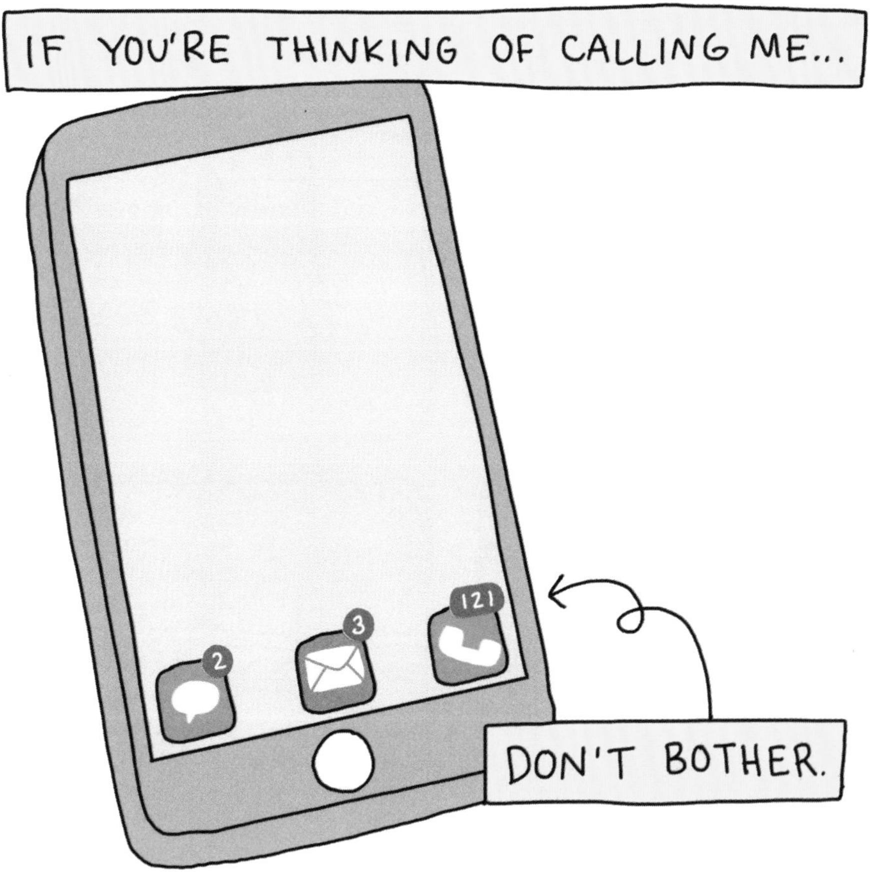
IF YOU'RE THINKING OF CALLING ME...
2
3
121
DON'T BOTHER.

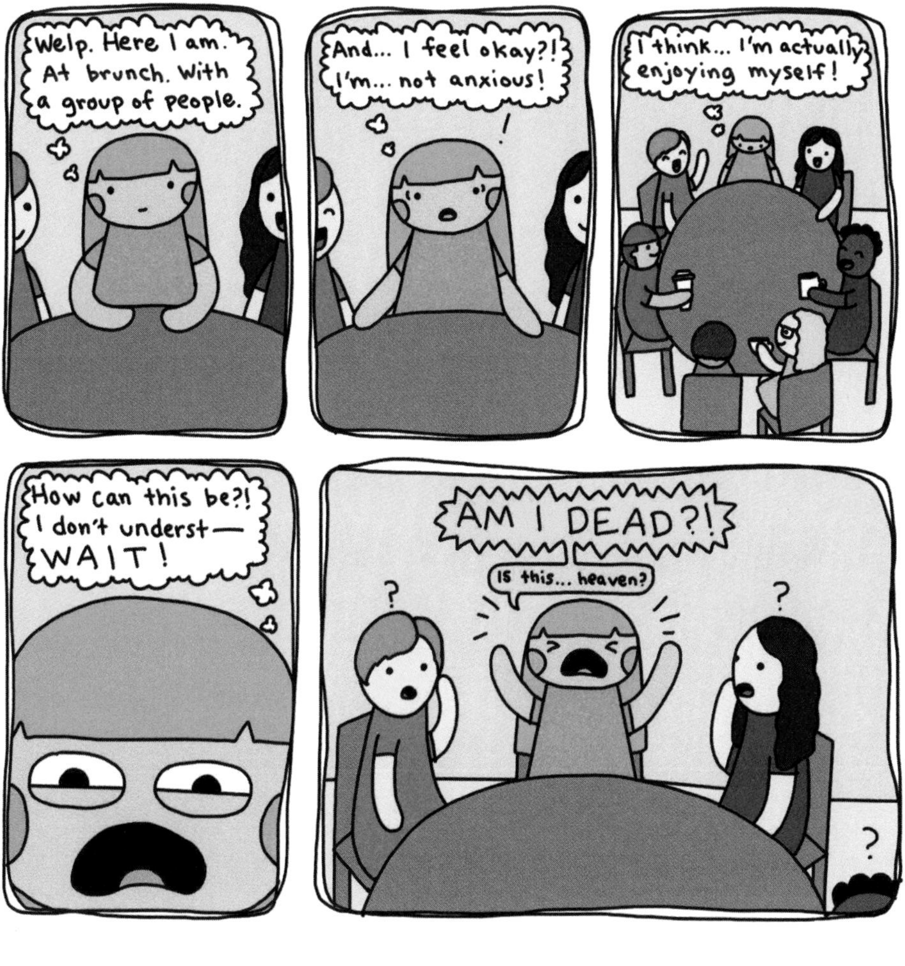
Welp. Here I am. At brunch. With a group of people.
And... I feel okay?! I'm... not anxious!
I think... I'm actually enjoying myself!
How can this be?! I don't underst— WAIT!
AM I DEAD?!
Is this... heaven?
?
?
?

DO I HAVE TO ?

-when responsibilities & anxiety collide-

Anxiety can make everyday tasks feel overwhelming. Replying to emails, going to the grocery store, paying bills... anxiety can make that to-do list seem impossible. When anxiety and responsibilities collide, things get messy!

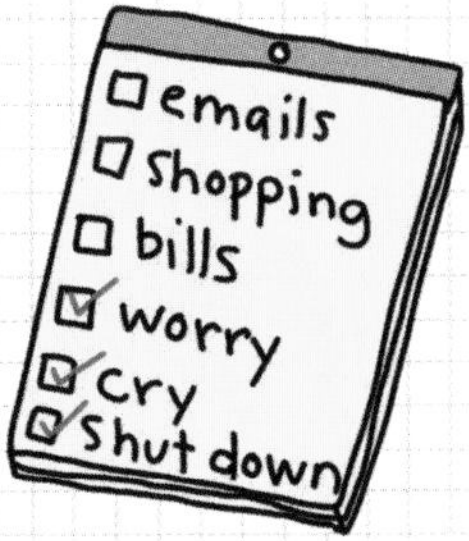
emails
shopping
bills
worry
cry
shut down

Sometimes I get frustrated with myself:

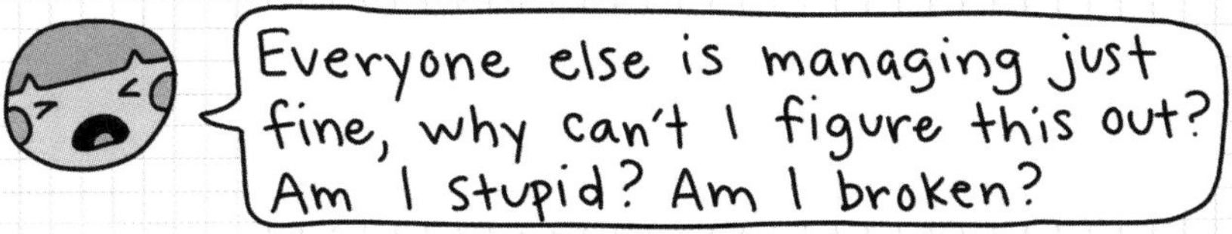
Everyone else is managing just fine, why can't I figure this out? Am I stupid? Am I broken?

It's true that I don't have it all figured out. But I'm beginning to realize that nobody does. We all deserve a little patience and a lot of self-compassion. After a hard day, these are the words I whisper to myself:

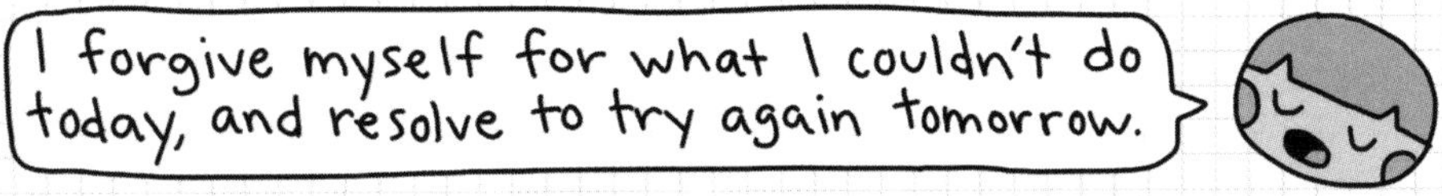
I forgive myself for what I couldn't do today, and resolve to try again tomorrow.

It is enough to just keep trying. I. Am. Enough.

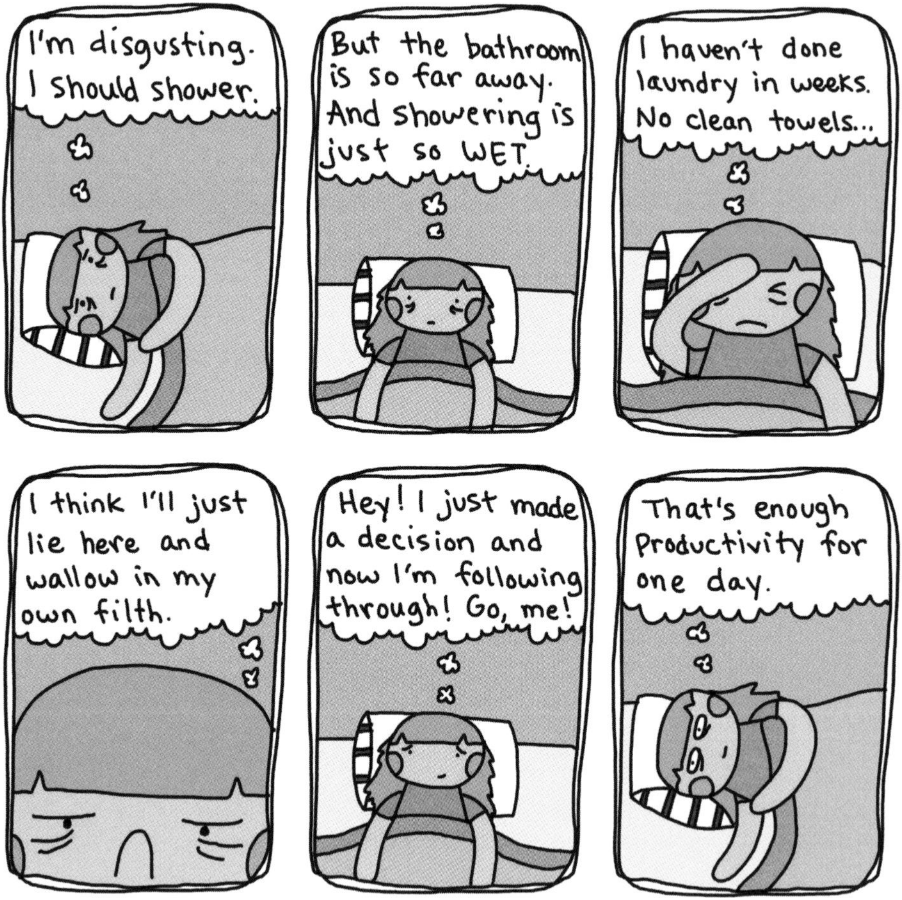
I'm disgusting. I should shower.
But the bathroom is so far away. And showering is just so WET.
I haven't done laundry in weeks. No clean towels...
I think I'll just lie here and wallow in my own filth.
Hey! I just made a decision and now I'm following through! Go, me!
That's enough productivity for one day.

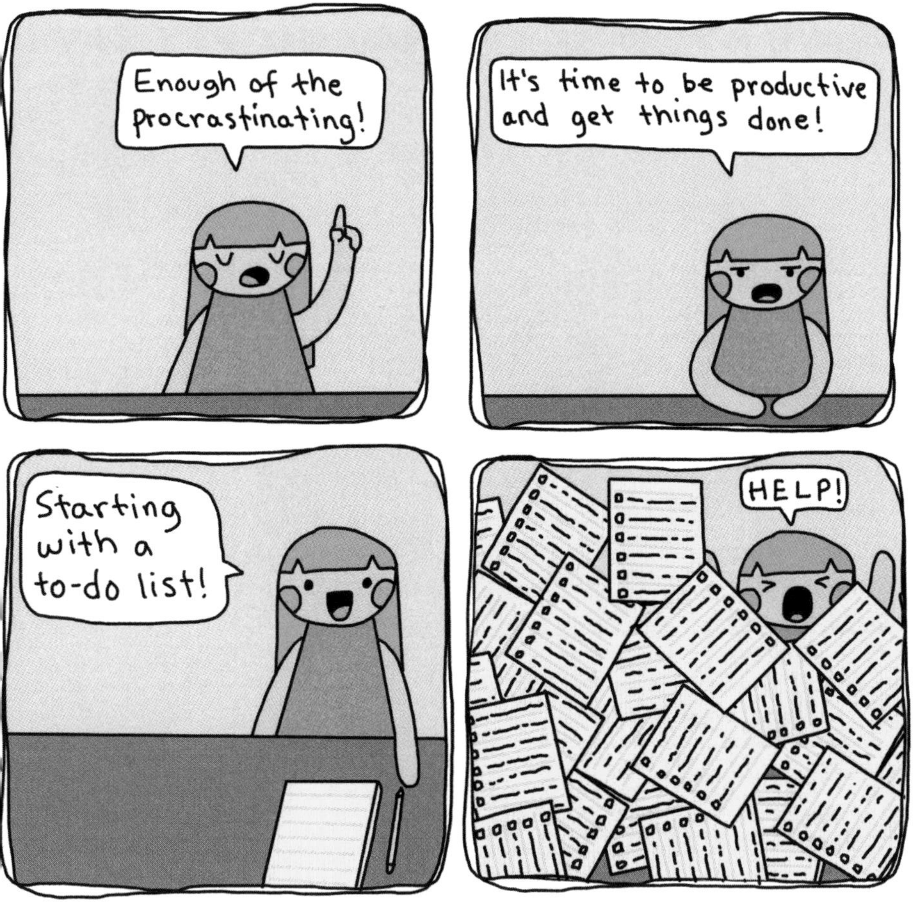
Enough of the procrastinating!
It's time to be productive and get things done!
Starting with a to-do list!
HELP!

LIST OF THINGS THAT WOULD CONVINCE ME TO LEAVE MY HOUSE ON A BAD ANXIETY DAY

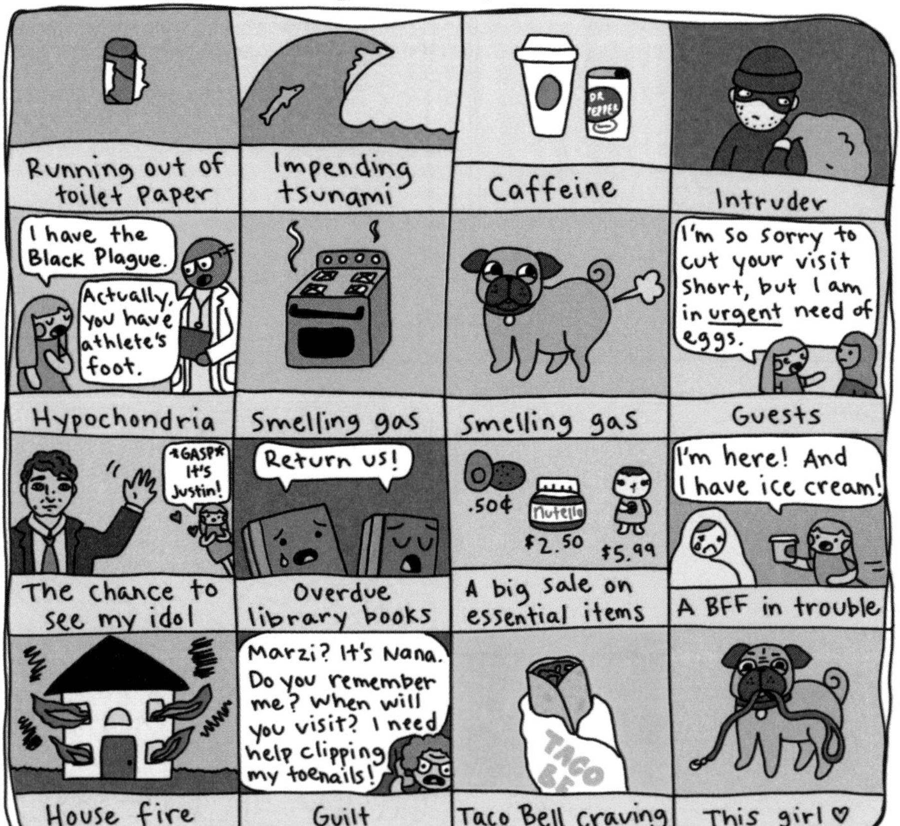
Running out of toilet paper
Impending tsunami
DR PEPPER
Caffeine
Intruder
I have the Black Plague.
Actually, you have athlete's foot.
Hypochondria
Smelling gas
Smelling gas
I'm so sorry to cut your visit short, but I am in urgent need of eggs.
Guests
GASP It's Justin!
The chance to see my idol
Return us!
Overdue library books
.50¢
Nutella
$2.50
$5.99
A big sale on essential items
I'm here! And I have ice cream!
A BFF in trouble
House fire
Marzi? It's Nana. Do you remember me? When will you visit? I need help clipping my toenails!
Guilt
TACO BE
Taco Bell craving
This girl ♡

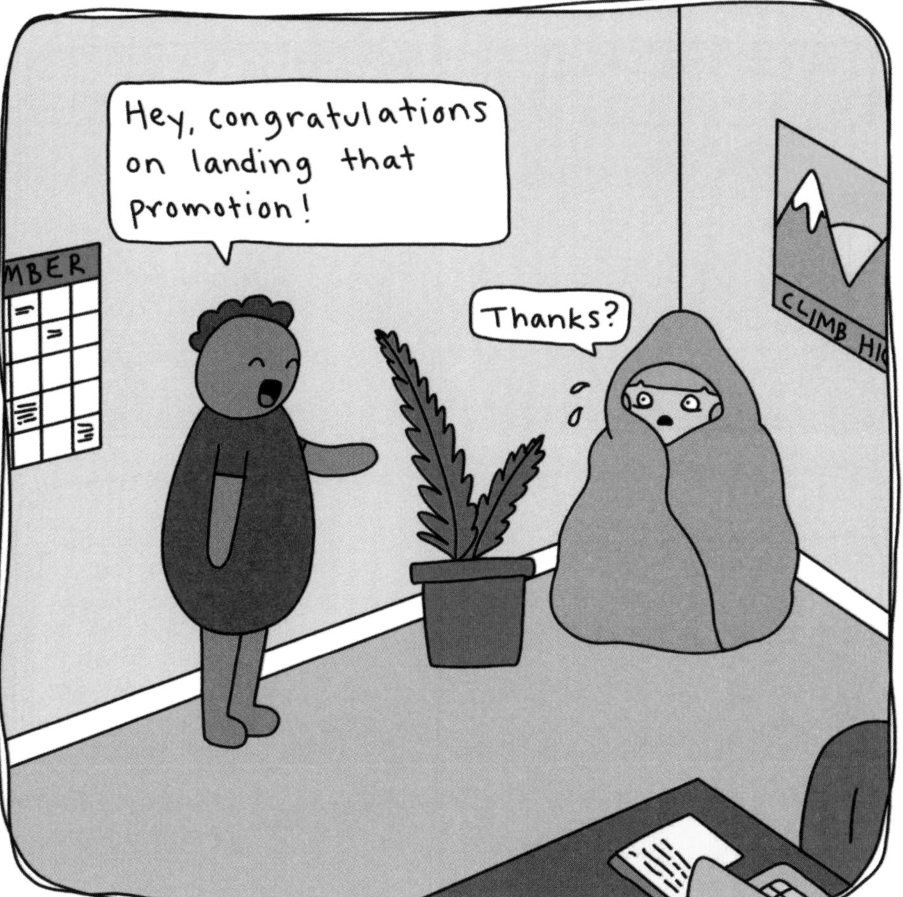
Hey, congratulations on landing that promotion!
Thanks?
MBER
CLIMB HI

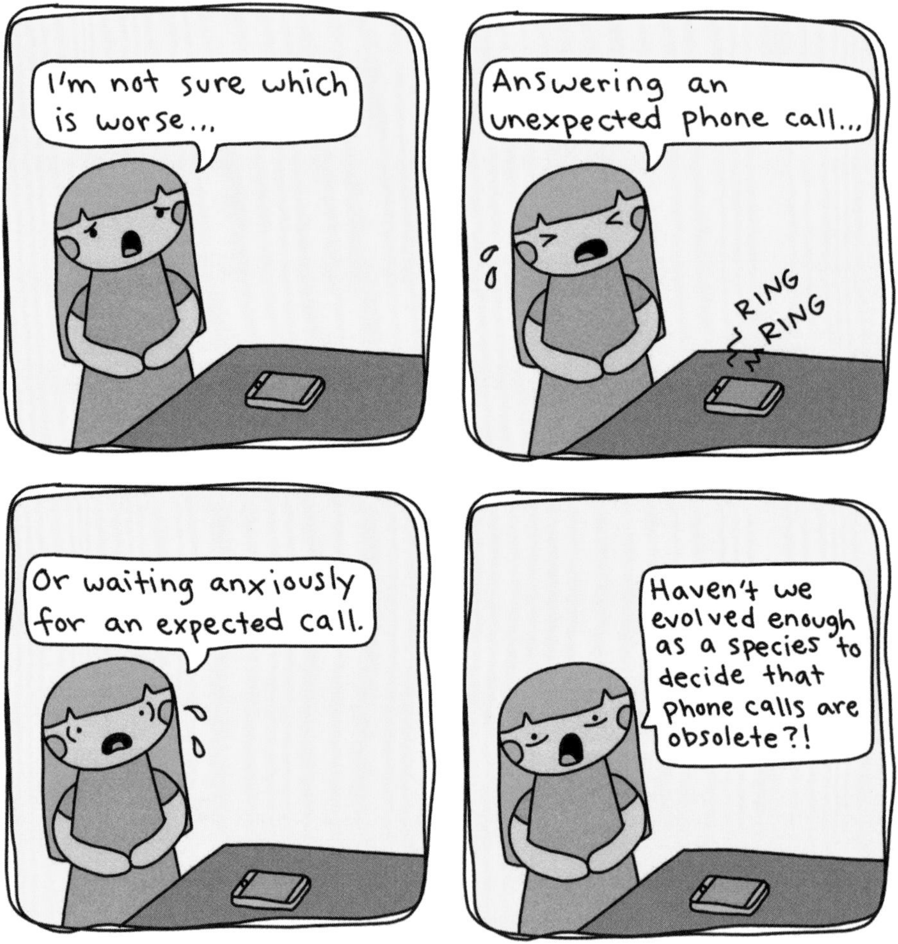
I'm not sure which is worse...
Answering an unexpected phone call...
RING
RING
Or waiting anxiously for an expected call.
Haven't we evolved enough as a species to decide that phone calls are obsolete?!

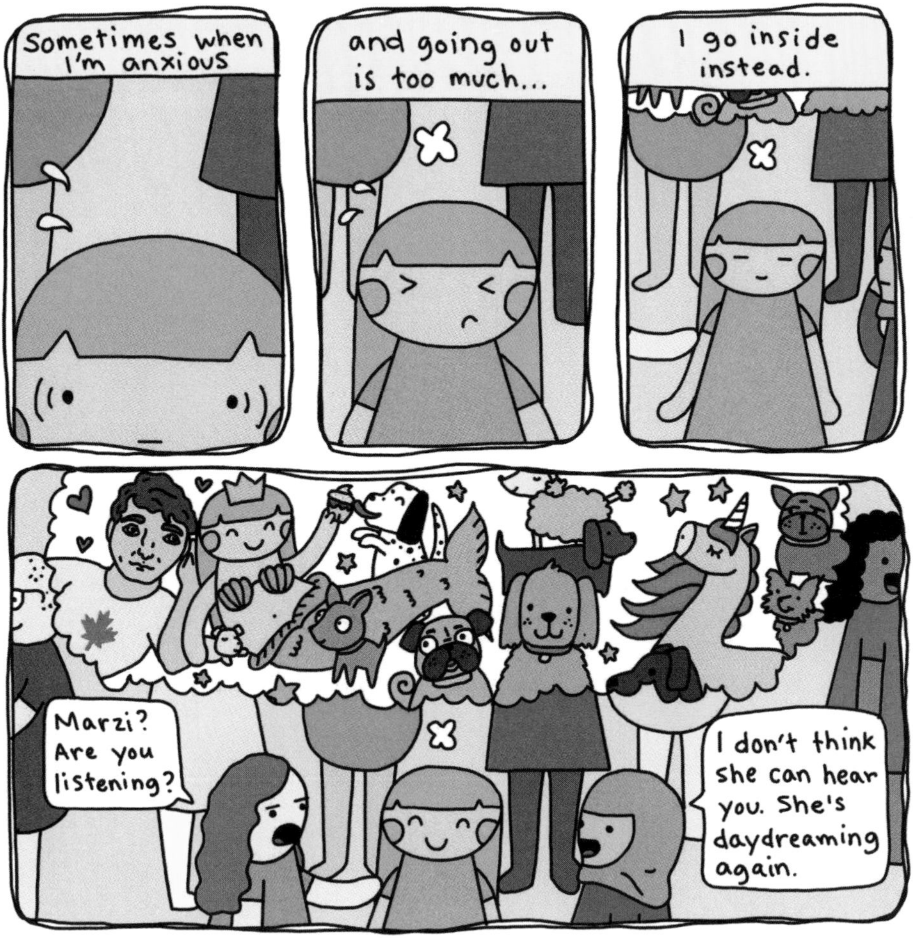
Sometimes when I'm anxious
and going out is too much...
I go inside instead.
Marzi? Are you listening?
I don't think she can hear you. She's daydreaming again.

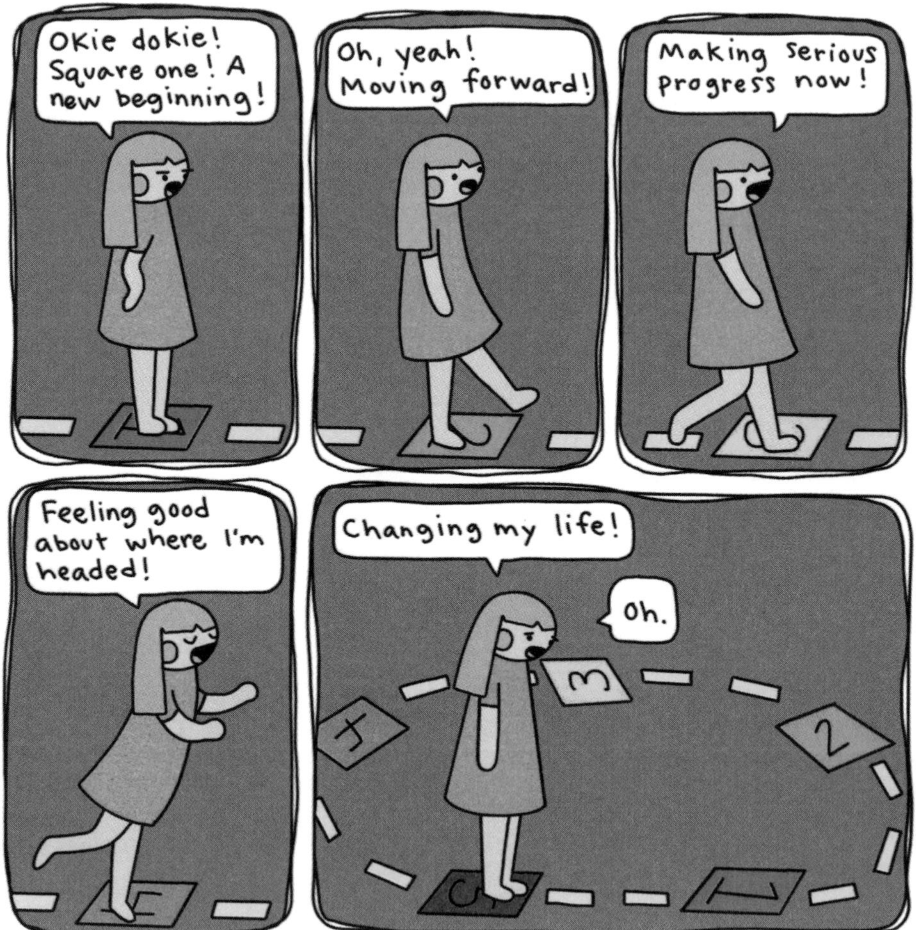
OKie dokie! Square one! A new beginning!
Oh, yeah! Moving forward!
Making serious progress now!
Feeling good about where I'm headed!
Changing my life!
Oh.

THINGS I'LL NEVER DO

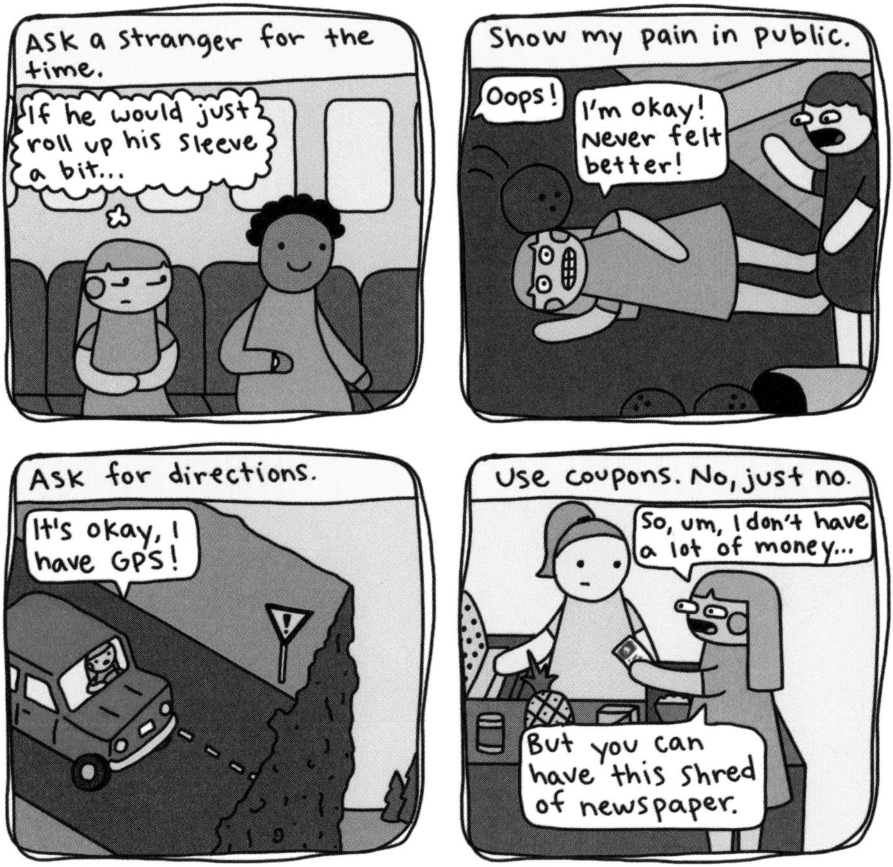

Ask a stranger for the time.
If he would just roll up his sleeve a bit...
Show my pain in public.
Oops!
I'm okay! Never felt better!
Ask for directions.
It's okay, I have GPS!
Use coupons. No, just no.
So, um, I don't have a lot of money...
But you can have this shred of newspaper.

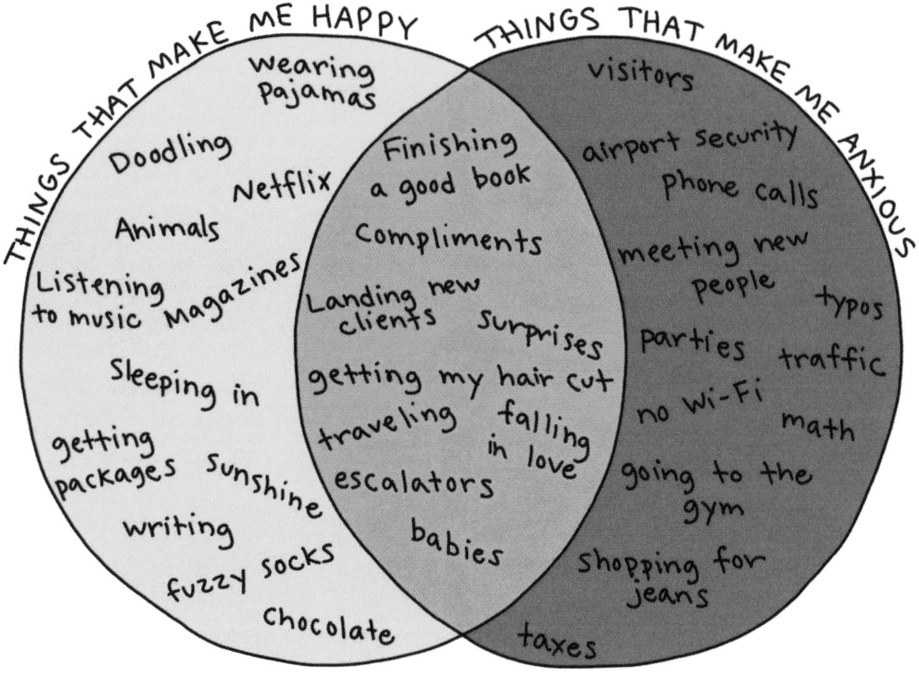
THINGS THAT MAKE ME HAPPY
THINGS THAT MAKE ME ANXIOUS
wearing pajamas
Doodling
Netflix
Animals
Listening to music
Magazines
Sleeping in
getting packages
Sunshine
writing
fuzzy socks
Chocolate
Finishing a good book
Compliments
Landing new clients
Surprises
getting my hair cut
traveling
falling in love
escalators
babies
visitors
airport security
Phone calls
meeting new people
typos
parties
traffic
no Wi-Fi
math
going to the gym
Shopping for jeans
taxes

STUFF I DON'T NOTICE UNTIL I HAVE GUESTS

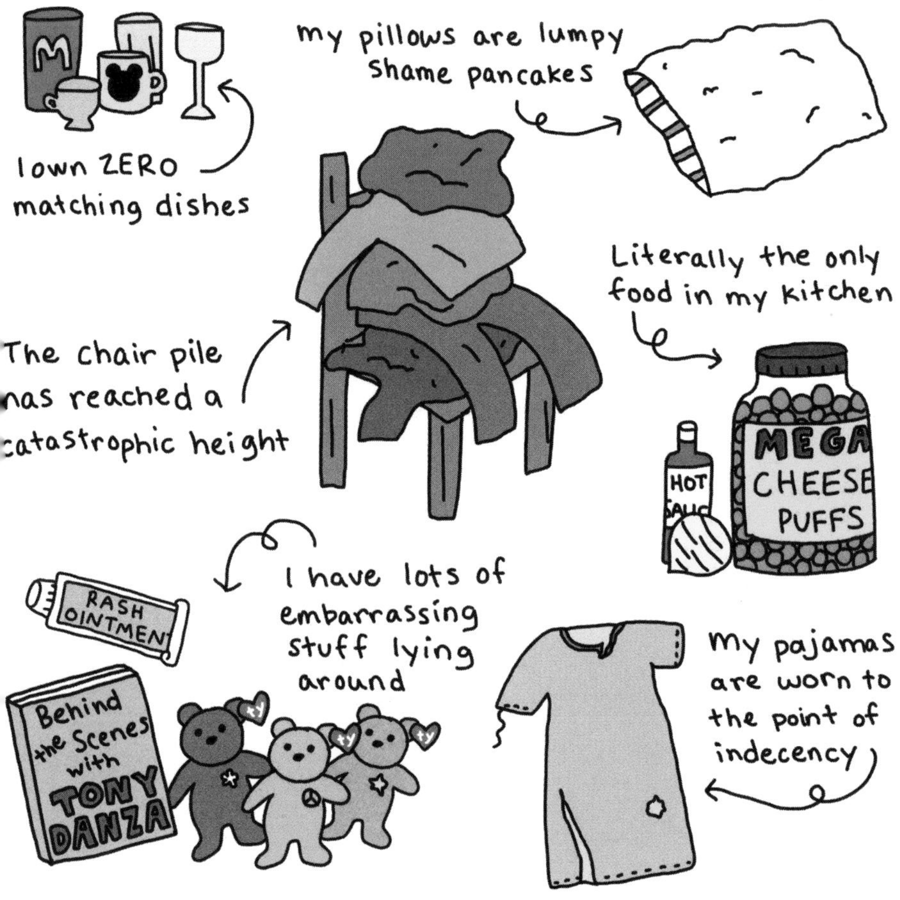
I own ZERO matching dishes
my pillows are lumpy shame pancakes
The chair pile has reached a catastrophic height
Literally the only food in my kitchen
HOT SAUC
MEGA CHEESE PUFFS
I have lots of embarrassing stuff lying around
RASH OINTMENT
Behind the Scenes with TONY DANZA
ty
My pajamas are worn to the point of indecency

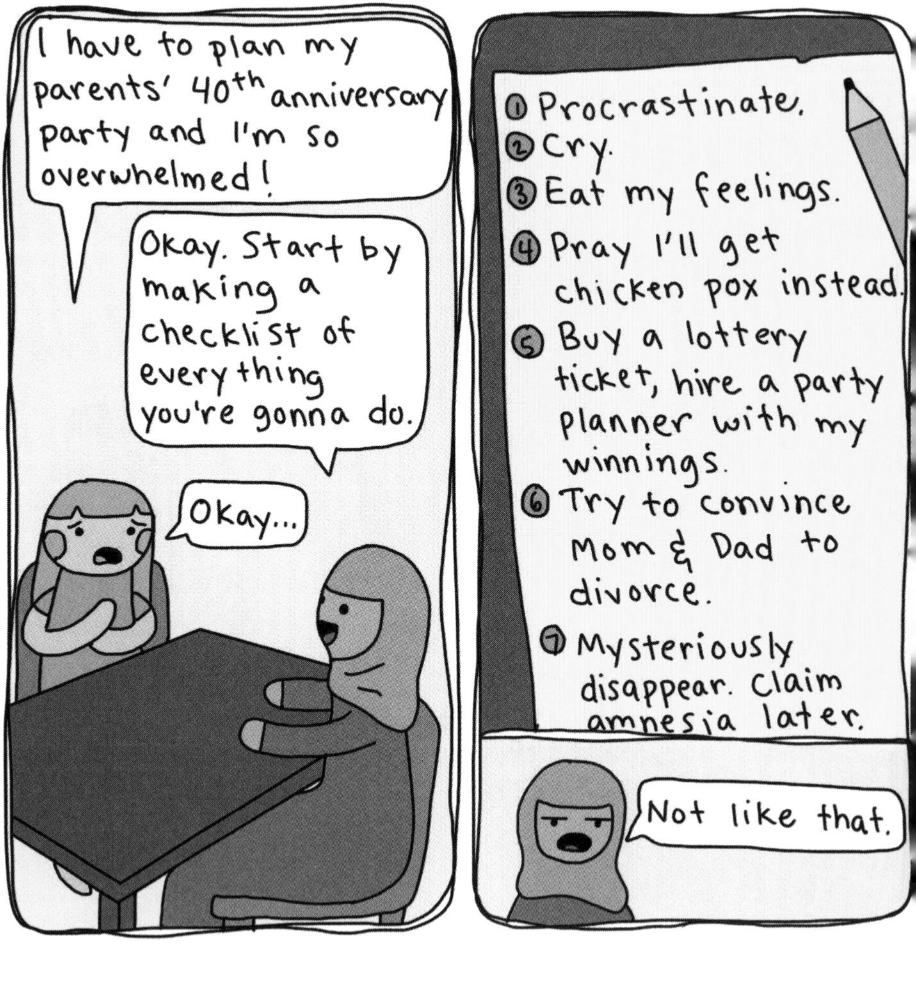

I have to plan my parents' 40th anniversary party and I'm so overwhelmed!
Okay. Start by making a checklist of everything you're gonna do.
Okay...
① Procrastinate.
② Cry.
③ Eat my feelings.
④ Pray I'll get chicken pox instead.
⑤ Buy a lottery ticket, hire a party planner with my winnings.
⑥ Try to convince Mom & Dad to divorce.
⑦ Mysteriously disappear. Claim amnesia later.
Not like that.

PLACES I FEEL UNCOMFORTABLE

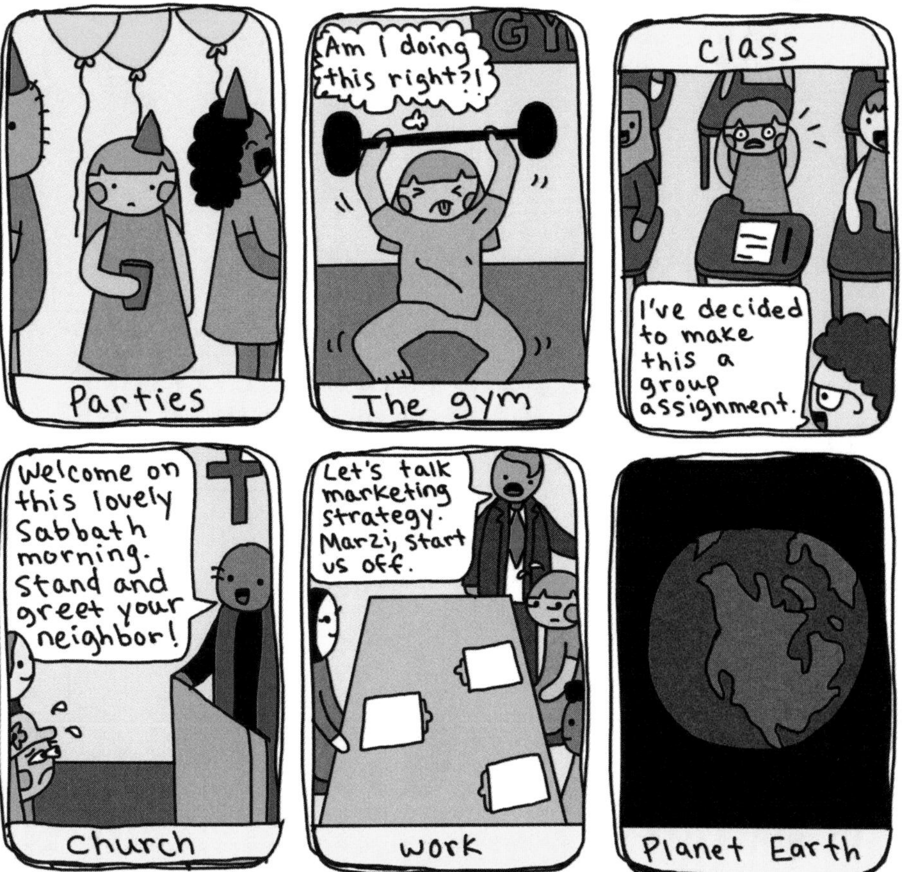
Parties
Am I doing this right?!
The gym
Class
I've decided to make this a group assignment.
Welcome on this lovely Sabbath morning. Stand and greet your neighbor!
Church
Let's talk marketing strategy. Marzi, start us off.
work
Planet Earth

CAREERS I WOULD SUCK AT

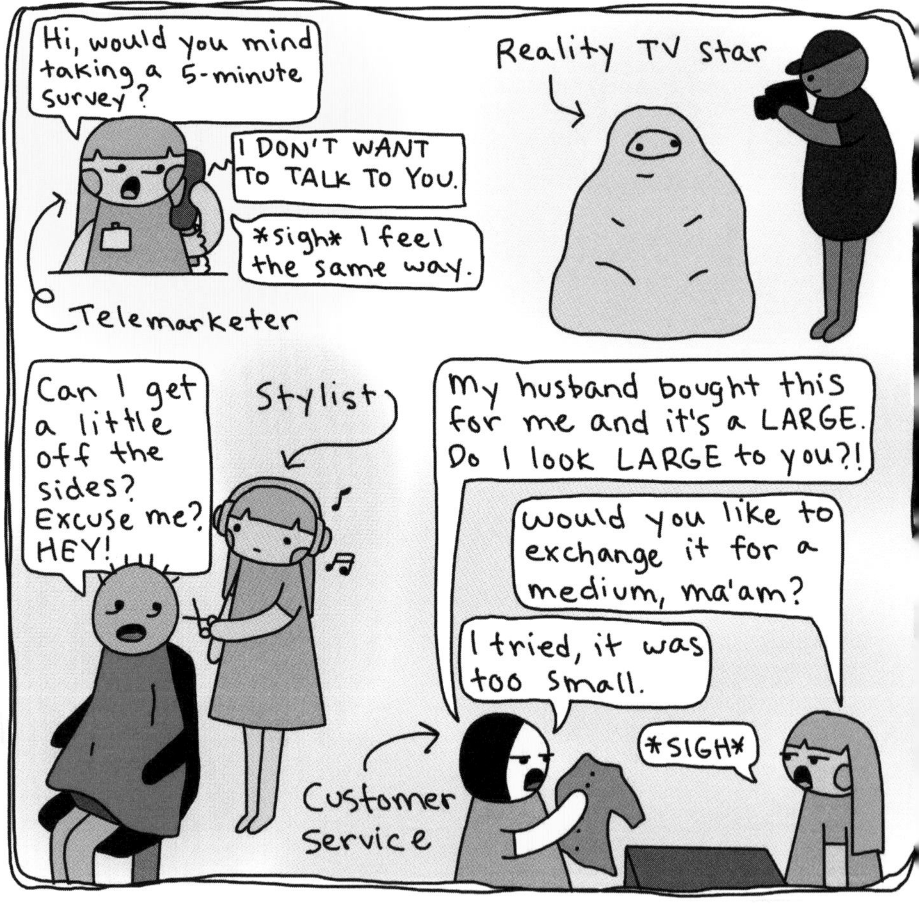
Hi, would you mind taking a 5-minute survey?
I DON'T WANT TO TALK TO YOU.
sigh I feel the same way.
Telemarketer
Reality TV star
Can I get a little off the sides? Excuse me? HEY!
Stylist
My husband bought this for me and it's a LARGE. Do I look LARGE to you?!
Would you like to exchange it for a medium, ma'am?
I tried, it was too small.
SIGH
Customer Service

SHOULD I SAY HELLO?

*a guide for the socially anxious

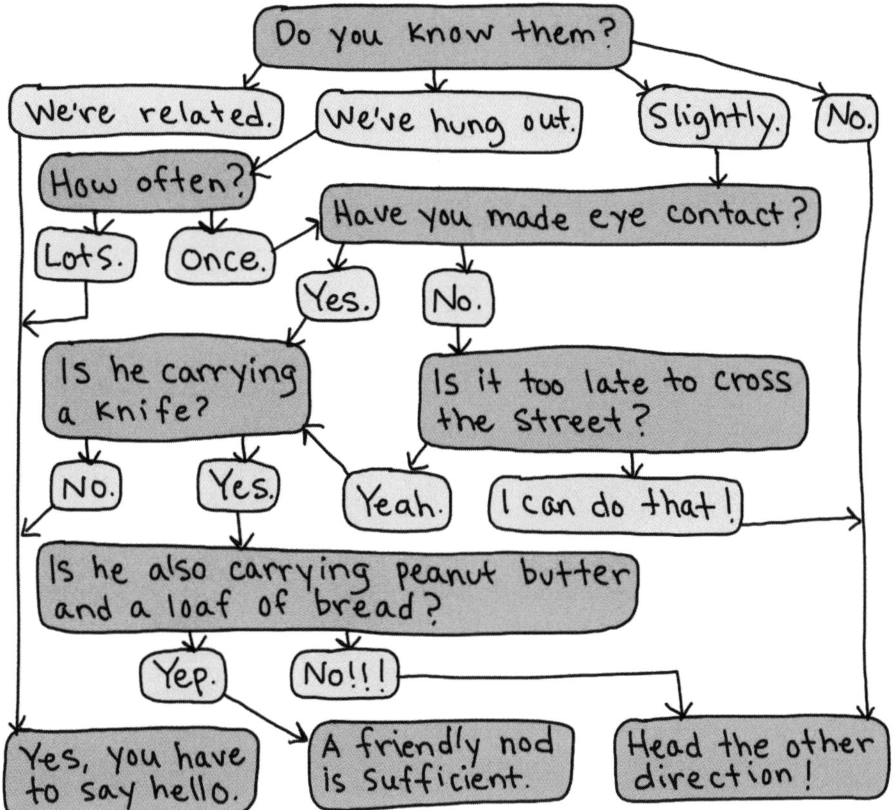
Do you know them?
We're related.
We've hung out.
Slightly.
No.
How often?
Lots.
Once.
Have you made eye contact?
Yes.
No.
Is he carrying a knife?
Is it too late to cross the street?
No.
Yes.
Yeah.
I can do that!
Is he also carrying peanut butter and a loaf of bread?
Yep.
No!!!
Yes, you have to say hello.
A friendly nod is sufficient.
Head the other direction!

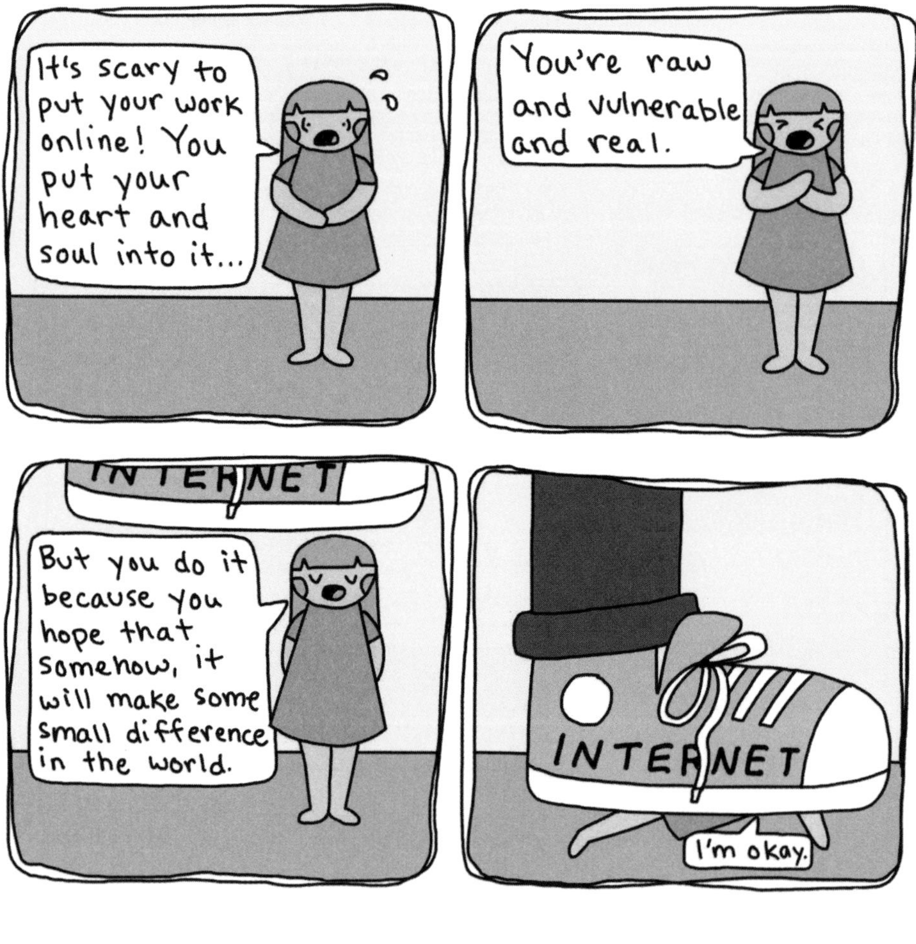
It's scary to put your work online! You put your heart and soul into it...
You're raw and vulnerable and real.
INTERNET
But you do it because you hope that somehow, it will make some small difference in the world.
INTERNET
I'm okay.

I HAVEN'T CALLED BECAUSE...

- ☐ I don't know what to say
- ☐ I was hoping you'd call first
- ☐ Phone calls make me anxious
- ☐ TBH I'm just not that into you
- ☐ I dropped my phone in the toilet

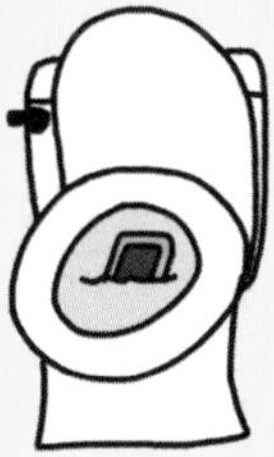

AND I WANT YOU TO KNOW...

- ☐ I'll try harder
- ☐ This is just how I roll
- ☐ It wasn't my fault
- ☐ I'm very sorry
- ☐ I'm not sorry

PLEASE TAKE THE FOLLOWING ACTION...

- ☐ Text instead
- ☐ Give me some time
- ☐ Make the first move
- ☐ Lower your expectations
- ☐ Leave me alone

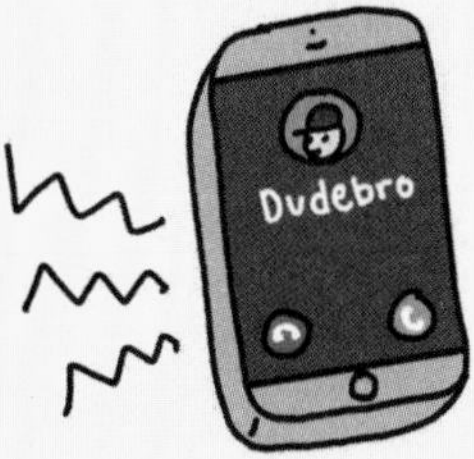
Dudebro

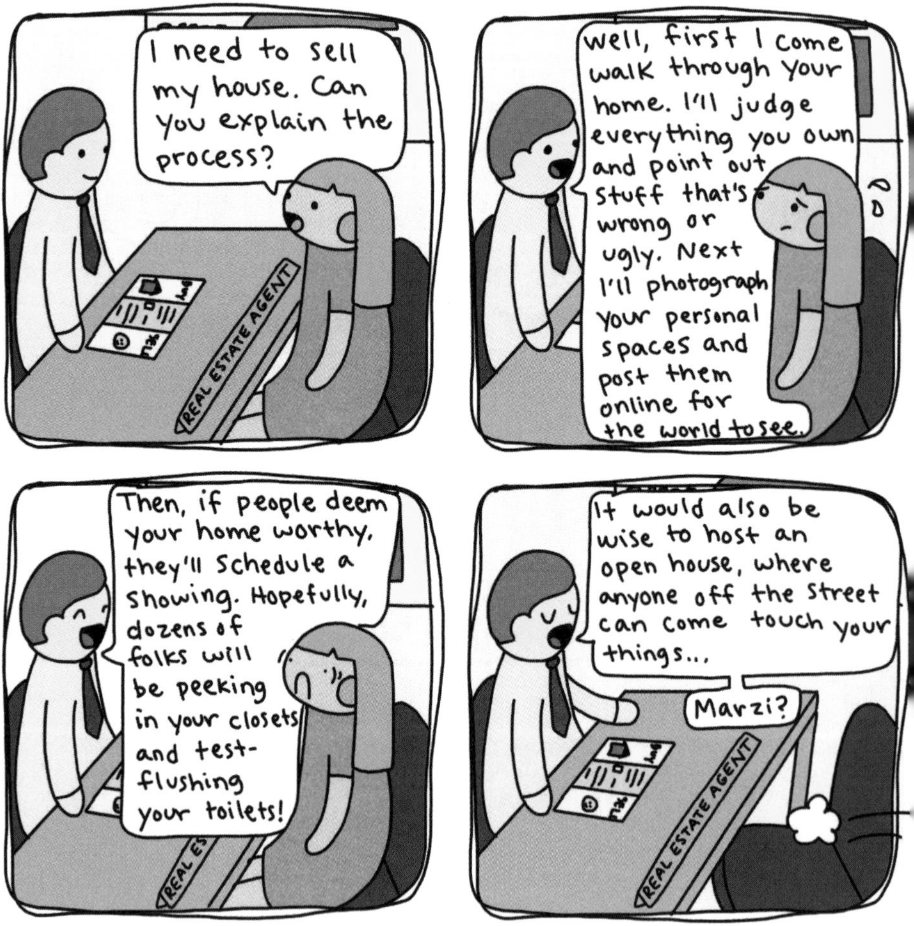
I need to sell my house. Can you explain the process?
REAL ESTATE AGENT
Well, first I come walk through your home. I'll judge everything you own and point out stuff that's wrong or ugly. Next I'll photograph your personal spaces and post them online for the world to see.
Then, if people deem your home worthy, they'll schedule a showing. Hopefully, dozens of folks will be peeking in your closets and test-flushing your toilets!
It would also be wise to host an open house, where anyone off the street can come touch your things...
Marzi?
REAL ESTATE AGENT

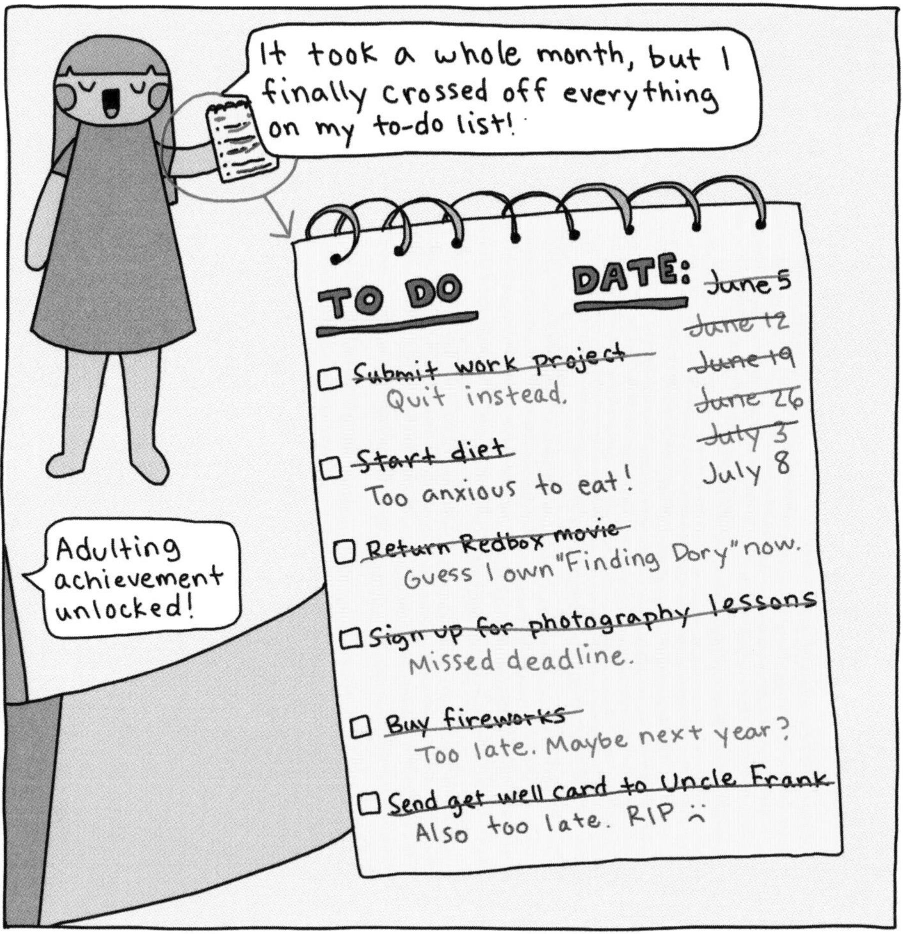
It took a whole month, but I finally crossed off everything on my to-do list!
TO DO
DATE: June 5
June 12
June 19
June 26
July 3
July 8
Submit work project
Quit instead.
Start diet
Too anxious to eat!
Return Redbox movie
Guess I own "Finding Dory" now.
Sign up for photography lessons
Missed deadline.
Buy fireworks
Too late. Maybe next year?
Send get well card to Uncle Frank
Also too late. RIP
Adulting achievement unlocked!

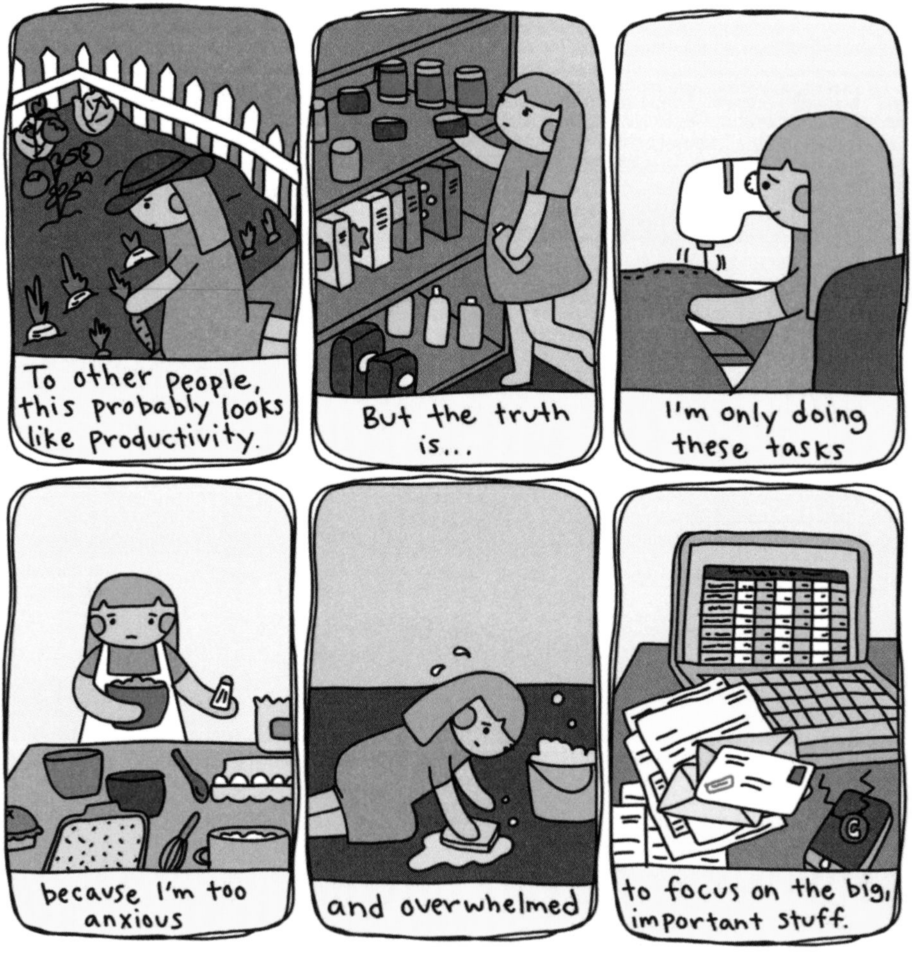
To other people, this probably looks like productivity.
But the truth is...
I'm only doing these tasks
because I'm too anxious
and overwhelmed
to focus on the big, important stuff.

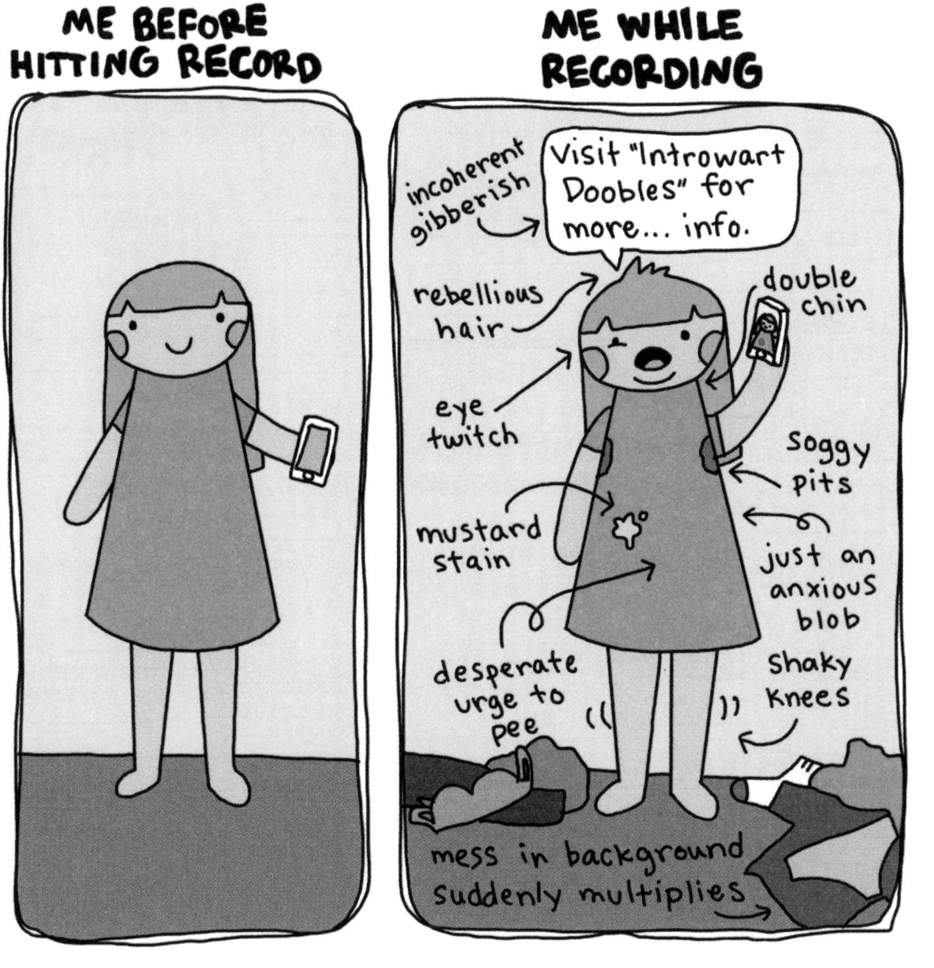
ME BEFORE HITTING RECORD
ME WHILE RECORDING
incoherent gibberish
Visit "Introwart Doobles" for more... info.
rebellious hair
double chin
eye twitch
soggy pits
mustard stain
just an anxious blob
desperate urge to pee
shaky knees
mess in background suddenly multiplies

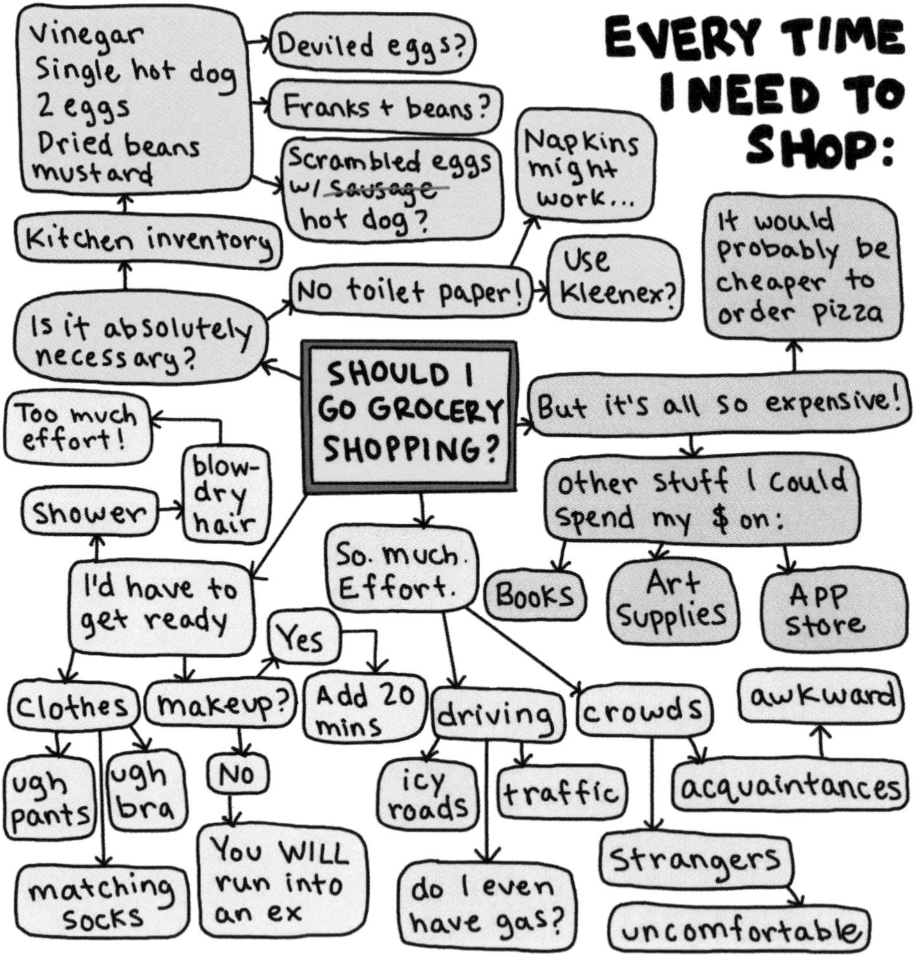
EVERY TIME I NEED TO SHOP:
SHOULD I GO GROCERY SHOPPING?
Is it absolutely necessary?
Kitchen inventory
Vinegar
Single hot dog
2 eggs
Dried beans
mustard
Deviled eggs?
Franks + beans?
Scrambled eggs w/ sausage hot dog?
No toilet paper!
Napkins might work...
Use Kleenex?
But it's all so expensive!
It would probably be cheaper to order pizza
other stuff I could spend my $ on:
Books
Art Supplies
App store
So. much. Effort.
driving
icy roads
traffic
do I even have gas?
crowds
acquaintances
awkward
Strangers
uncomfortable
I'd have to get ready
Shower
blow-dry hair
Too much effort!
Clothes
ugh pants
ugh bra
matching socks
makeup?
Yes
Add 20 mins
No
You WILL run into an ex

WHEN YOU DON'T WANT TO INCONVENIENCE ANYONE

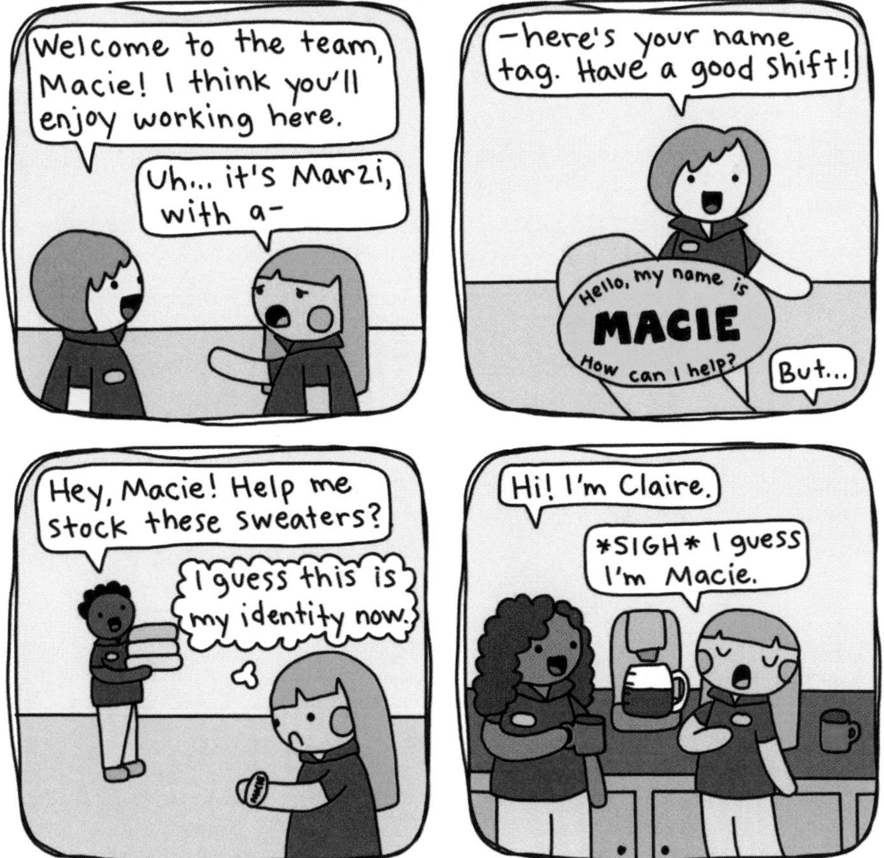
Welcome to the team, Macie! I think you'll enjoy working here.
Uh... it's Marzi, with a-
-here's your name tag. Have a good shift!
Hello, my name is
MACIE
How can I help?
But...
Hey, Macie! Help me stock these sweaters?
I guess this is my identity now.
Hi! I'm Claire.
SIGH I guess I'm Macie.

HOW I FEEL ABOUT SALES "PARTIES"

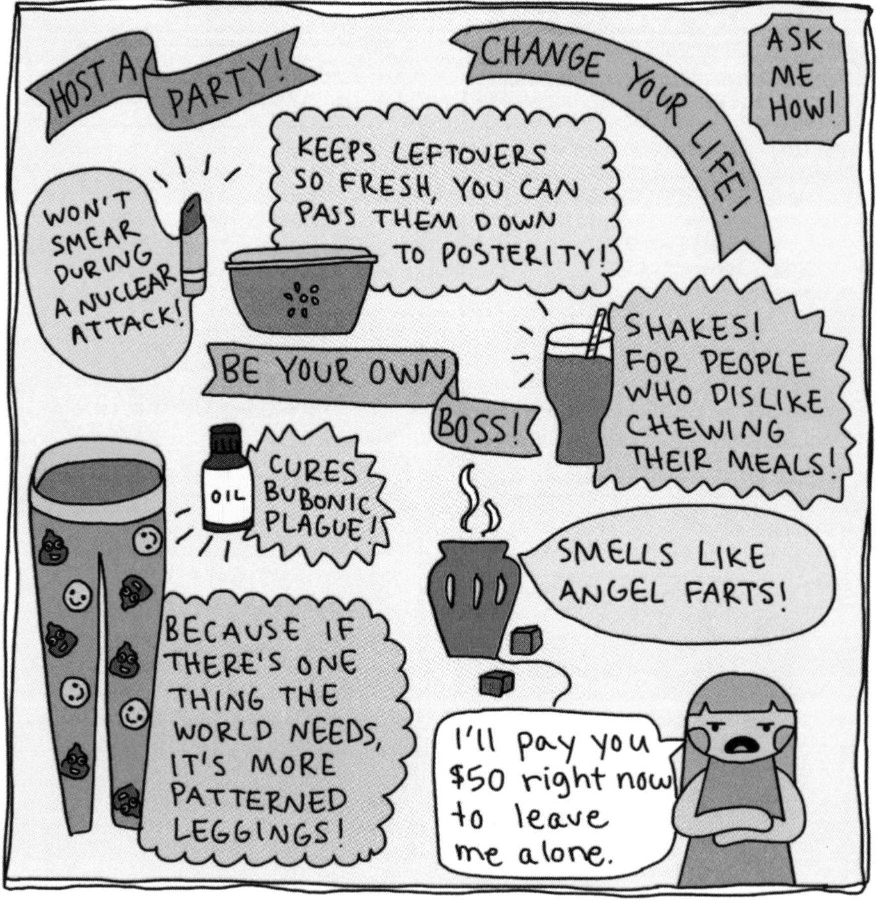
HOST A PARTY!
CHANGE YOUR LIFE!
ASK ME HOW!
KEEPS LEFTOVERS SO FRESH, YOU CAN PASS THEM DOWN TO POSTERITY!
WON'T SMEAR DURING A NUCLEAR ATTACK!
SHAKES! FOR PEOPLE WHO DISLIKE CHEWING THEIR MEALS!
BE YOUR OWN BOSS!
OIL
CURES BUBONIC PLAGUE!
SMELLS LIKE ANGEL FARTS!
BECAUSE IF THERE'S ONE THING THE WORLD NEEDS, IT'S MORE PATTERNED LEGGINGS!
I'll pay you $50 right now to leave me alone.

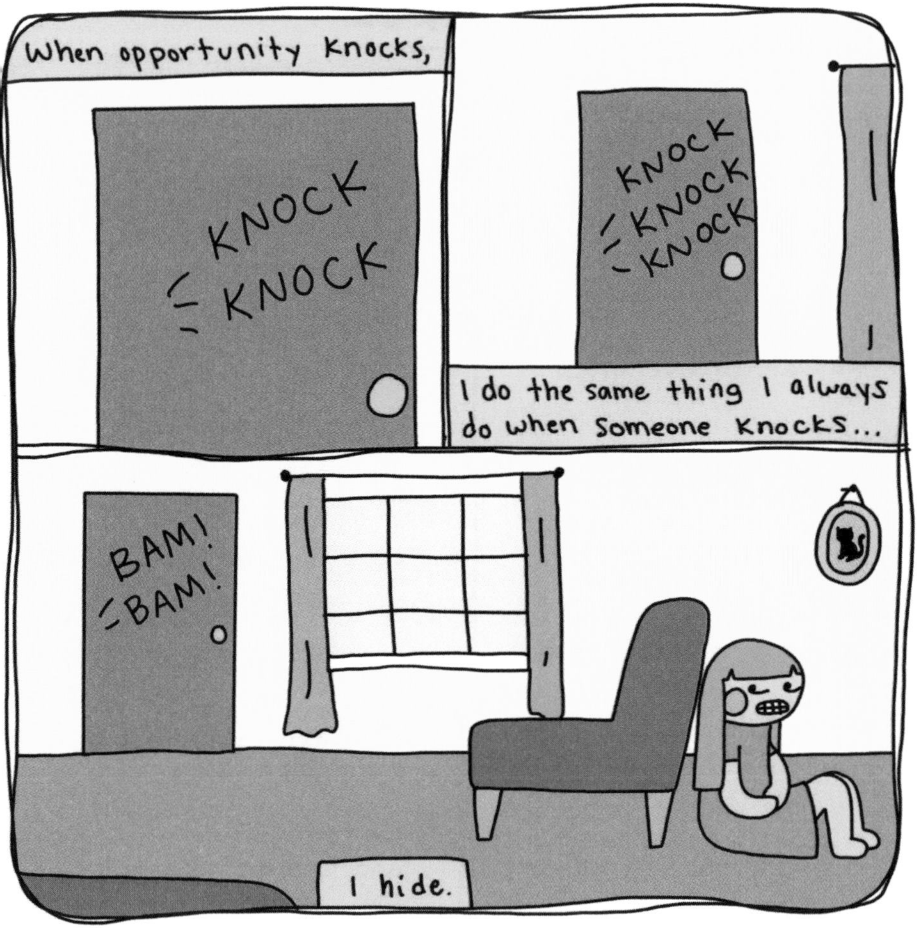
When opportunity knocks,
KNOCK
KNOCK
KNOCK
KNOCK
KNOCK
I do the same thing I always do when someone knocks...
BAM!
BAM!
I hide.

ADULTHOOD

PROS	CONS
* Driving 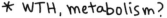	* Car payment 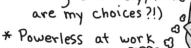
* Cake for breakfast	* WTH, metabolism?
* Voting ← sigh 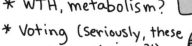	* Voting (seriously, these are my choices?!)
* Power over the remote	* Powerless at work
* Romantic evenings ← HA!	* Gynecologist (I'm wearing paper.)
* No school	* Student loans
* Staying up late	* What happened to naptime?
* Credit cards 	* Credit cards (what have I done?!)
* Away from parents	* Want my mommy
* Spending my money on whatever I want LOL →	* Taxes, rent, insurance, gas, utilities, groceries
* A fulfilling career and a bright future ← naïve	* A bottomless spiral of stress and despair that ends only in death

THINGS THAT ARE CURRENTLY BREAKING DOWN

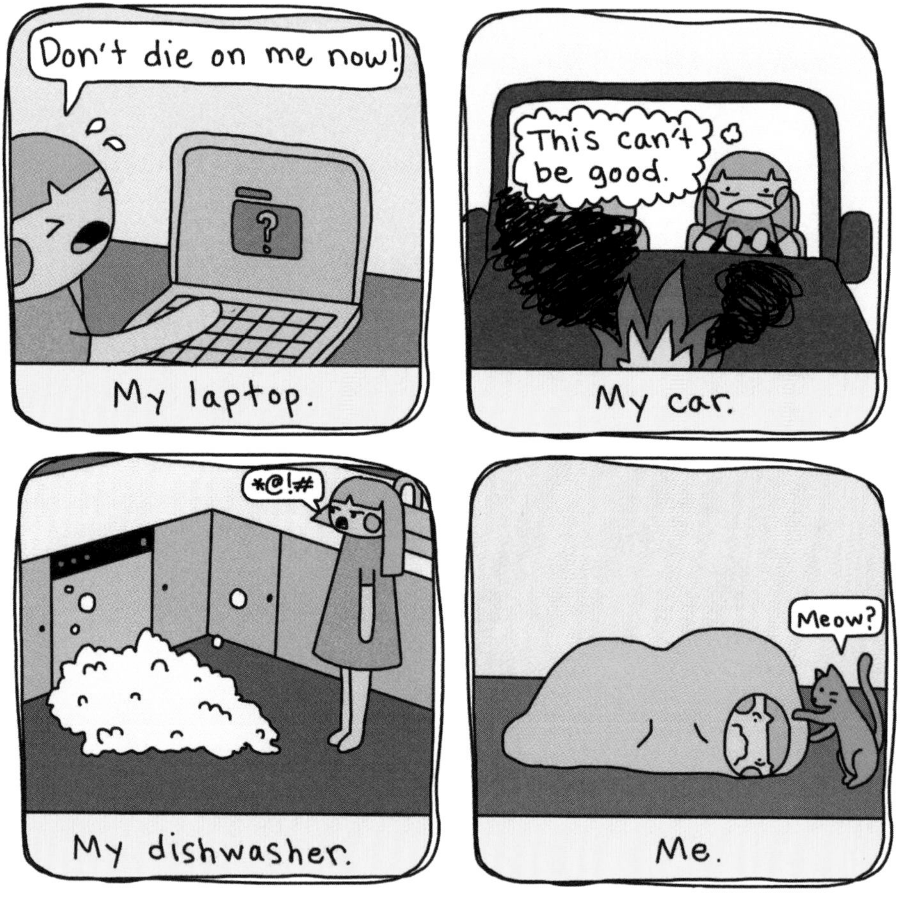
Don't die on me now!
My laptop.
This can't be good.
My car.
*@!#
My dishwasher.
Meow?
Me.

SET GOALS... BUT ADJUST AS NEEDED

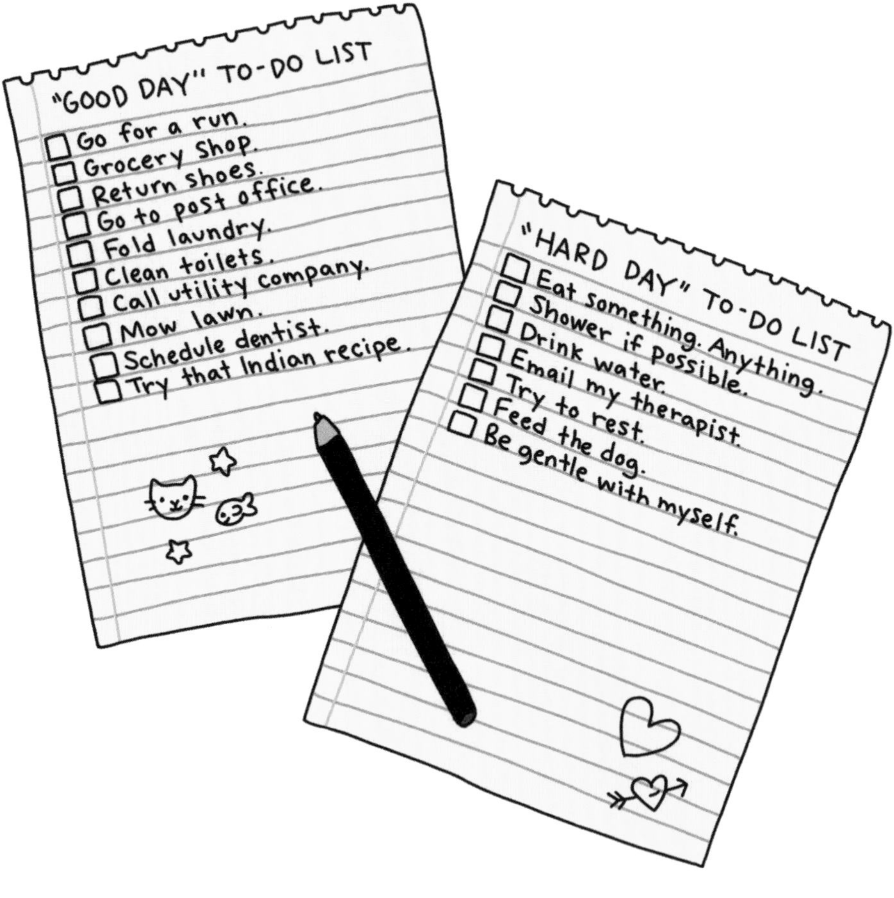

"GOOD DAY" TO-DO LIST
Go for a run.
Grocery Shop.
Return shoes.
Go to post office.
Fold laundry.
Clean toilets.
Call utility company.
Mow lawn.
Schedule dentist.
Try that Indian recipe.
"HARD DAY" TO-DO LIST
Eat something. Anything.
Shower if possible.
Drink water.
Email my therapist.
Try to rest.
Feed the dog.
Be gentle with myself.

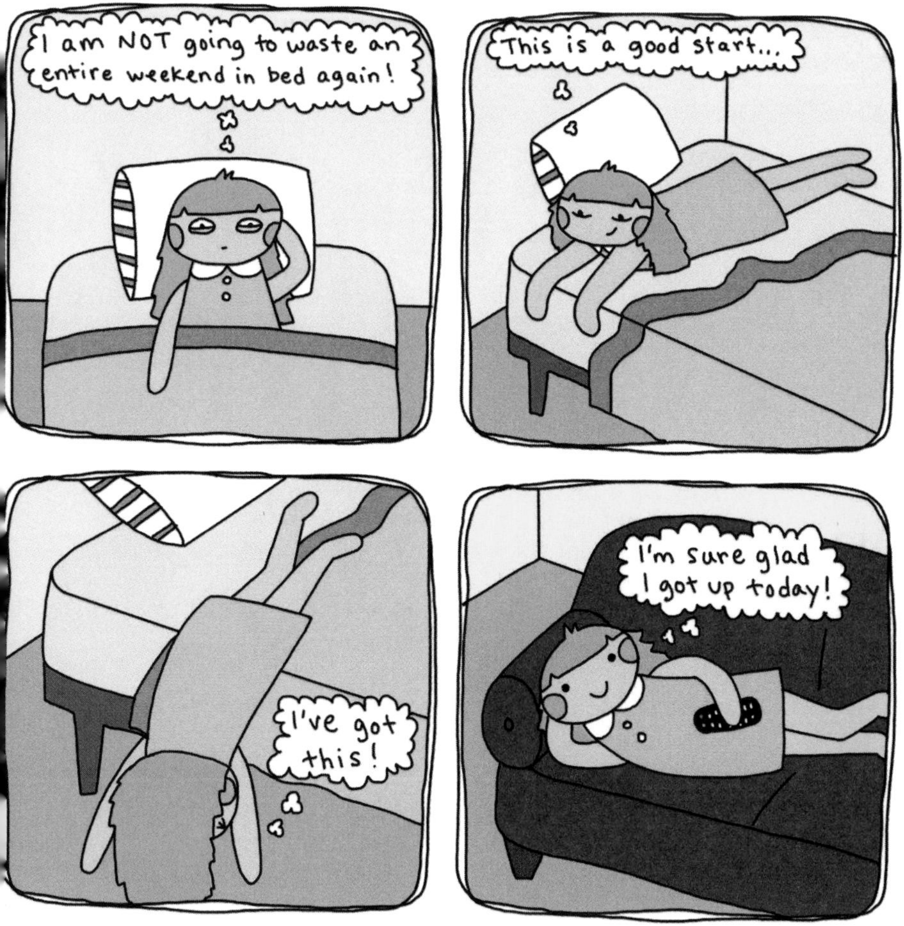
I am NOT going to waste an entire weekend in bed again!
This is a good start...
I've got this!
I'm sure glad I got up today!

OVERTHINK ALL THE THINGS

-when my brain misbehaves-

Anxiety, by its very nature, is irrational. I like to believe I'm a somewhat intelligent person. But when anxiety creeps in, logic goes out the window. My brain goes into overdrive, racing through hundreds of potential outcomes, most of them disastrous.

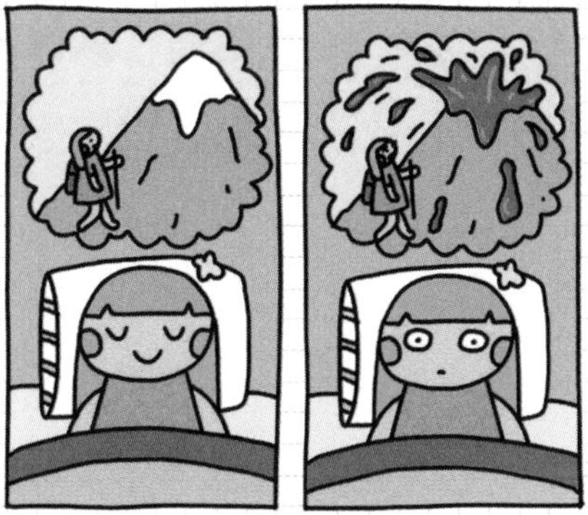

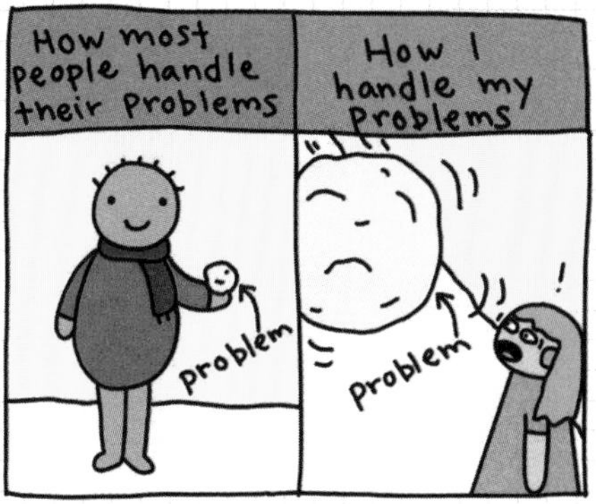
How most people handle their problems
problem
How I handle my problems
problem
!

Small problems snowball into seemingly insurmountable obstacles. Sometimes the fear is paralyzing; I don't dare make a move, because

WHAT IF I MAKE THE WRONG CHOICE?

Am I the only one who thinks this way, feels this way?

THE ANXIETY CYCLE

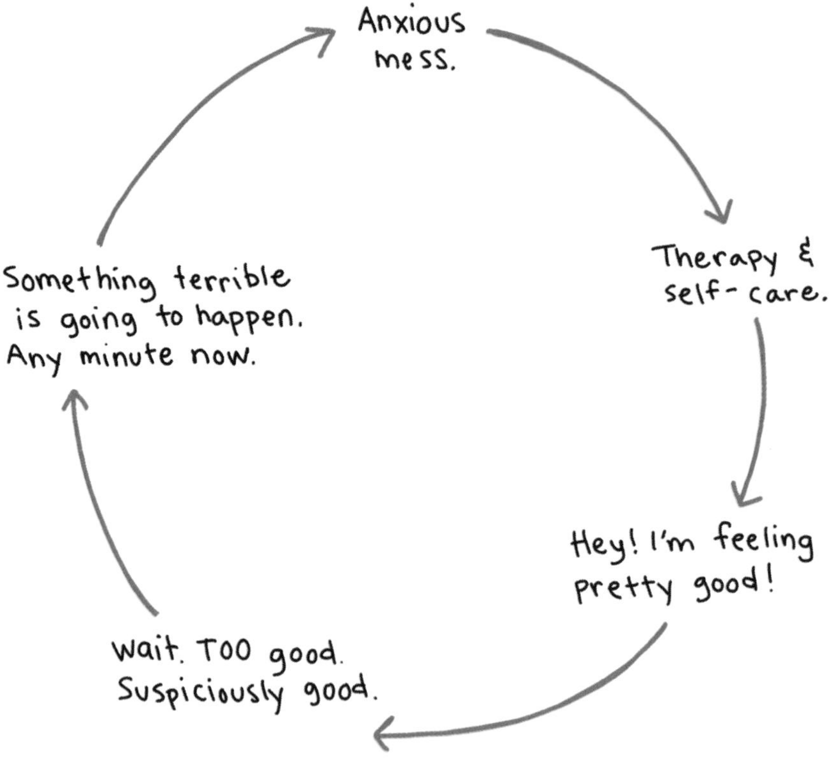
Anxious mess.
Therapy & self-care.
Hey! I'm feeling pretty good!
Wait. TOO good. Suspiciously good.
Something terrible is going to happen. Any minute now.

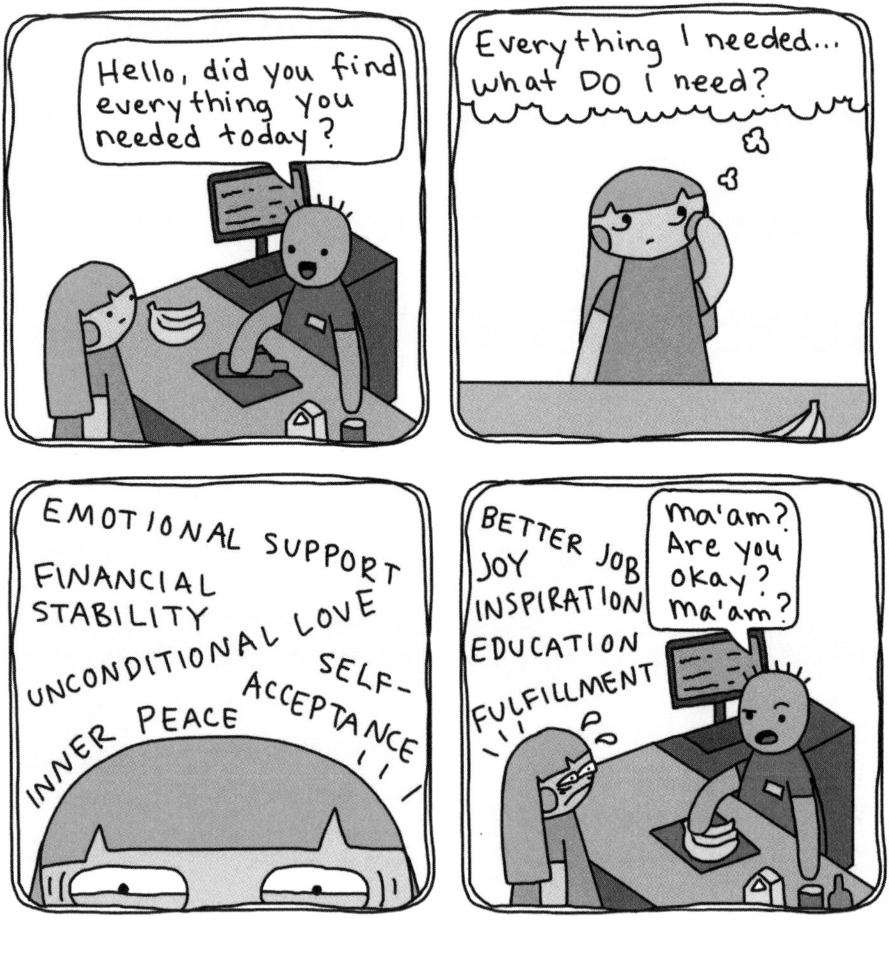
Hello, did you find everything you needed today?
Everything I needed... what DO I need?
EMOTIONAL SUPPORT
FINANCIAL STABILITY
UNCONDITIONAL LOVE
SELF-ACCEPTANCE
INNER PEACE
BETTER JOB
JOY
INSPIRATION
EDUCATION
FULFILLMENT
ma'am? Are you okay? ma'am?

POSSIBLE REASONS HE HASN'T REPLIED

1. He thinks I'm boring.

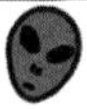

2. He was abducted by aliens.
3. He's taken a vow of silence that extends to texting.
4. I'm not worth his time.
5. He's mad at me.

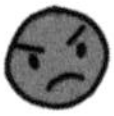

6. He's made new, cooler friends.
7. I said something offensive.
8. He's busy.
9. A software glitch is deleting all his replies.
10. He has amnesia and forgot we're friends.
11. He hates me.

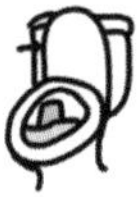

12. He dropped his phone in the toilet.
13. He's in the Witness Protection Program and is forbidden from communicating with former contacts.

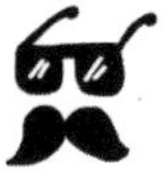

14. I'm not worth the emotional energy.

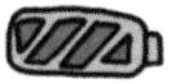

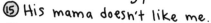

15. His mama doesn't like me.
16. He broke his fingers & thumbs and is physically incapable of texting.
17. He joined a cult.
18. I'm too negative & I'm killing his vibe.
19. He's fallen for someone & is too lovesick to think about anything else.

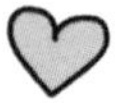

20. ~~He doesn't think my puns are funny.~~ IMPOSSIBLE!
21. A wizard cursed him with a Full-Body Bind spell.

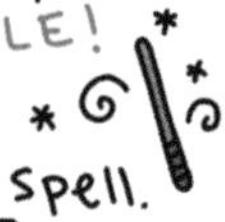

22. He ran away to join the circus.

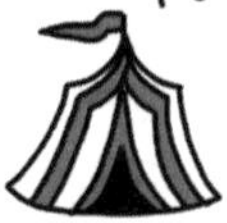

23. He knows I'm going through a hard time but doesn't know what to say.
24. He's dead.
OMG, HE'S DEAD!!

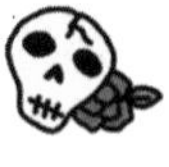

WHY TRAVEL MAKES ME ANXIOUS

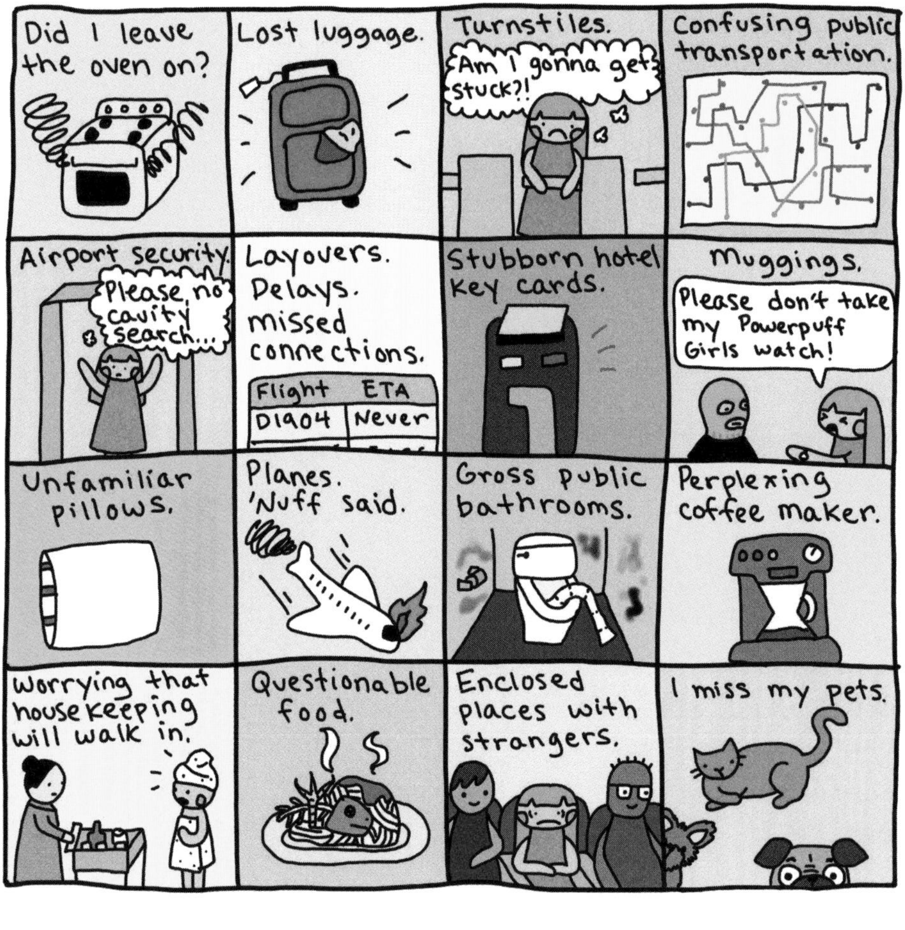
Did I leave the oven on?
Lost luggage.
Turnstiles.
Am I gonna get stuck?!
Confusing public transportation.
Airport security.
Please, no cavity search...
Layovers. Delays. missed connections.
Flight ETA
D1904 Never
Stubborn hotel key cards.
Muggings.
Please don't take my Powerpuff Girls watch!
Unfamiliar pillows.
Planes. 'Nuff said.
Gross public bathrooms.
Perplexing coffee maker.
Worrying that housekeeping will walk in.
Questionable food.
Enclosed places with strangers.
I miss my pets.

THOUGHTS I HAVE AT THE BANK

Don't make a joke about robbery, don't make a joke about robbery— "Hey, what's the HOLD-UP?"

Do I look suspicious? Maybe I shouldn't have worn a hat & sunglasses.

It's so hushed in here... Should I whisper?

Why is this line so long?

Can the teller see my transaction history? I can explain!

I would have gone through the drive-thru, but the vacuum tubes kinda freak me out.

I'm not sure I know what to do in the event of a bank robbery.

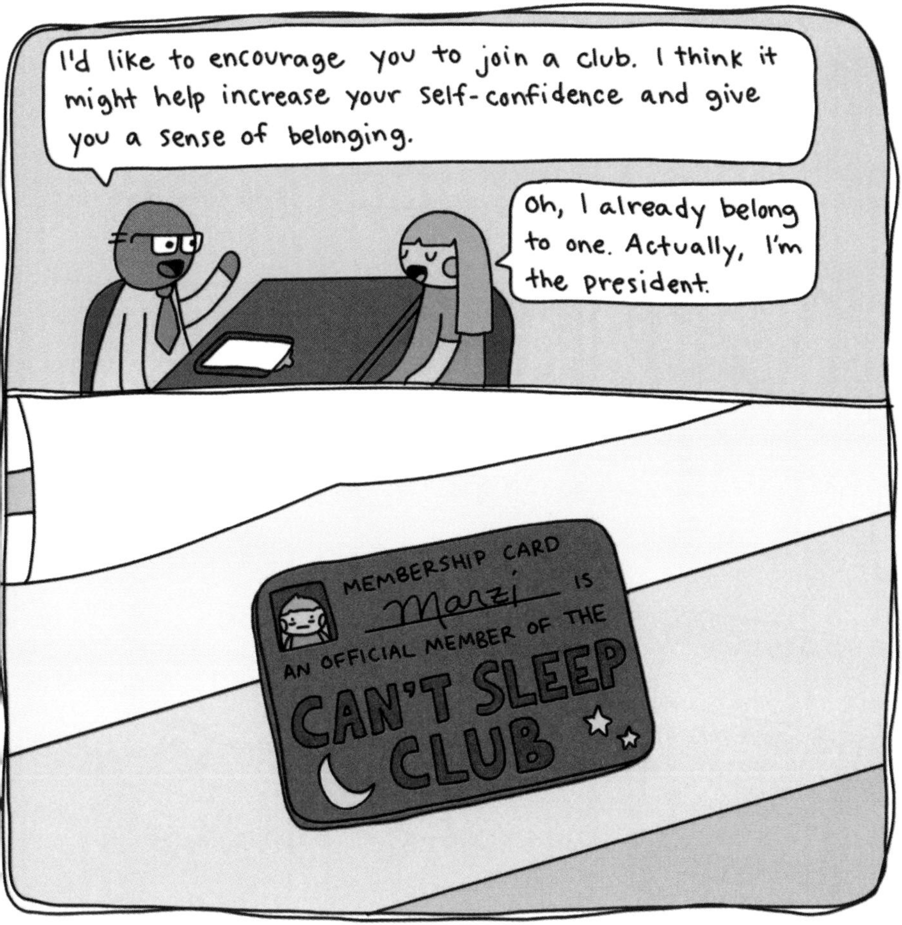
I'd like to encourage you to join a club. I think it might help increase your self-confidence and give you a sense of belonging.
Oh, I already belong to one. Actually, I'm the president.
MEMBERSHIP CARD
Marzi IS
AN OFFICIAL MEMBER OF THE
CAN'T SLEEP CLUB

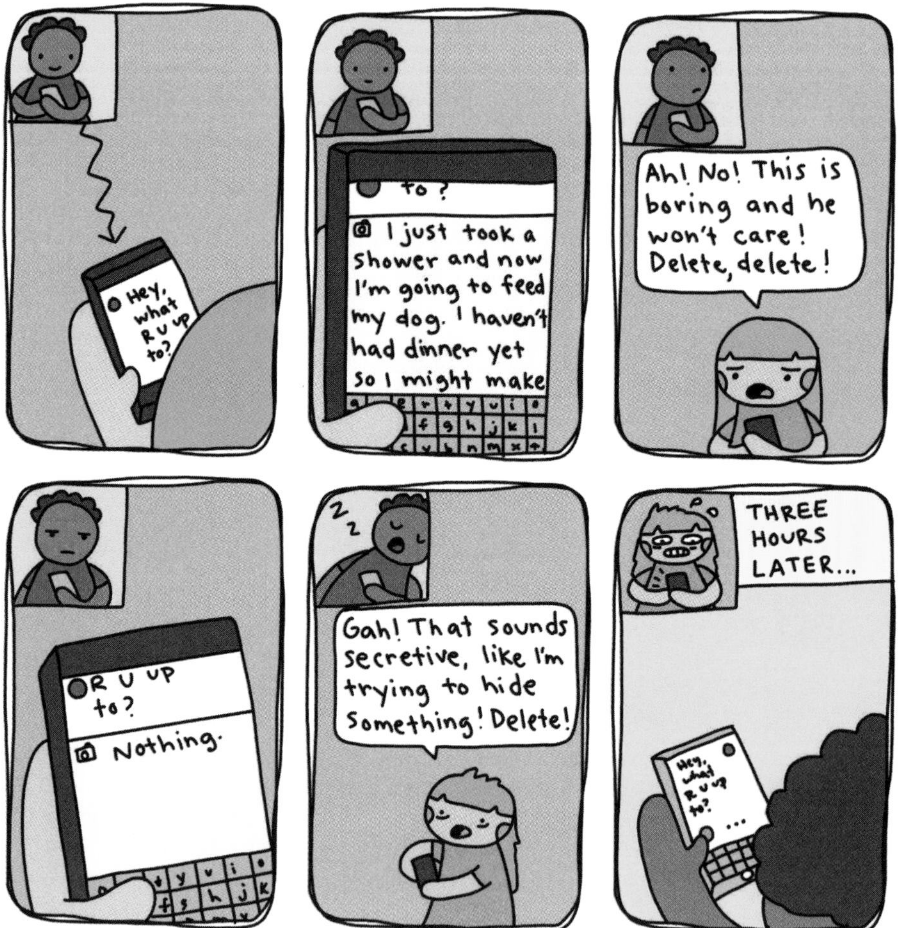
Hey, what R U up to?
to ?
I just took a shower and now I'm going to feed my dog. I haven't had dinner yet so I might make
Ah! No! This is boring and he won't care! Delete, delete!
R U up to?
Nothing.
Z Z
Gah! That sounds secretive, like I'm trying to hide Something! Delete!
THREE HOURS LATER...
Hey, what R U up to?
...

ANXIOUS BUS THOUGHTS

why doesn't this seat have a functional seatbelt? Is this even legal?!

Please don't sit by me...

How can I be sure I'm actually on the right bus?

Please, please, please don't sit by me!!!

Is there a bathroom on this bus? Is it clean? Does the door lock? will people be able to hear me go?

Oh! A pregnant lady! Should I offer my seat? But wait, what if she's just curvy, and I insult her...?

Please don't sit by me...

Please don't sit by me!

Will people be less likely to sit by me if I pick an aisle seat?

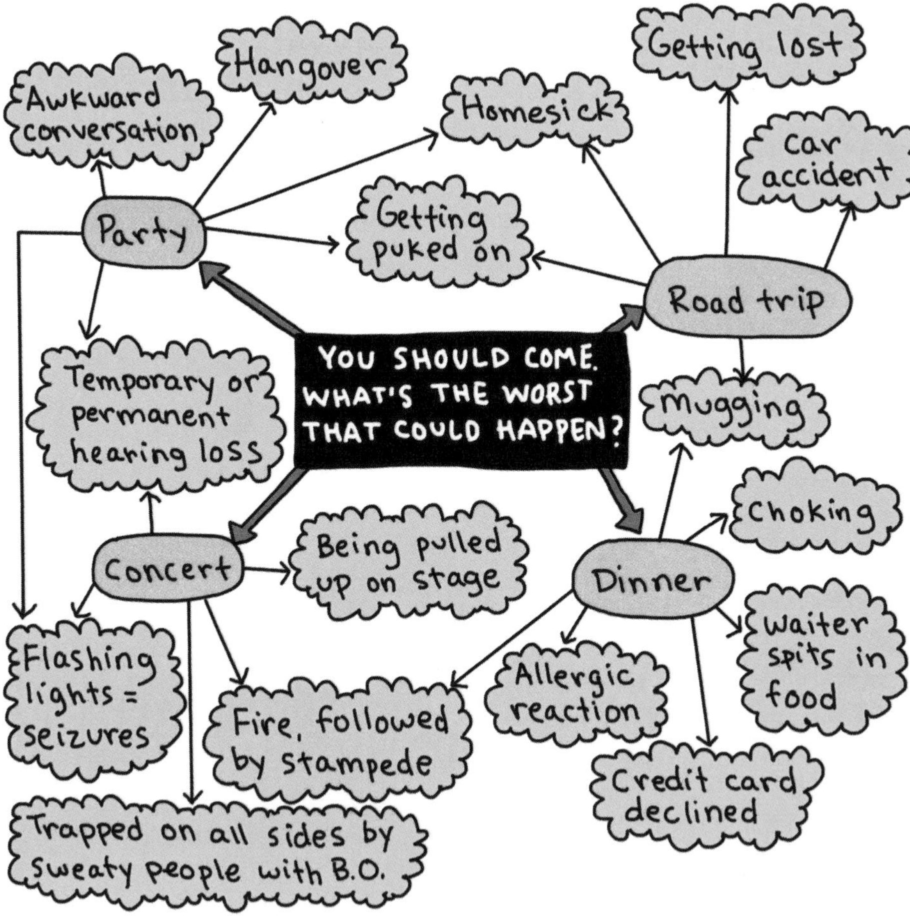
YOU SHOULD COME. WHAT'S THE WORST THAT COULD HAPPEN?
Party
Awkward conversation
Hangover
Homesick
Getting puked on
Temporary or permanent hearing loss
Flashing lights = seizures
Road trip
Getting lost
Car accident
Mugging
Concert
Being pulled up on stage
Fire, followed by stampede
Trapped on all sides by sweaty people with B.O.
Dinner
Choking
Waiter spits in food
Allergic reaction
Credit card declined

WHEN YOU'RE AN ANXIOUS GIFTER

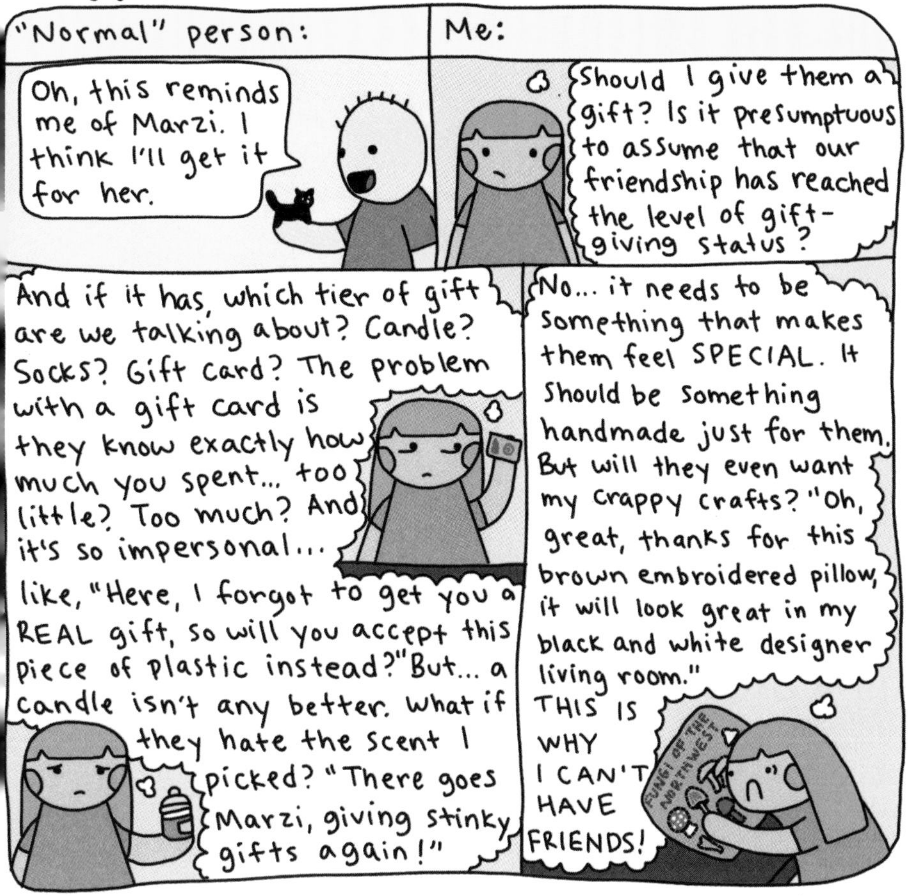
"Normal" person:
Me:
Oh, this reminds me of Marzi. I think I'll get it for her.
Should I give them a gift? Is it presumptuous to assume that our friendship has reached the level of gift-giving status?
And if it has, which tier of gift are we talking about? Candle? Socks? Gift card? The problem with a gift card is they know exactly how much you spent... too little? Too much? And it's so impersonal...
like, "Here, I forgot to get you a REAL gift, so will you accept this piece of plastic instead?" But... a candle isn't any better. What if they hate the scent I picked? "There goes Marzi, giving stinky gifts again!"
No... it needs to be something that makes them feel SPECIAL. It should be something handmade just for them. But will they even want my crappy crafts? "Oh, great, thanks for this brown embroidered pillow, it will look great in my black and white designer living room."
THIS IS WHY I CAN'T HAVE FRIENDS!
FUNGI OF THE NORTHWEST

GYM THOUGHTS

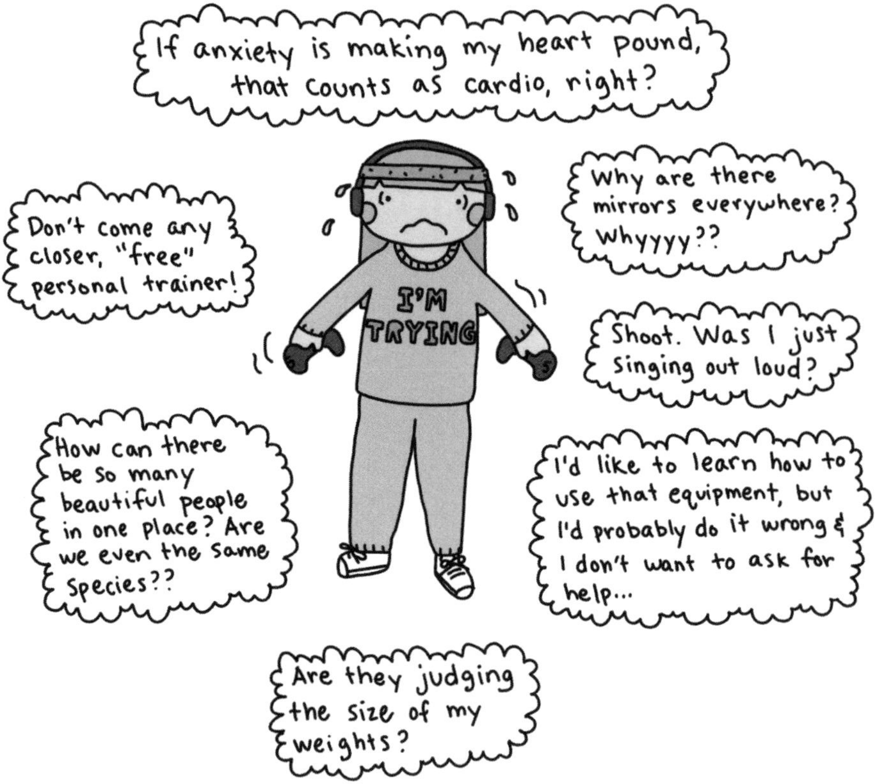
If anxiety is making my heart pound, that counts as cardio, right?
Don't come any closer, "free" personal trainer!
Why are there mirrors everywhere? Whyyyy??
I'M TRYING
Shoot. Was I just singing out loud?
How can there be so many beautiful people in one place? Are we even the same species??
I'd like to learn how to use that equipment, but I'd probably do it wrong & I don't want to ask for help...
Are they judging the size of my weights?

AT THE MOVIE THEATER

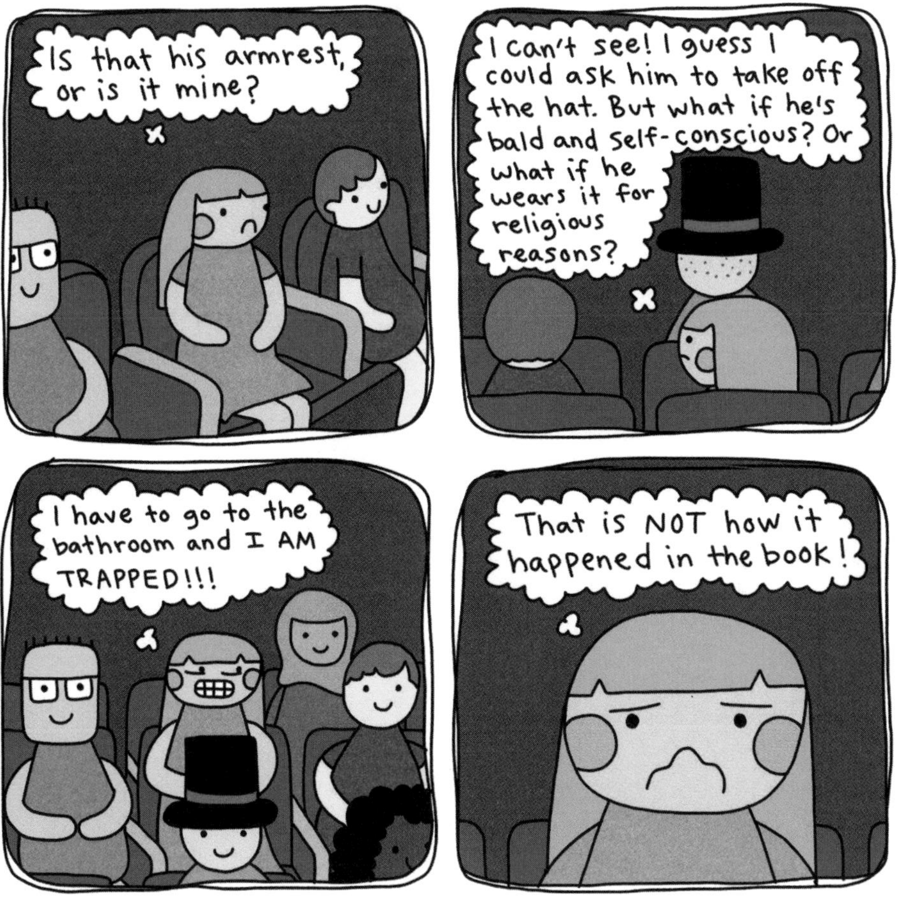
Is that his armrest, or is it mine?
I can't see! I guess I could ask him to take off the hat. But what if he's bald and self-conscious? Or what if he wears it for religious reasons?
I have to go to the bathroom and I AM TRAPPED!!!
That is NOT how it happened in the book!

WHEN A REPAIRMAN COMES

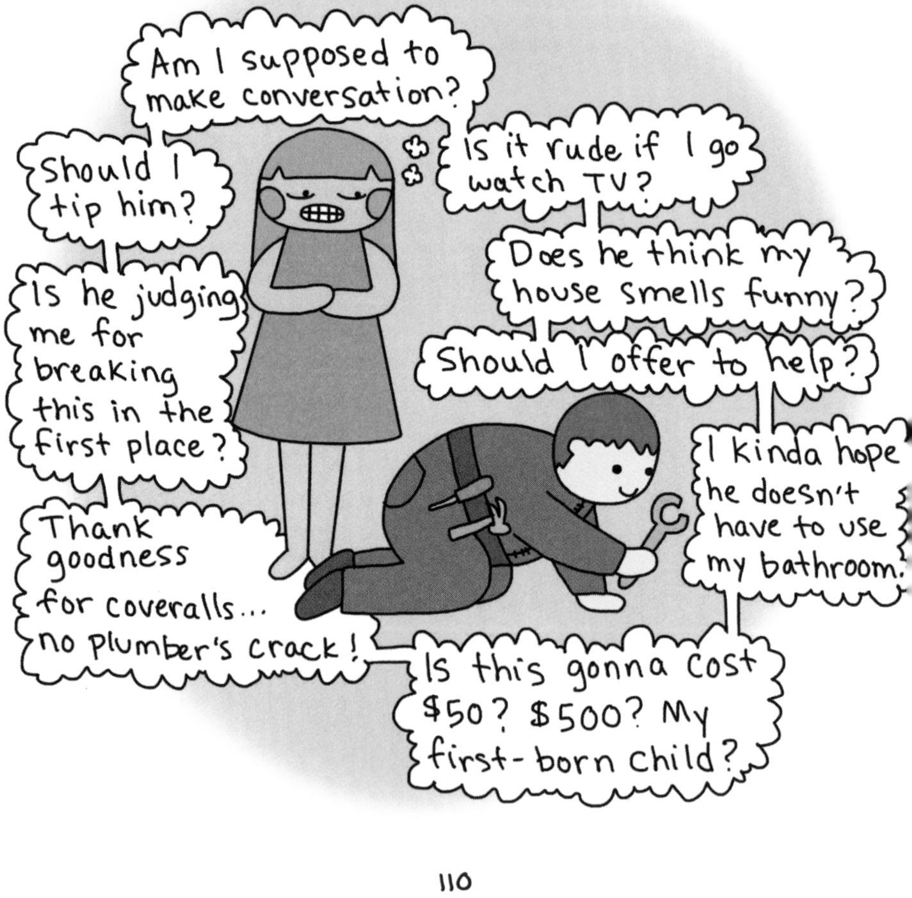
Am I supposed to make conversation?
Should I tip him?
Is it rude if I go watch TV?
Does he think my house smells funny?
Is he judging me for breaking this in the first place?
Should I offer to help?
I kinda hope he doesn't have to use my bathroom.
Thank goodness for coveralls... no plumber's crack!
Is this gonna cost $50? $500? My first-born child?

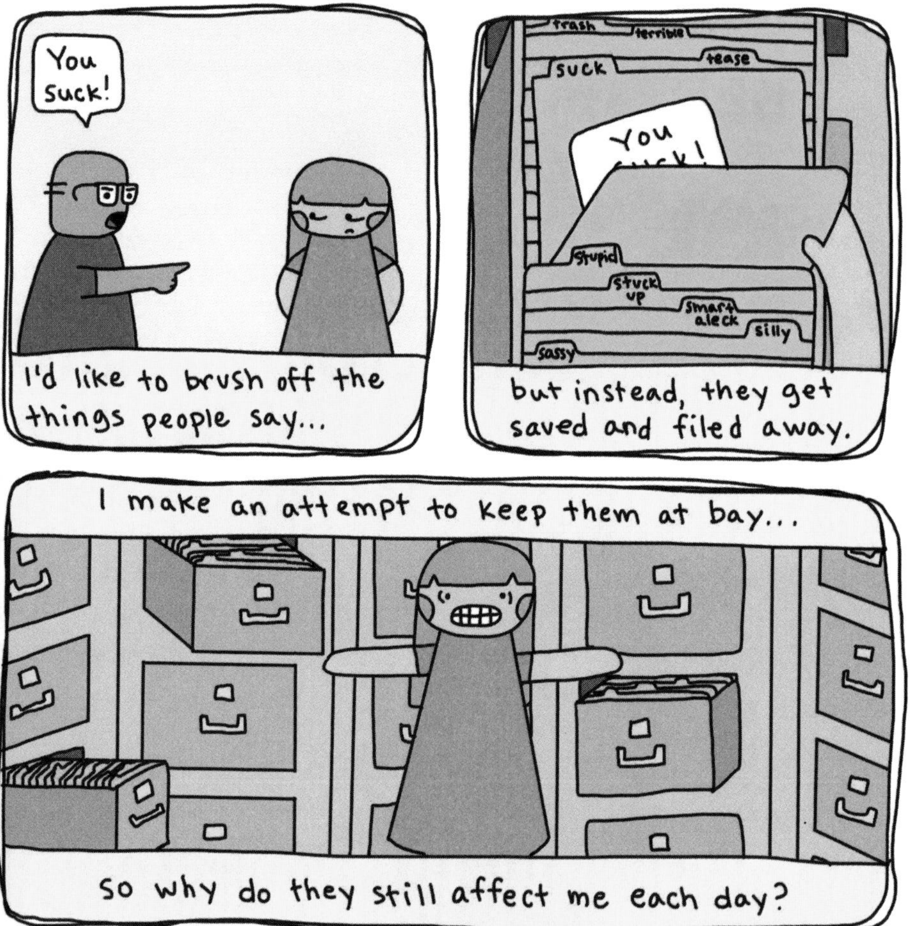
You suck!
I'd like to brush off the things people say...
trash
terrible
suck
tease
You
stupid
stuck up
smart aleck
silly
sassy
but instead, they get saved and filed away.
I make an attempt to keep them at bay...
So why do they still affect me each day?

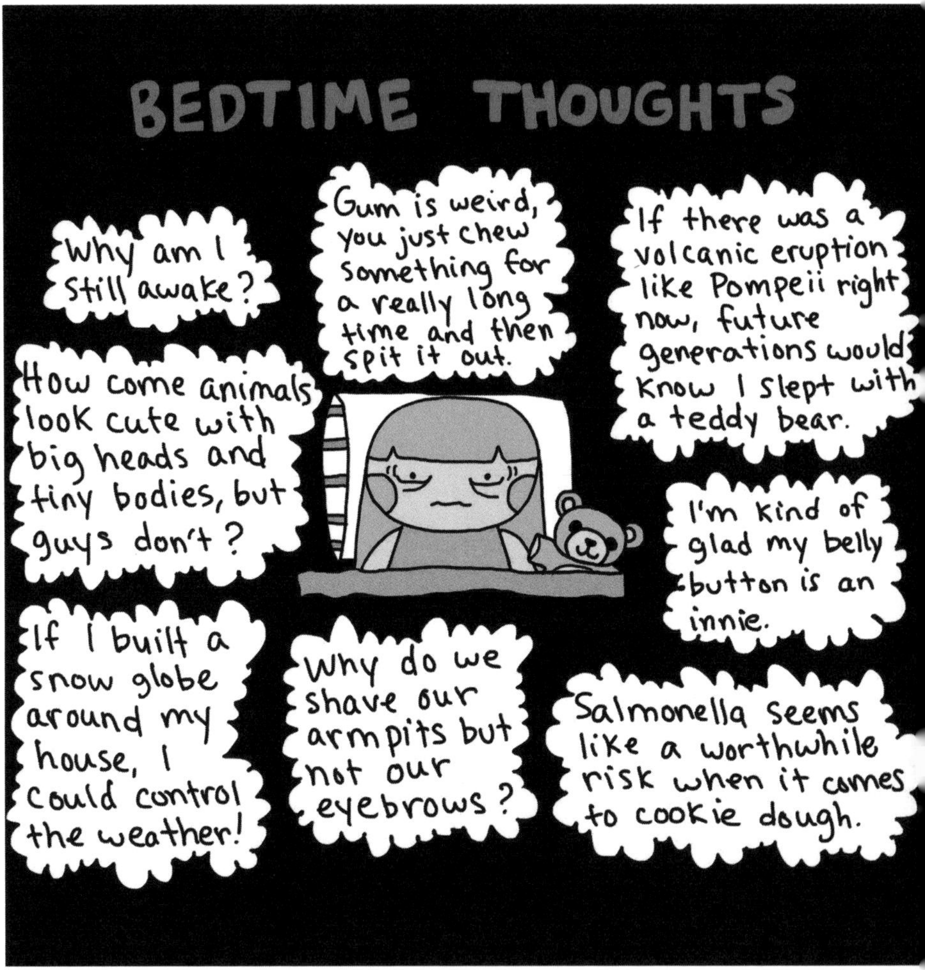
BEDTIME THOUGHTS
Why am I still awake?
Gum is weird, you just chew something for a really long time and then spit it out.
If there was a volcanic eruption like Pompeii right now, future generations would know I slept with a teddy bear.
How come animals look cute with big heads and tiny bodies, but guys don't?
I'm kind of glad my belly button is an innie.
If I built a snow globe around my house, I could control the weather!
Why do we shave our armpits but not our eyebrows?
Salmonella seems like a worthwhile risk when it comes to cookie dough.

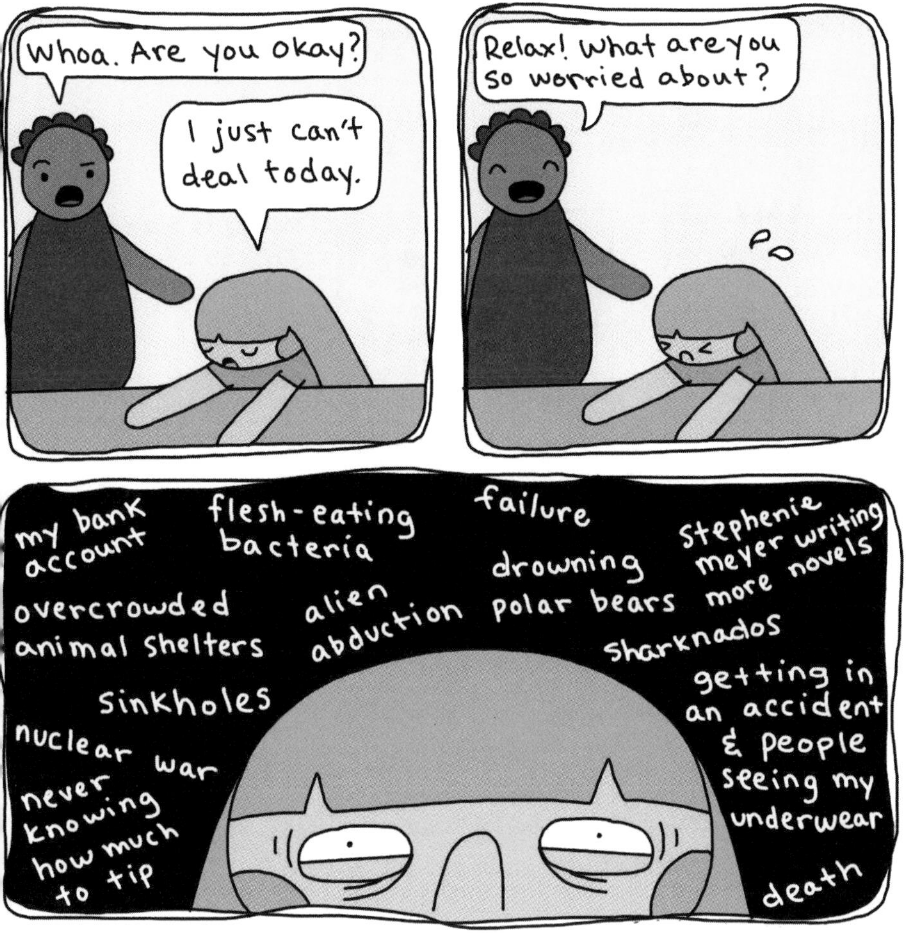
Whoa. Are you okay?
I just can't deal today.
Relax! What are you so worried about?
my bank account
flesh-eating bacteria
failure
stephenie meyer writing more novels
drowning
overcrowded animal shelters
alien abduction
polar bears
sharknados
sinkholes
getting in an accident & people seeing my underwear
nuclear war
never knowing how much to tip
death

ELEVATOR THOUGHTS

Just think of this like a fair ride. It will be fun!

Why is the door so slow? Close already!

What if it gets stuck? Is there adequate ventilation?

Wait. This is NOT a ride! This is a COFFIN!

I hope that red call button isn't just decorative.

Too many people! What's the weight capacity in here?

Please don't talk to me...

But the silence is so awkward!

Somebody smells.

OMG, is it ME? Do I smell?

Why is the door so slow? Open already!

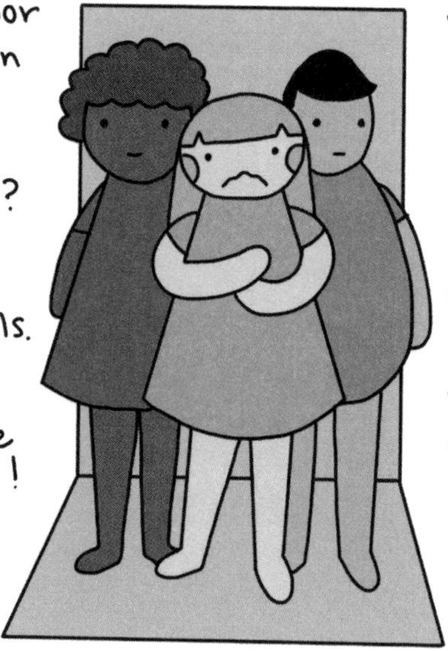

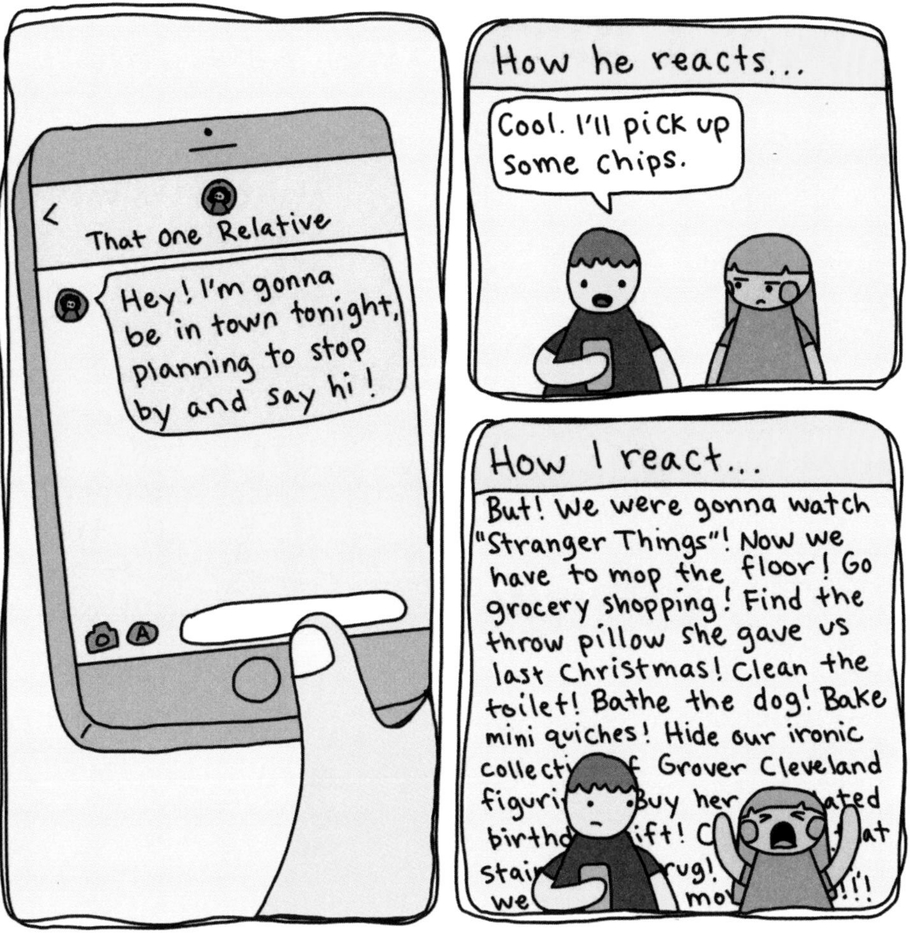

That One Relative
Hey! I'm gonna be in town tonight, planning to stop by and say hi!
How he reacts...
Cool. I'll pick up some chips.
How I react...
But! We were gonna watch "Stranger Things"! Now we have to mop the floor! Go grocery shopping! Find the throw pillow she gave us last Christmas! Clean the toilet! Bathe the dog! Bake mini quiches! Hide our ironic
Grover Cleveland
Buy her
rug!

WHY I HATE THE CAR WASH

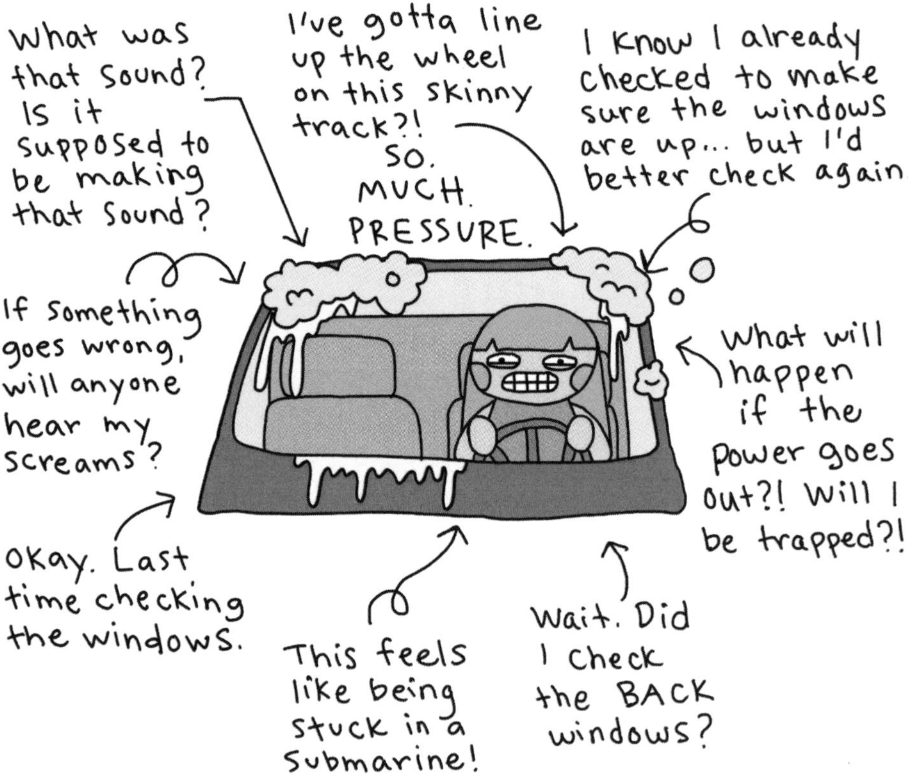
What was that sound? Is it supposed to be making that sound?
I've gotta line up the wheel on this skinny track?! SO. MUCH. PRESSURE.
I know I already checked to make sure the windows are up... but I'd better check again.
If something goes wrong, will anyone hear my screams?
What will happen if the power goes out?! Will I be trapped?!
Okay. Last time checking the windows.
This feels like being stuck in a submarine!
Wait. Did I check the BACK windows?

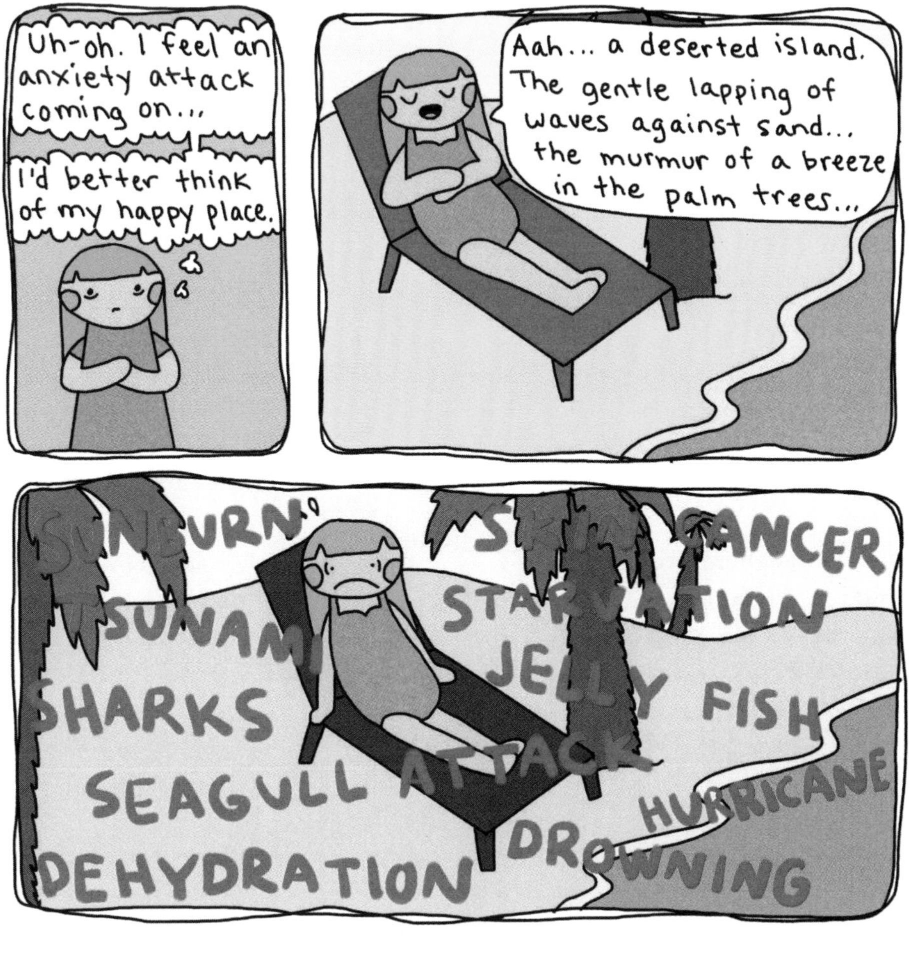
Uh-oh. I feel an anxiety attack coming on...
I'd better think of my happy place.
Aah... a deserted island. The gentle lapping of waves against sand... the murmur of a breeze in the palm trees...
SUNBURN
SKIN CANCER
TSUNAMI
STARVATION
SHARKS
JELLY FISH
SEAGULL ATTACK
HURRICANE
DROWNING
DEHYDRATION

WHEN I HAVE TO FLY

will they search my suitcase? My handbag? My orifices?

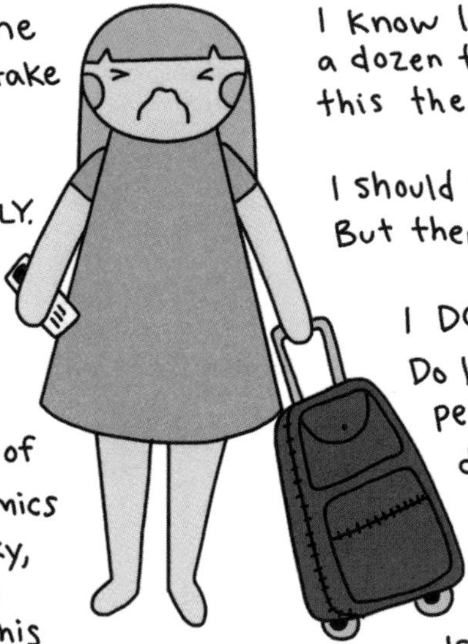

If I die in a plane crash, who will take care of my dog?

I know I already checked a dozen times, but... is this the right gate?

I have to pee SO BADLY. I can hold it for 3 hours, 22 minutes, right?

I should stay hydrated. But then I'll have to pee.

I DO have to pee. Do I have time to pee? What will I do with my carry-on suitcase?

My comprehension of physics & aerodynamics may be a bit shaky, but... I really don't understand how this plane could possibly stay airborne.

Why is stuffing my bag in the overhead bin so DIFFICULT? Are my armpits wet?

Is it acceptable to ask to see the pilot's credentials?

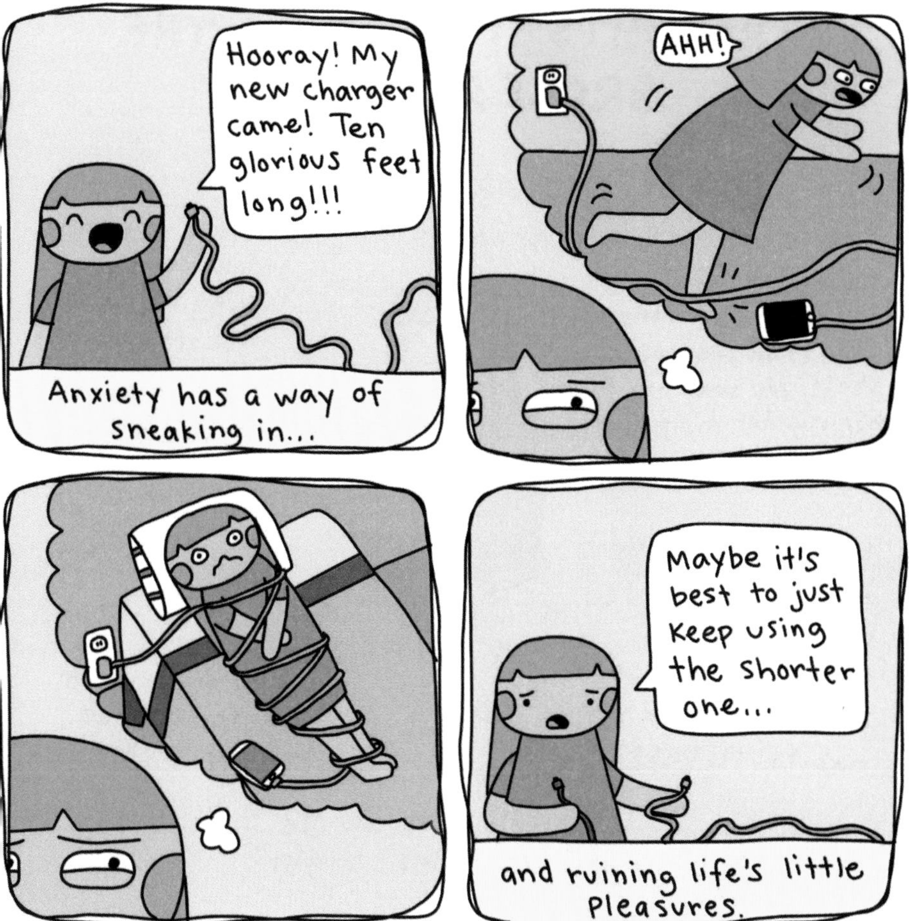
Hooray! My new charger came! Ten glorious feet long!!!
Anxiety has a way of sneaking in...
AHH!
Maybe it's best to just keep using the shorter one...
and ruining life's little pleasures.

THOUGHTS I HAVE AT THE GROCERY STORE

why are the lights so bright? Why is it so crowded?

Will the cashier judge me for buying an XL Snickers bar?

I can't reach the cereal on the top shelf. No way am I asking for help. Curse my stubby legs!

There's someone I know! Have I been spotted? Is there still time to hide?

Loyalty program? As in, I'm supposed to give you my phone number so you can track my habits? I'll pass.

Am I too old to ask for a free bakery cookie?

Definitely not too old for Lunchables... right?

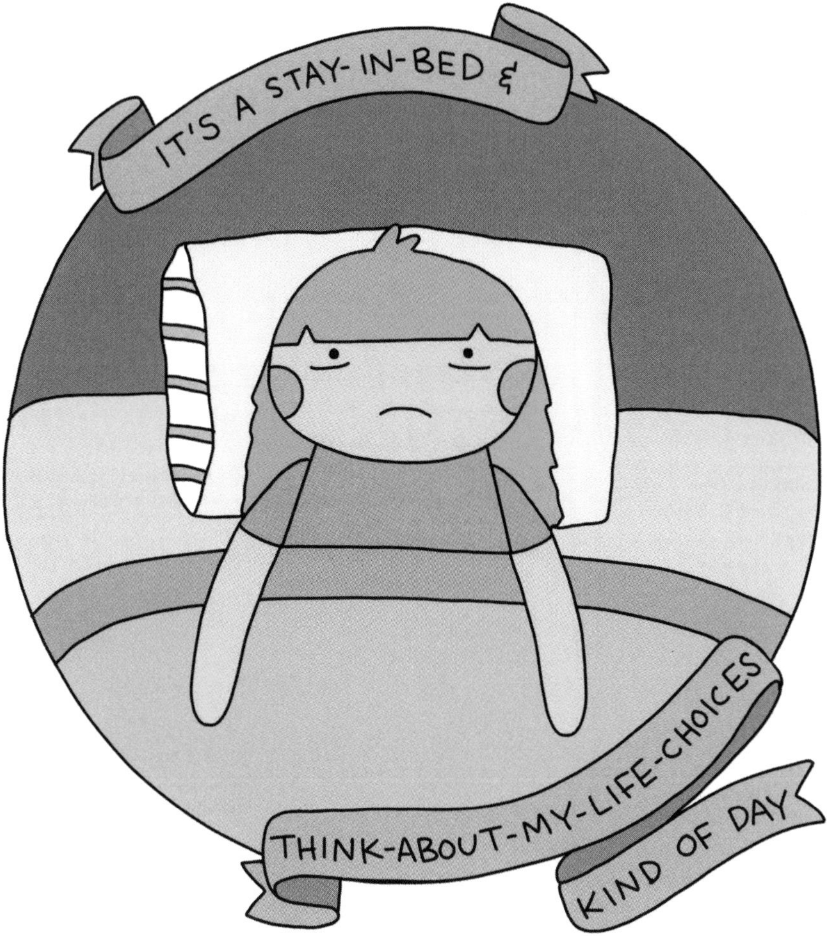
IT'S A STAY-IN-BED &
THINK-ABOUT-MY-LIFE-CHOICES
KIND OF DAY

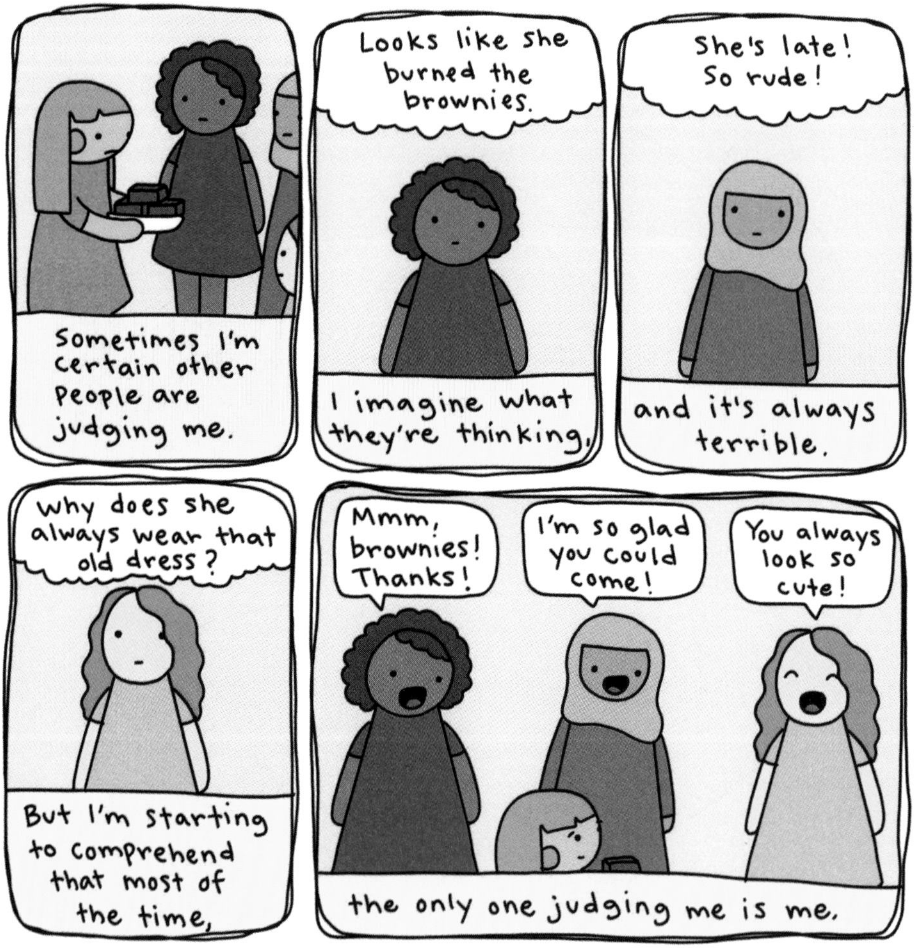

Sometimes I'm certain other people are judging me.
Looks like she burned the brownies.
I imagine what they're thinking,
She's late! So rude!
and it's always terrible.
Why does she always wear that old dress?
But I'm starting to comprehend that most of the time,
Mmm, brownies! Thanks!
I'm so glad you could come!
You always look so cute!
the only one judging me is me.

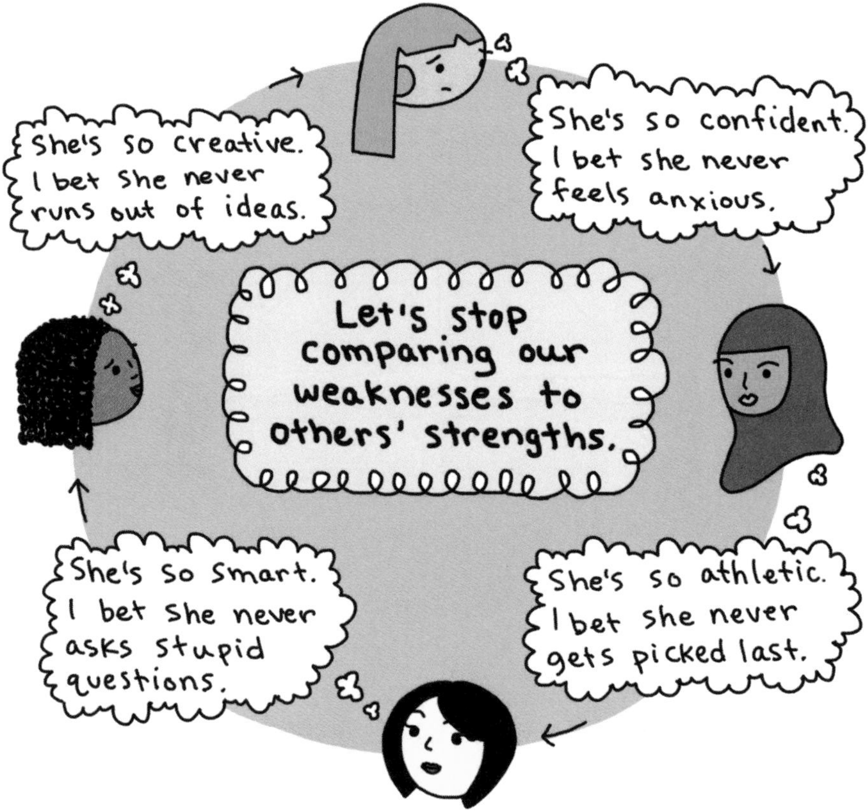
She's so creative. I bet she never runs out of ideas.
She's so confident. I bet she never feels anxious.
She's so athletic. I bet she never gets picked last.
She's so smart. I bet she never asks stupid questions.
Let's stop comparing our weaknesses to others' strengths.

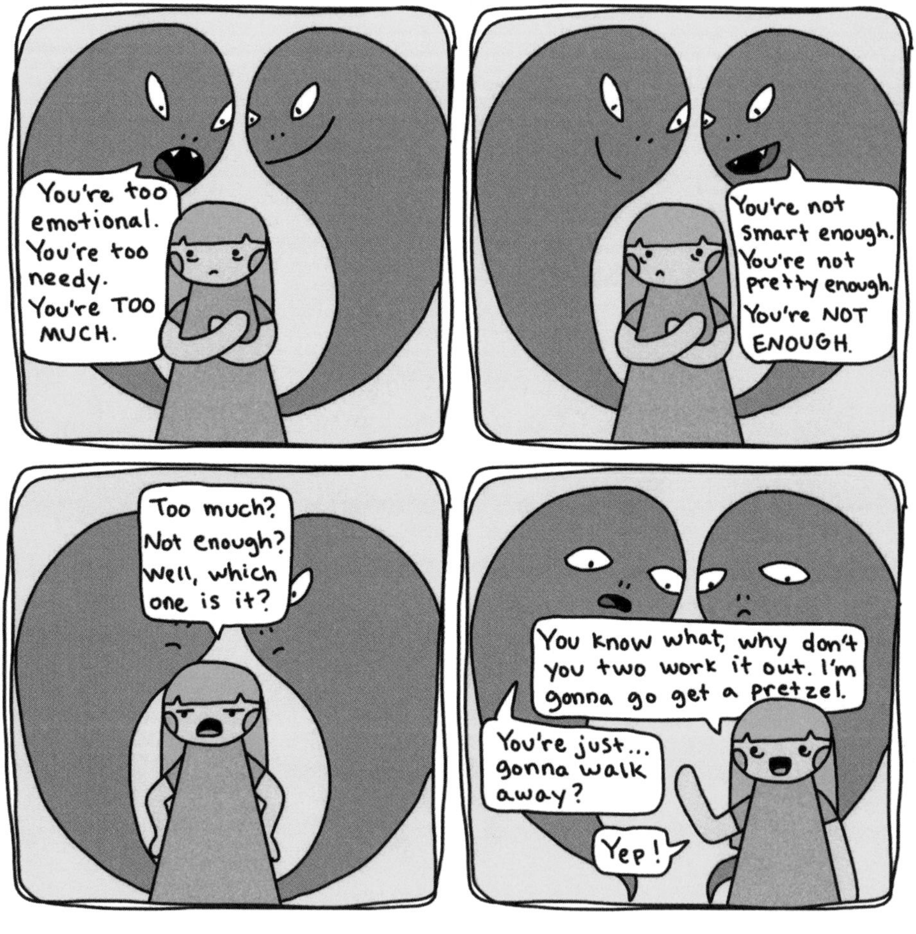
You're too emotional. You're too needy. You're TOO MUCH.
You're not smart enough. You're not pretty enough. You're NOT ENOUGH.
Too much? Not enough? Well, which one is it?
You know what, why don't you two work it out. I'm gonna go get a pretzel.
You're just... gonna walk away?
Yep!

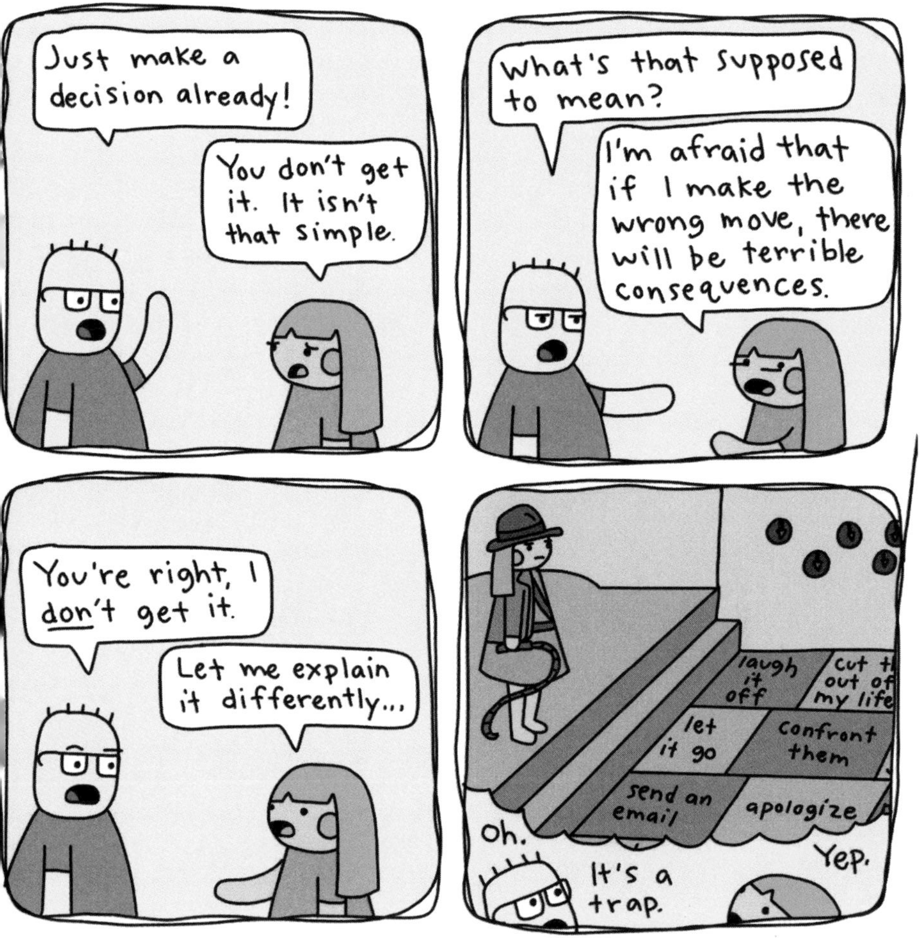
Just make a decision already!
You don't get it. It isn't that simple.
What's that supposed to mean?
I'm afraid that if I make the wrong move, there will be terrible consequences.
You're right, I don't get it.
Let me explain it differently...
laugh it off
cut out of my life
let it go
confront them
send an email
apologize
Oh.
It's a trap.
Yep.

A LITTLE HELP?

-recognizing the need for support-

Although I'm a very introverted person, I've come to realize that I still need a support team to help me manage my anxiety in a healthy way. There have been times when people close to me haven't said or done helpful things, but I know they care about me and mean well. So it's important for me to help them understand how to help me. It's okay for me to ask for the things I need.

MY SUPPORT TEAM

doctor

therapist

friend

My support team includes my therapist. I've stayed flexible in my approach to therapy: at times I've had multiple therapists at once, attended group therapy, or engaged in online therapy sessions. Sometimes it's hard work, other times it's a lifeline. I stick with it because I see progress.

I don't expect my support team to cure me, but with their help, I'm figuring out how to cope.

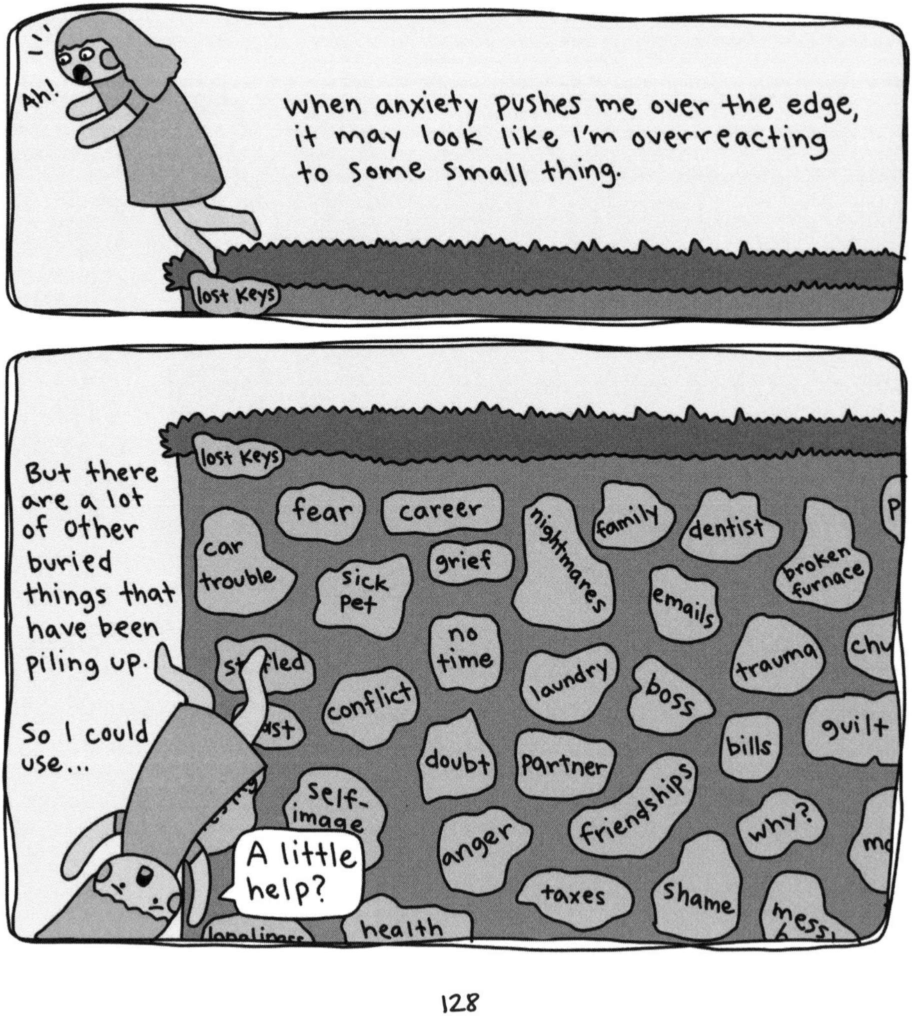
Ah!
When anxiety pushes me over the edge, it may look like I'm overreacting to some small thing.
lost keys
But there are a lot of other buried things that have been piling up.
lost keys
fear
career
nightmares
family
dentist
car trouble
sick pet
grief
broken furnace
emails
no time
trauma
laundry
conflict
boss
guilt
bills
doubt
partner
self-image
friendships
why?
anger
taxes
shame
health
So I could use...
A little help?

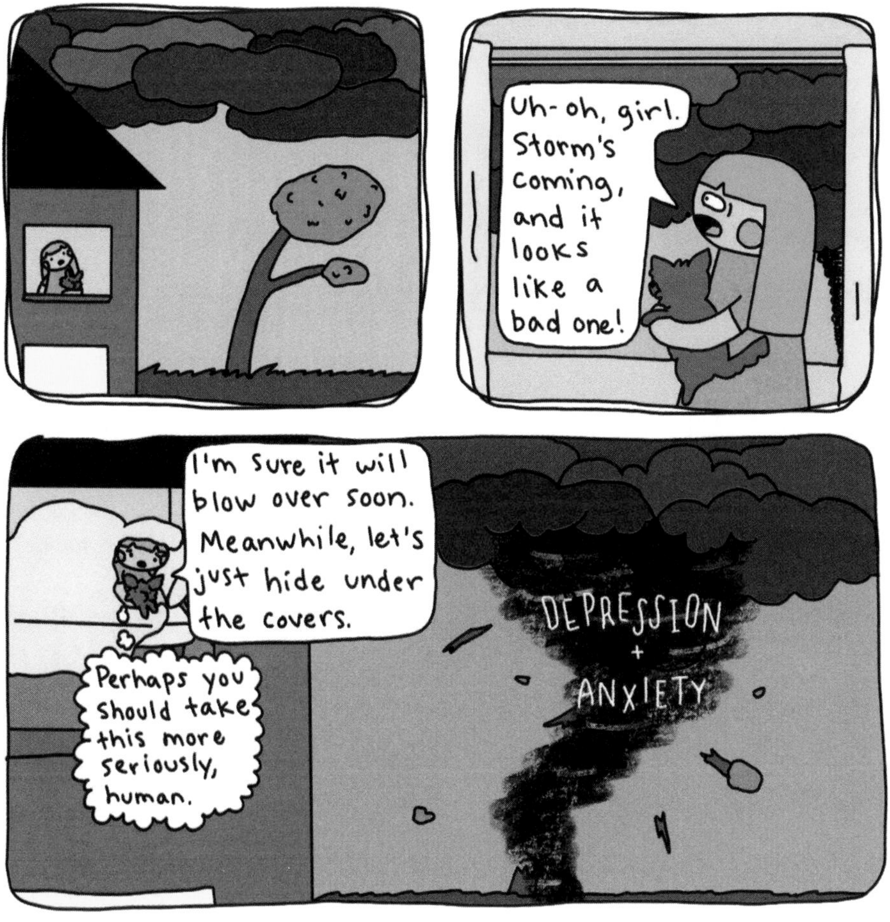
Uh-oh, girl. Storm's coming, and it looks like a bad one!
I'm sure it will blow over soon. Meanwhile, let's just hide under the covers.
Perhaps you should take this more seriously, human.
DEPRESSION + ANXIETY

BE THAT FRIEND

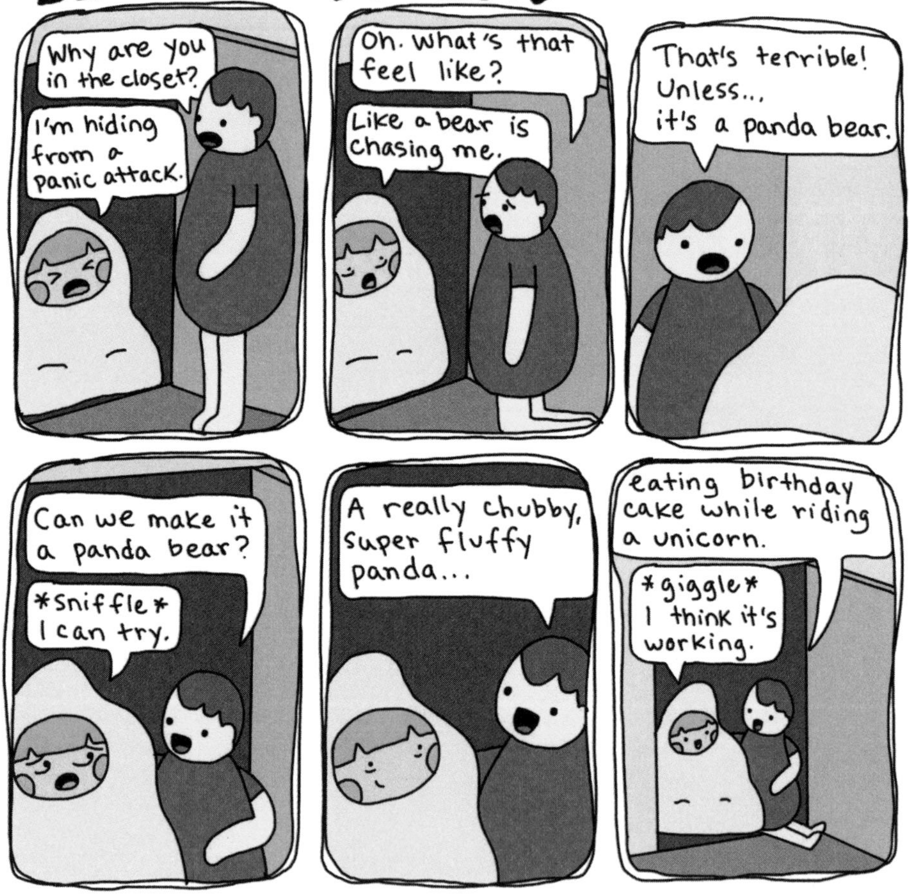

Why are you in the closet?
I'm hiding from a panic attack.
Oh. What's that feel like?
Like a bear is chasing me.
That's terrible! Unless..., it's a panda bear.
Can we make it a panda bear?
sniffle I can try.
A really chubby, super fluffy panda...
eating birthday cake while riding a unicorn.
giggle I think it's working.

WHAT NOT TO SAY TO SOMEONE WITH ANXIETY:

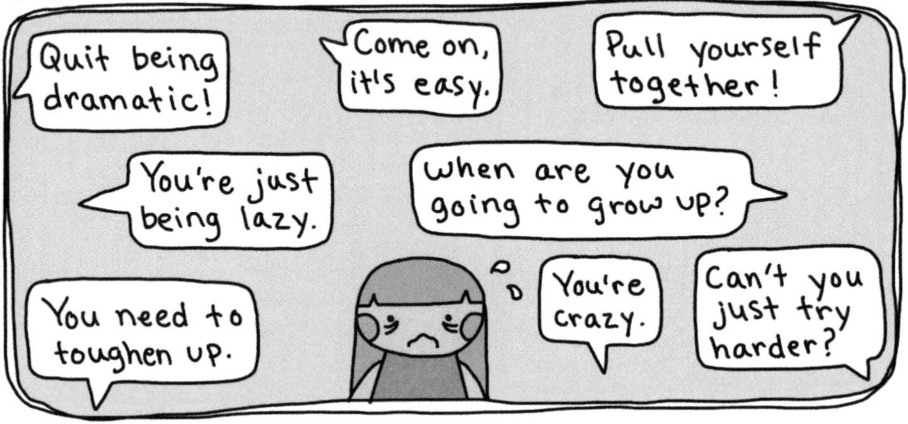
Quit being dramatic!
Come on, it's easy.
Pull yourself together!
You're just being lazy.
When are you going to grow up?
You need to toughen up.
You're crazy.
Can't you just try harder?

TRY ONE OF THESE INSTEAD:

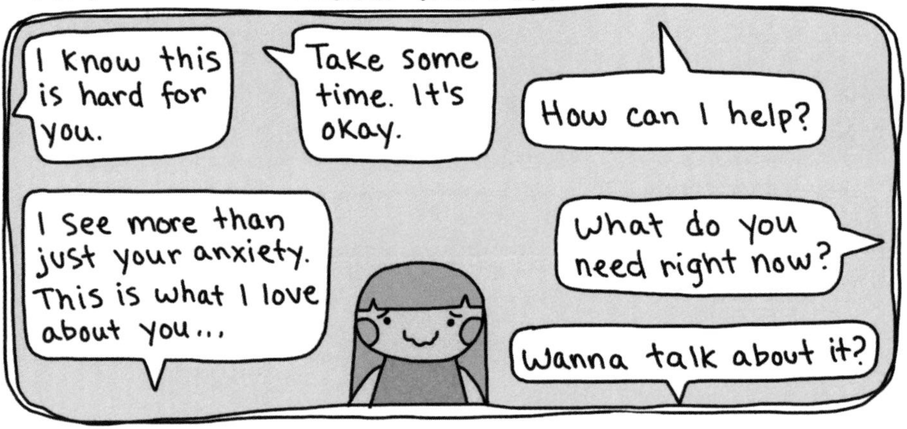
I know this is hard for you.
Take some time. It's okay.
How can I help?
I see more than just your anxiety. This is what I love about you...
What do you need right now?
Wanna talk about it?

FINDING A NEW THERAPIST

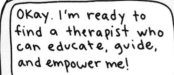

OKay. I'm ready to find a therapist who can educate, guide, and empower me!

That's great. Just... don't be too picky. You Know how you get sometimes.

Too picky? I'm not too picky! I am just the right amount of picky! Let's check out the websites of some local clinics.

Cutesy font. Hard pass.

Feel Good Therapy

In a shopping mall? Questionable.

NEW DAY

Their phone number seems... ominous. Better Keep looking.

FRESH START
call us today!
666-1313

Slow to load... what if their approach is as outdated as their web server?

So... how's it going?

It appears my process of elimination has worked! Only one clinic left.

132

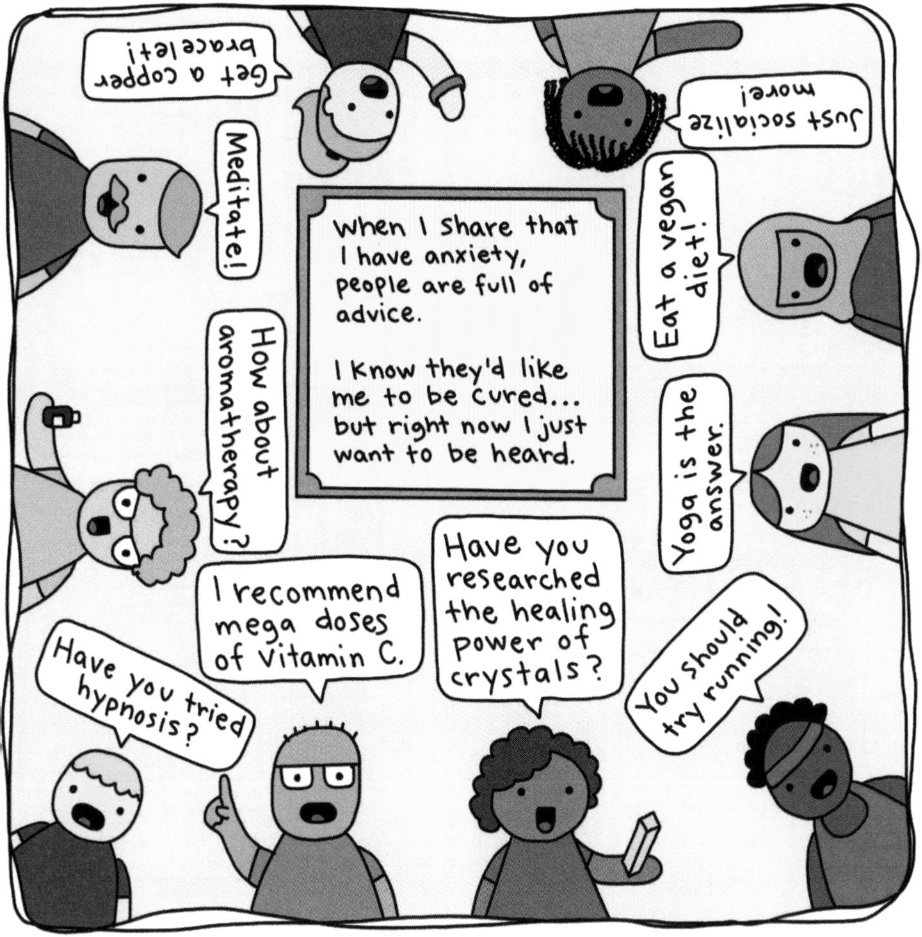

When I share that I have anxiety, people are full of advice.
I know they'd like me to be cured... but right now I just want to be heard.
Get a copper bracelet!
Just socialize more!
Meditate!
Eat a vegan diet!
How about aromatherapy?
Yoga is the answer.
Have you tried hypnosis?
I recommend mega doses of vitamin C.
Have you researched the healing power of crystals?
You should try running!

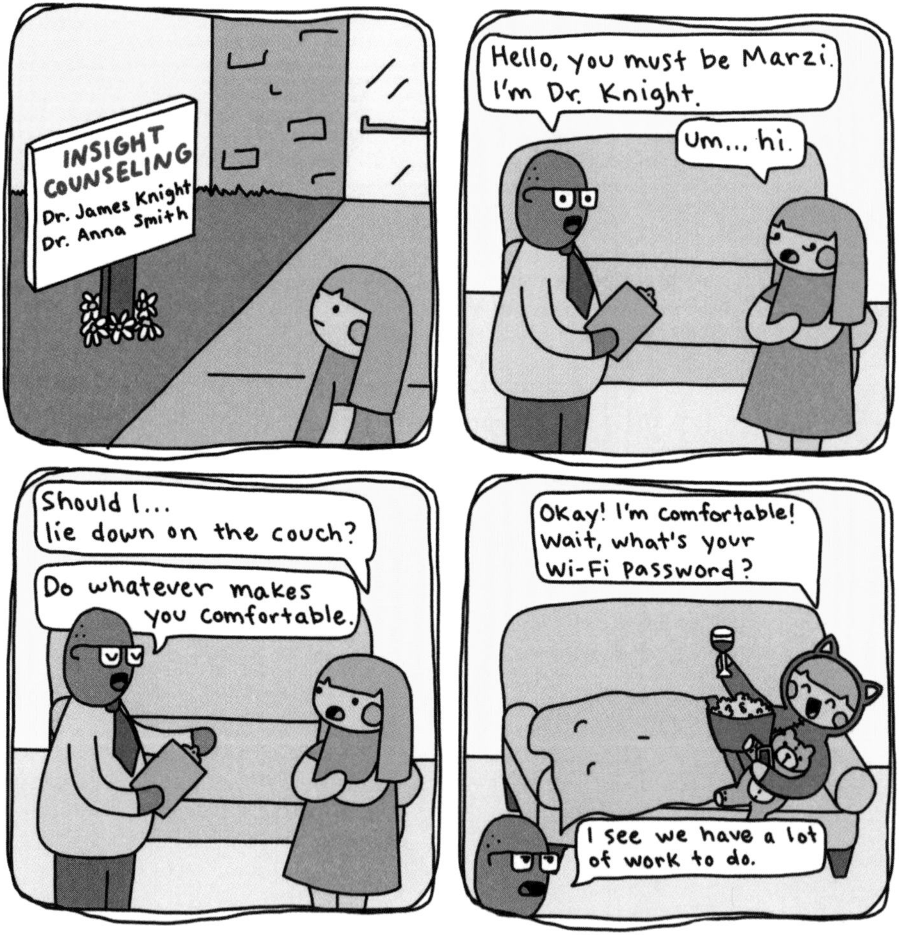
INSIGHT COUNSELING
Dr. James Knight
Dr. Anna Smith
Hello, you must be Marzi. I'm Dr. Knight.
Um... hi.
Should I... lie down on the couch?
Do whatever makes you comfortable.
Okay! I'm comfortable! Wait, what's your Wi-Fi password?
I see we have a lot of work to do.

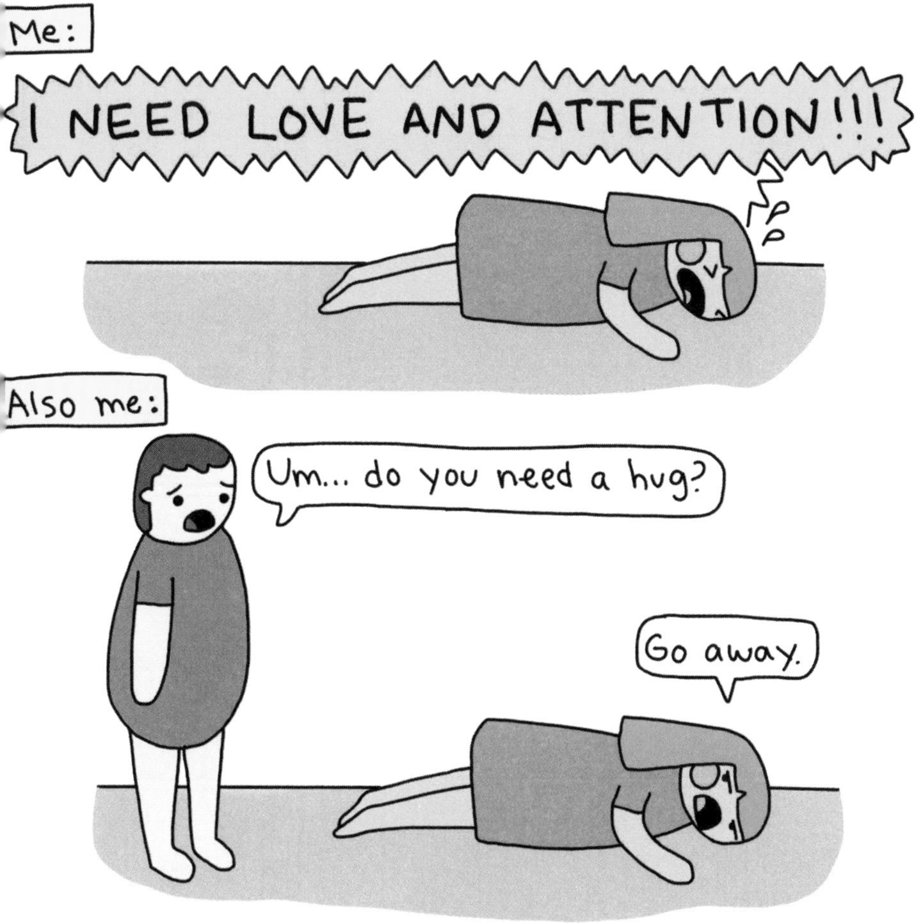

Me:
I NEED LOVE AND ATTENTION!!!
Also me:
Um... do you need a hug?
Go away.

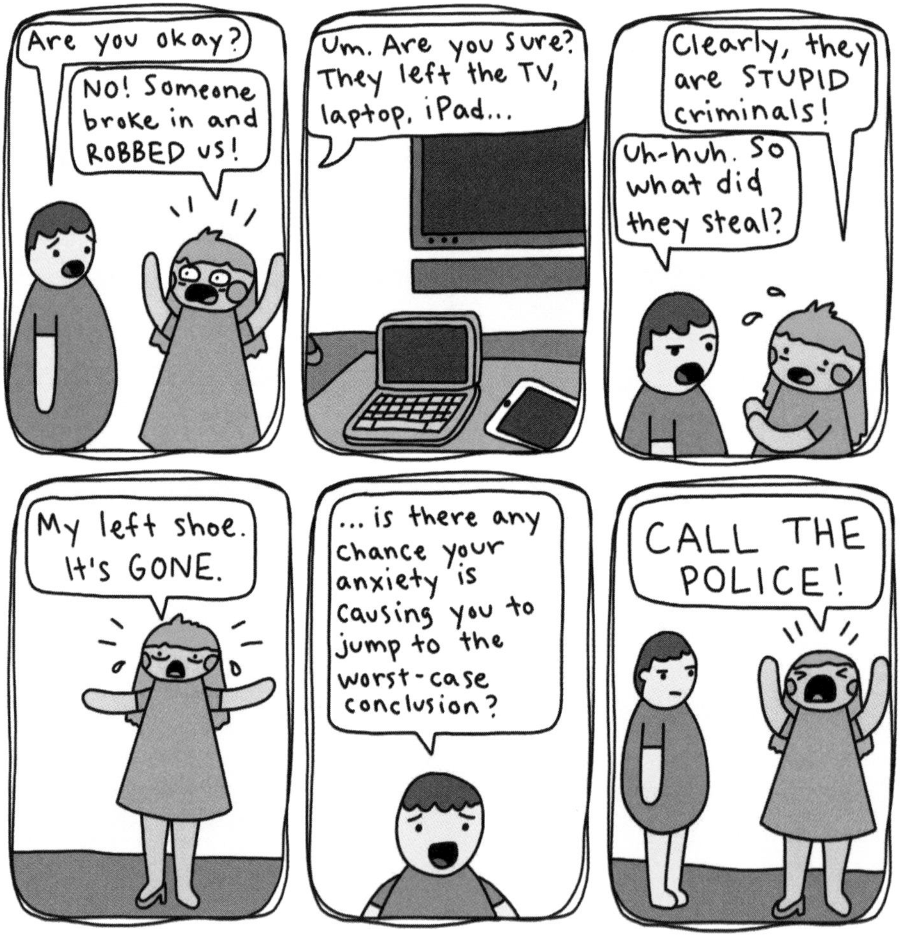
Are you okay?
No! Someone broke in and ROBBED us!
Um. Are you sure? They left the TV, laptop, iPad...
Clearly, they are STUPID criminals!
Uh-huh. So what did they steal?
My left shoe. It's GONE.
... is there any chance your anxiety is causing you to jump to the worst-case conclusion?
CALL THE POLICE!

NOTE TO SELF:

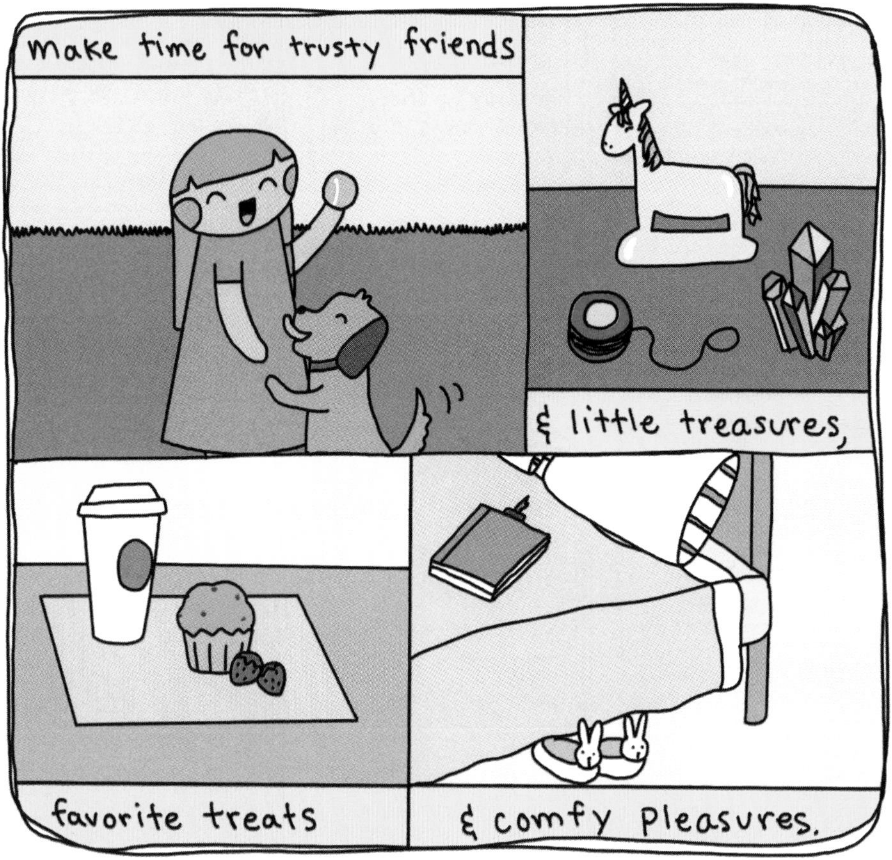
make time for trusty friends
& little treasures,
favorite treats
& comfy pleasures.

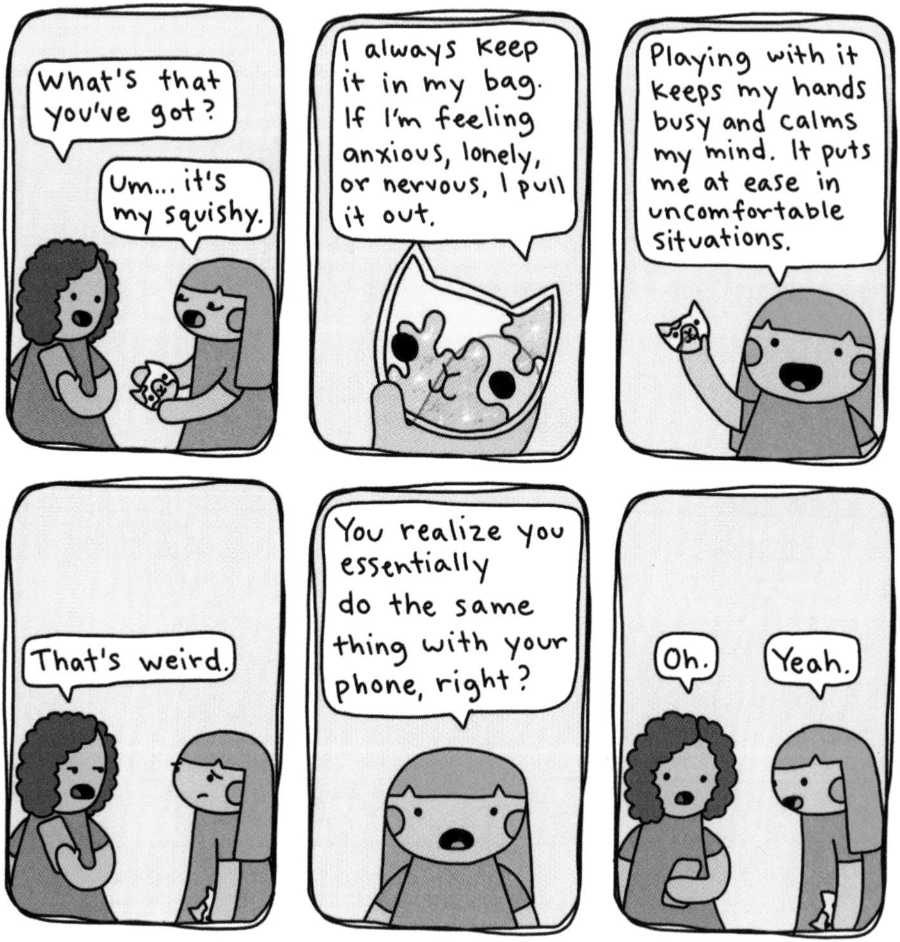
What's that you've got?
Um... it's my squishy.
I always keep it in my bag. If I'm feeling anxious, lonely, or nervous, I pull it out.
Playing with it keeps my hands busy and calms my mind. It puts me at ease in uncomfortable situations.
That's weird.
You realize you essentially do the same thing with your phone, right?
Oh.
Yeah.

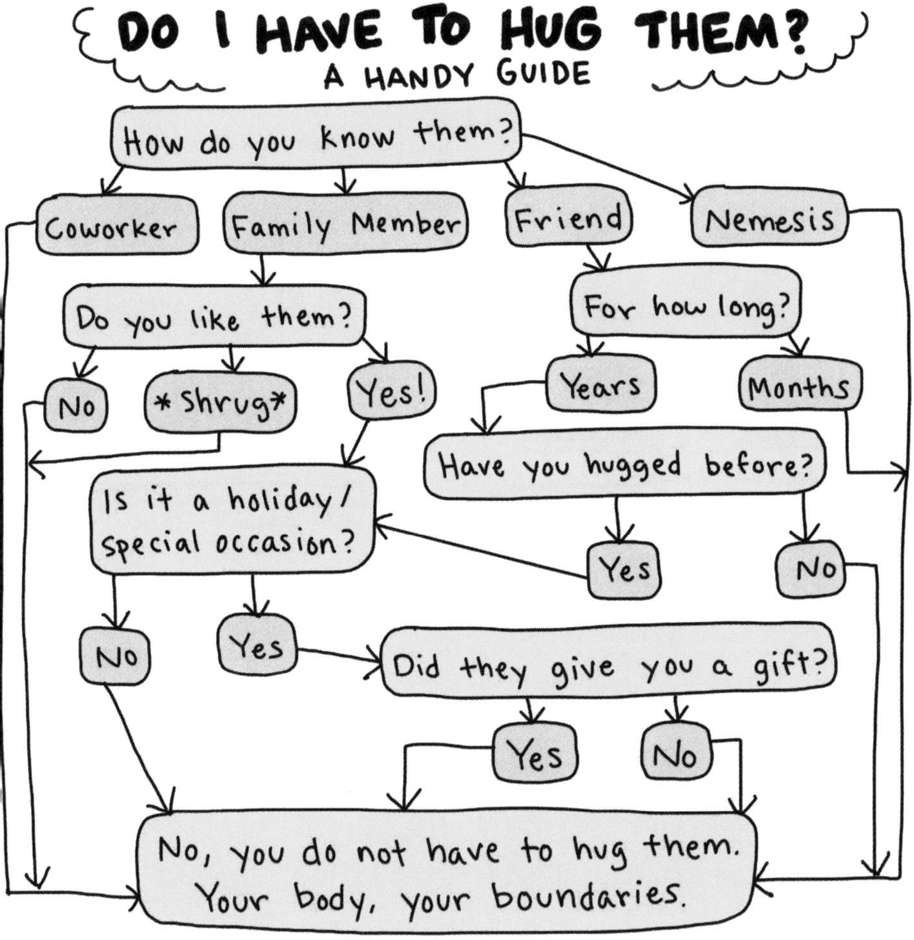
DO I HAVE TO HUG THEM?
A HANDY GUIDE
How do you know them?
Coworker
Family Member
Friend
Nemesis
Do you like them?
No
Shrug
Yes!
For how long?
Years
Months
Have you hugged before?
Yes
No
Is it a holiday / special occasion?
No
Yes
Did they give you a gift?
Yes
No
No, you do not have to hug them.
Your body, your boundaries.

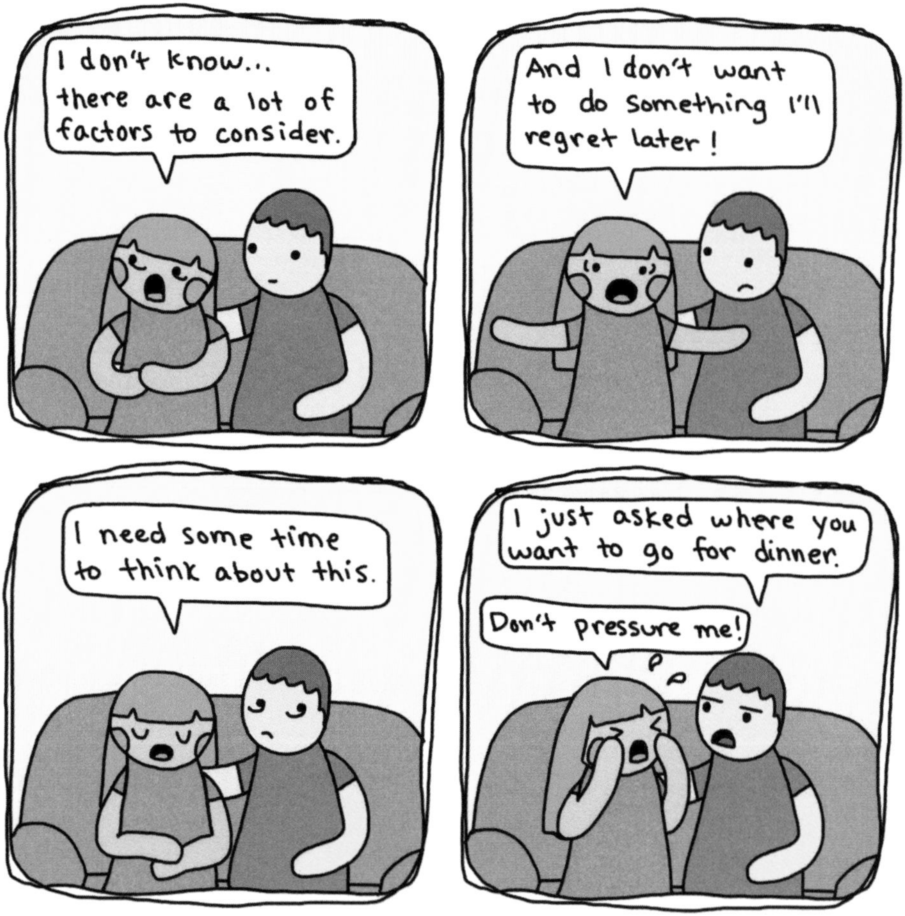
I don't know...
there are a lot of
factors to consider.
And I don't want
to do something I'll
regret later!
I need some time
to think about this.
I just asked where you
want to go for dinner.
Don't pressure me!

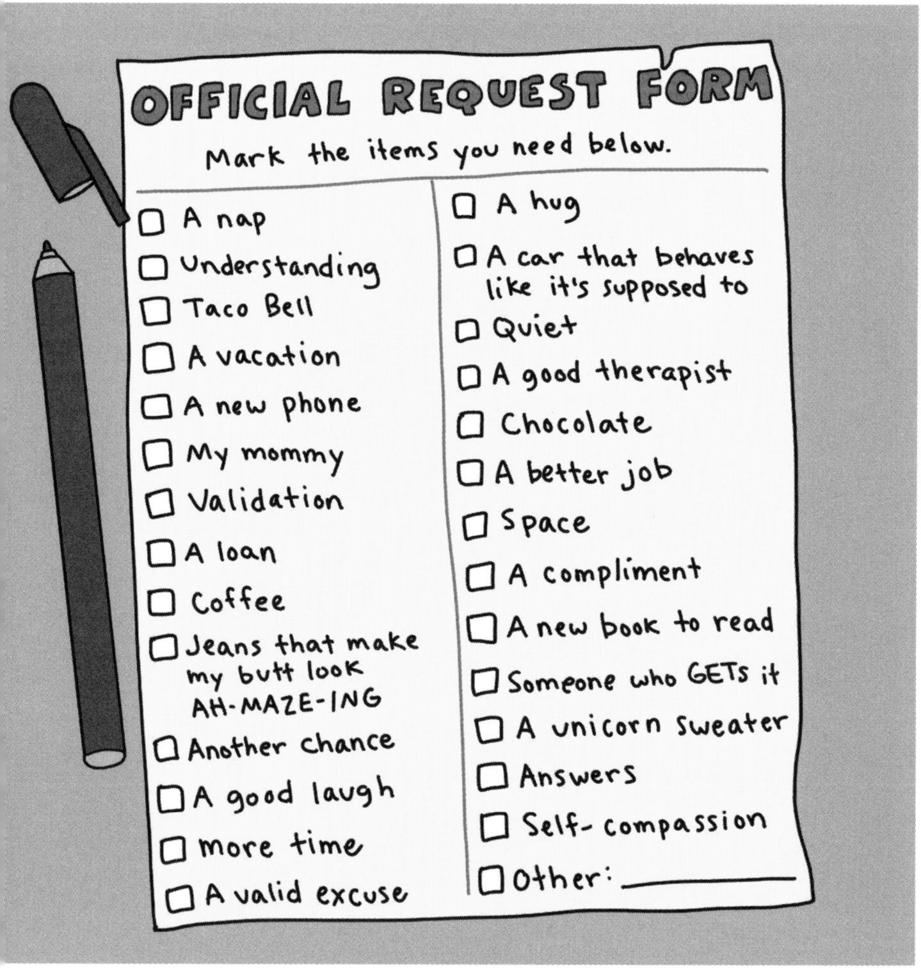

OFFICIAL REQUEST FORM

Mark the items you need below.

- ☐ A nap
- ☐ Understanding
- ☐ Taco Bell
- ☐ A vacation
- ☐ A new phone
- ☐ My mommy
- ☐ Validation
- ☐ A loan
- ☐ Coffee
- ☐ Jeans that make my butt look AH-MAZE-ING
- ☐ Another chance
- ☐ A good laugh
- ☐ more time
- ☐ A valid excuse
- ☐ A hug
- ☐ A car that behaves like it's supposed to
- ☐ Quiet
- ☐ A good therapist
- ☐ Chocolate
- ☐ A better job
- ☐ Space
- ☐ A compliment
- ☐ A new book to read
- ☐ Someone who GETs it
- ☐ A unicorn sweater
- ☐ Answers
- ☐ Self-compassion
- ☐ Other: ____________

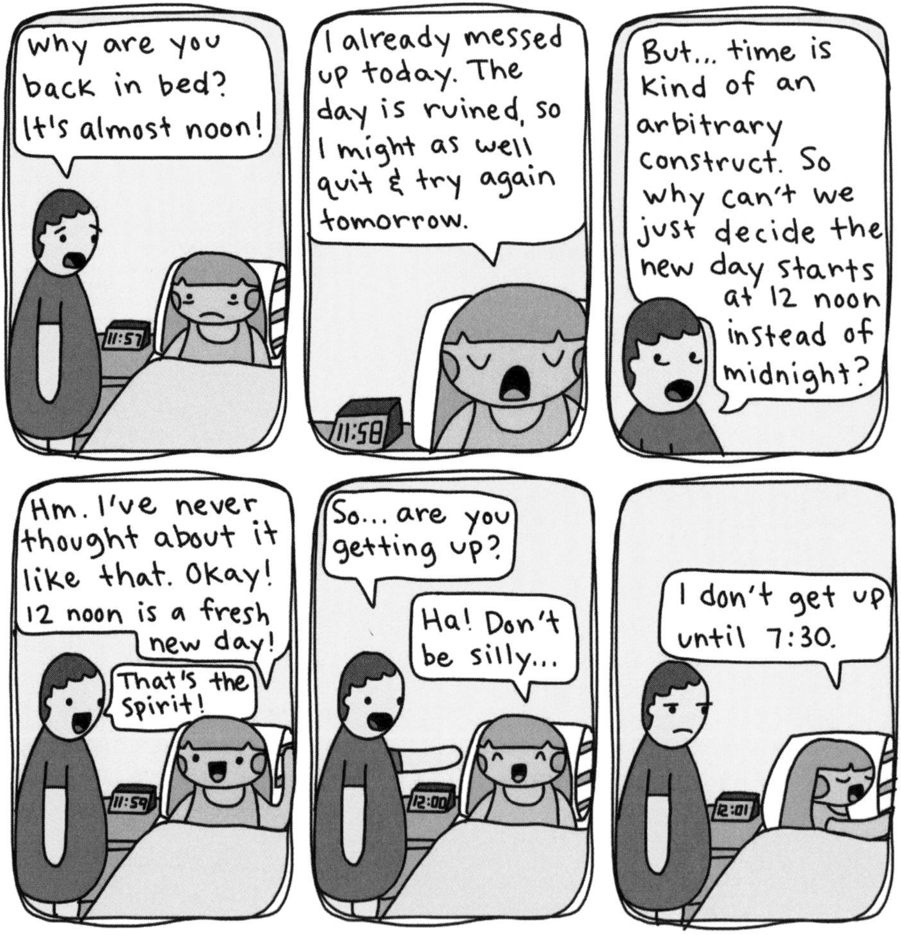
Why are you back in bed? It's almost noon!
11:57
I already messed up today. The day is ruined, so I might as well quit & try again tomorrow.
11:58
But... time is kind of an arbitrary construct. So why can't we just decide the new day starts at 12 noon instead of midnight?
Hm. I've never thought about it like that. Okay! 12 noon is a fresh new day!
That's the Spirit!
11:59
So... are you getting up?
Ha! Don't be silly...
12:00
I don't get up until 7:30.
12:01

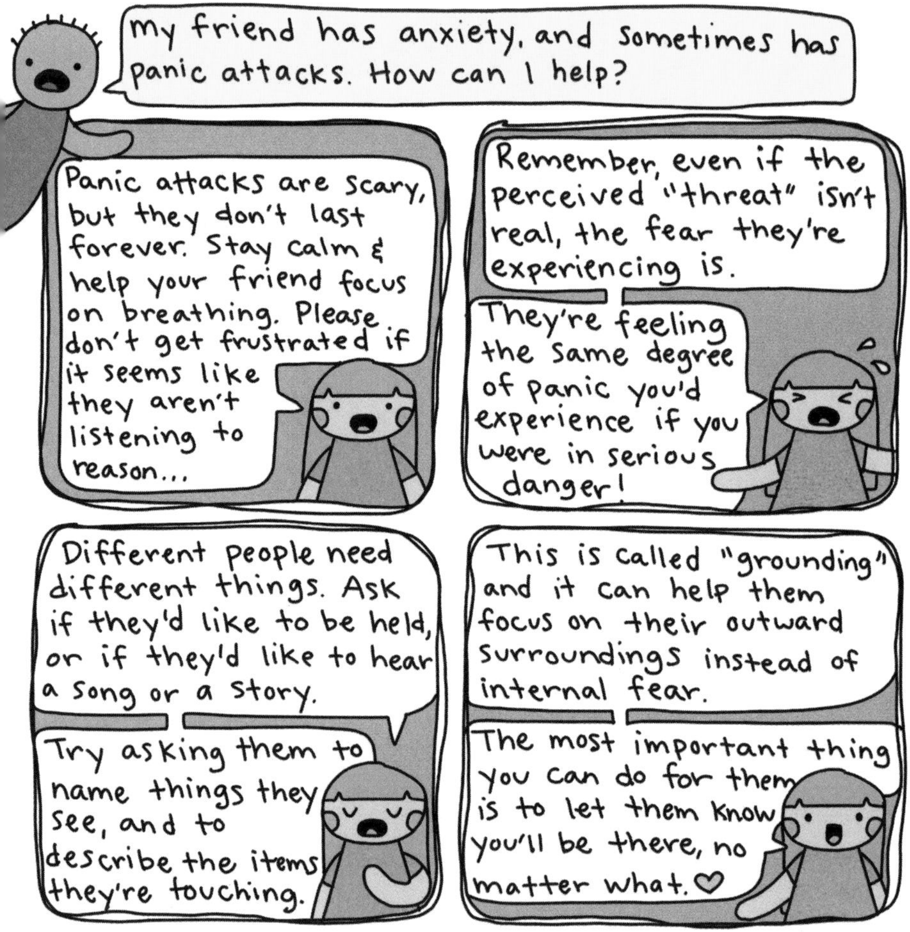
My friend has anxiety, and sometimes has panic attacks. How can I help?
Panic attacks are scary, but they don't last forever. Stay calm & help your friend focus on breathing. Please don't get frustrated if it seems like they aren't listening to reason...
Remember, even if the perceived "threat" isn't real, the fear they're experiencing is.
They're feeling the same degree of panic you'd experience if you were in serious danger!
Different people need different things. Ask if they'd like to be held, or if they'd like to hear a song or a story.
Try asking them to name things they see, and to describe the items they're touching.
This is called "grounding" and it can help them focus on their outward surroundings instead of internal fear.
The most important thing you can do for them is to let them know you'll be there, no matter what. ♡

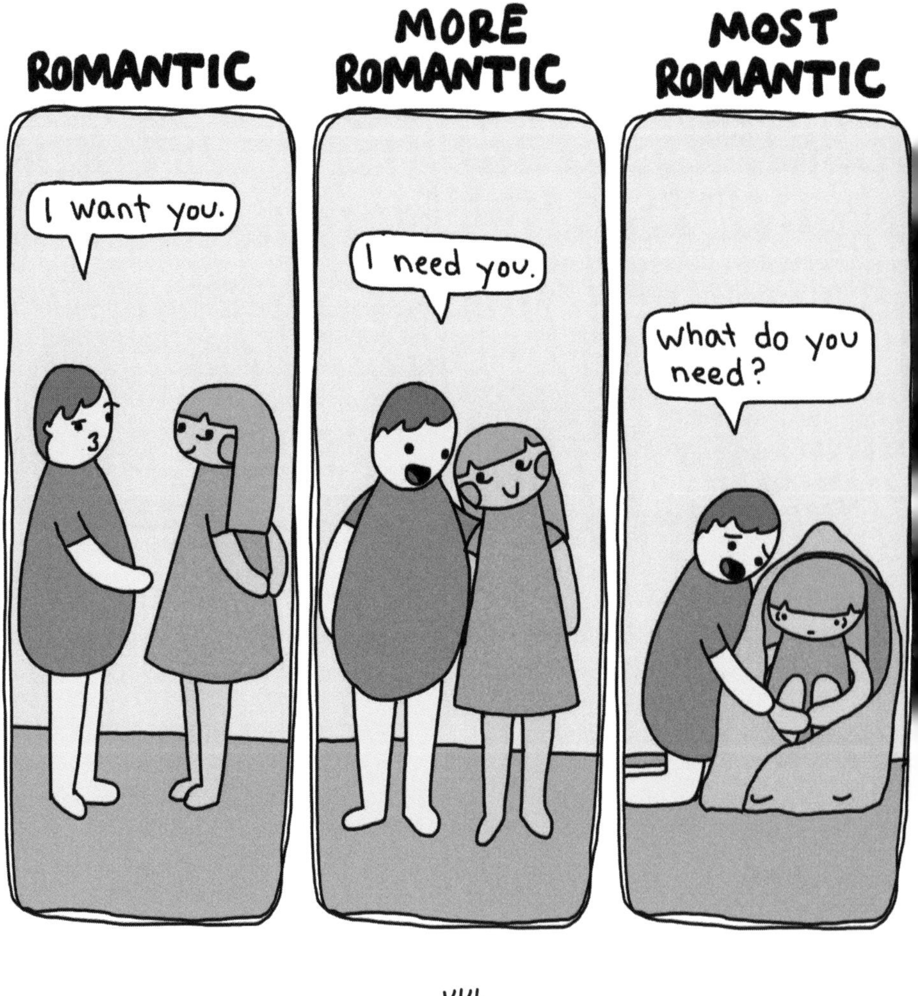
ROMANTIC
I want you.
MORE ROMANTIC
I need you.
MOST ROMANTIC
What do you need?

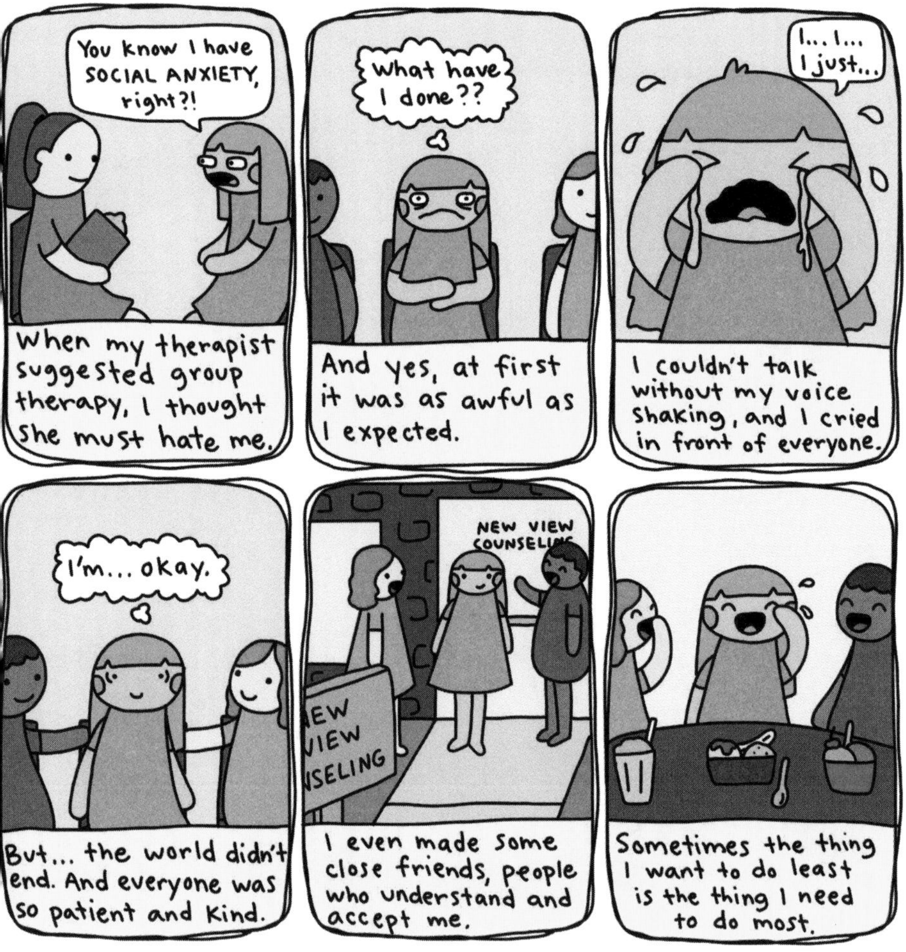
You know I have SOCIAL ANXIETY, right?!
When my therapist suggested group therapy, I thought she must hate me.
What have I done??
And yes, at first it was as awful as I expected.
I... I... I just...
I couldn't talk without my voice shaking, and I cried in front of everyone.
I'm... okay.
But... the world didn't end. And everyone was so patient and kind.
NEW VIEW COUNSEL
EW VIEW NSELING
I even made some close friends, people who understand and accept me.
Sometimes the thing I want to do least is the thing I need to do most.

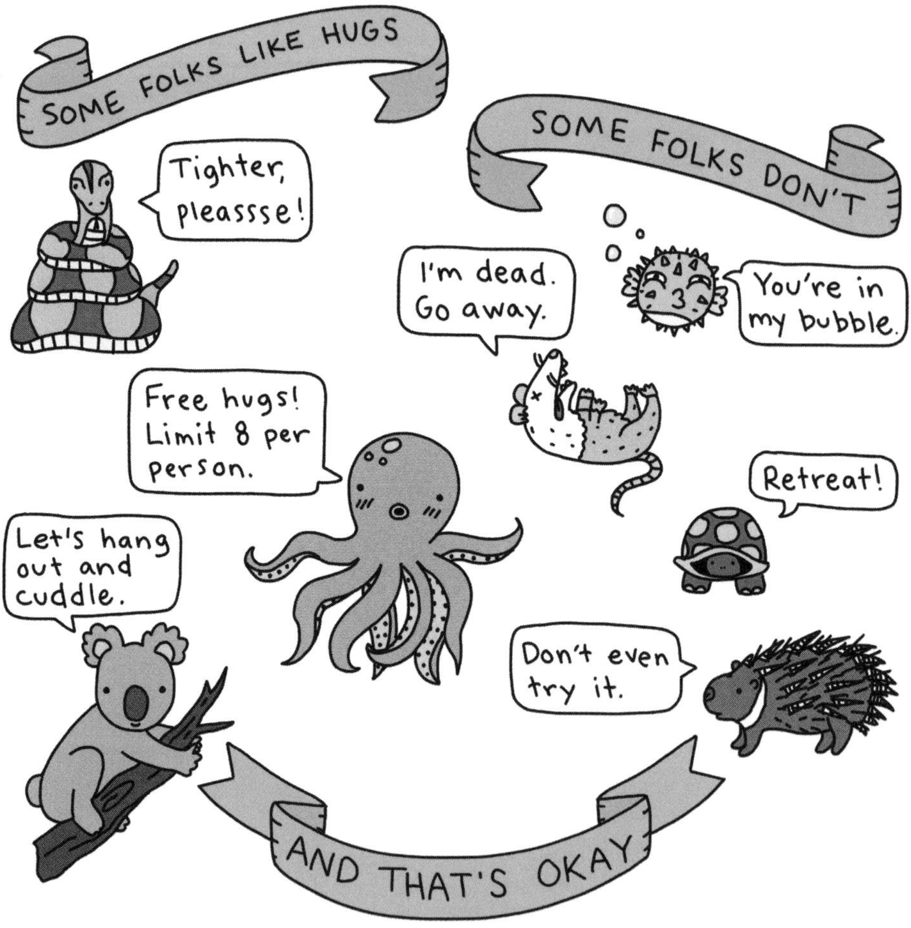
SOME FOLKS LIKE HUGS
SOME FOLKS DON'T
Tighter, pleassse!
You're in my bubble.
I'm dead. Go away.
Free hugs! Limit 8 per person.
Retreat!
Let's hang out and cuddle.
Don't even try it.
AND THAT'S OKAY

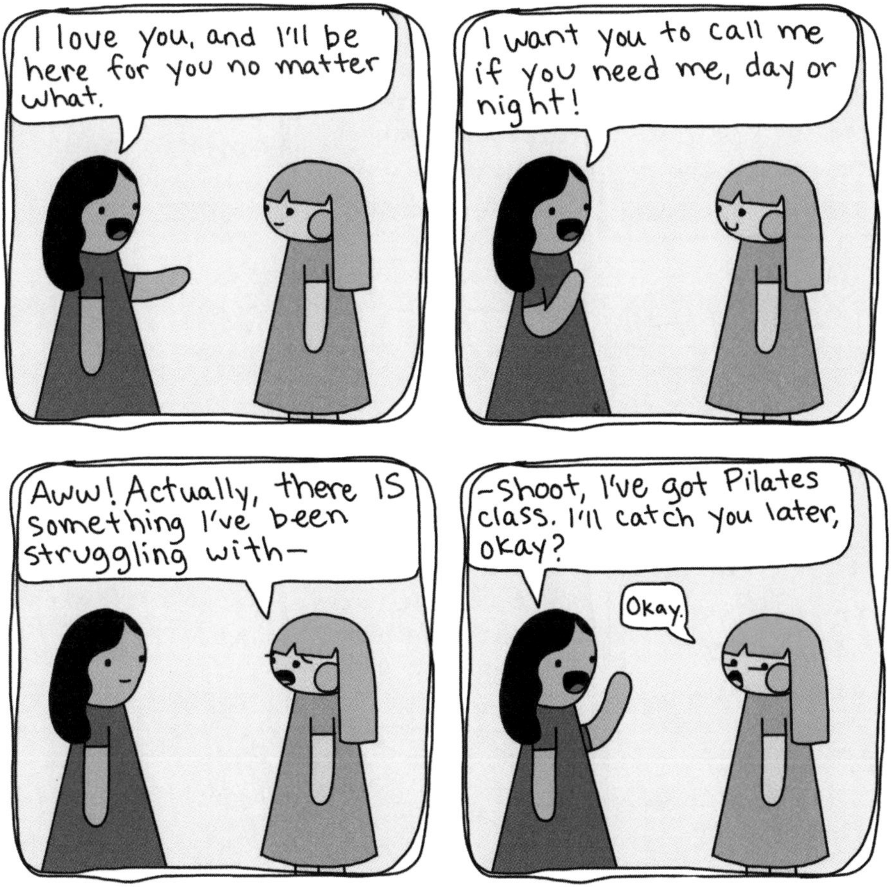
I love you, and I'll be here for you no matter what.
I want you to call me if you need me, day or night!
Aww! Actually, there IS something I've been struggling with—
—Shoot, I've got Pilates class. I'll catch you later, okay?
Okay.

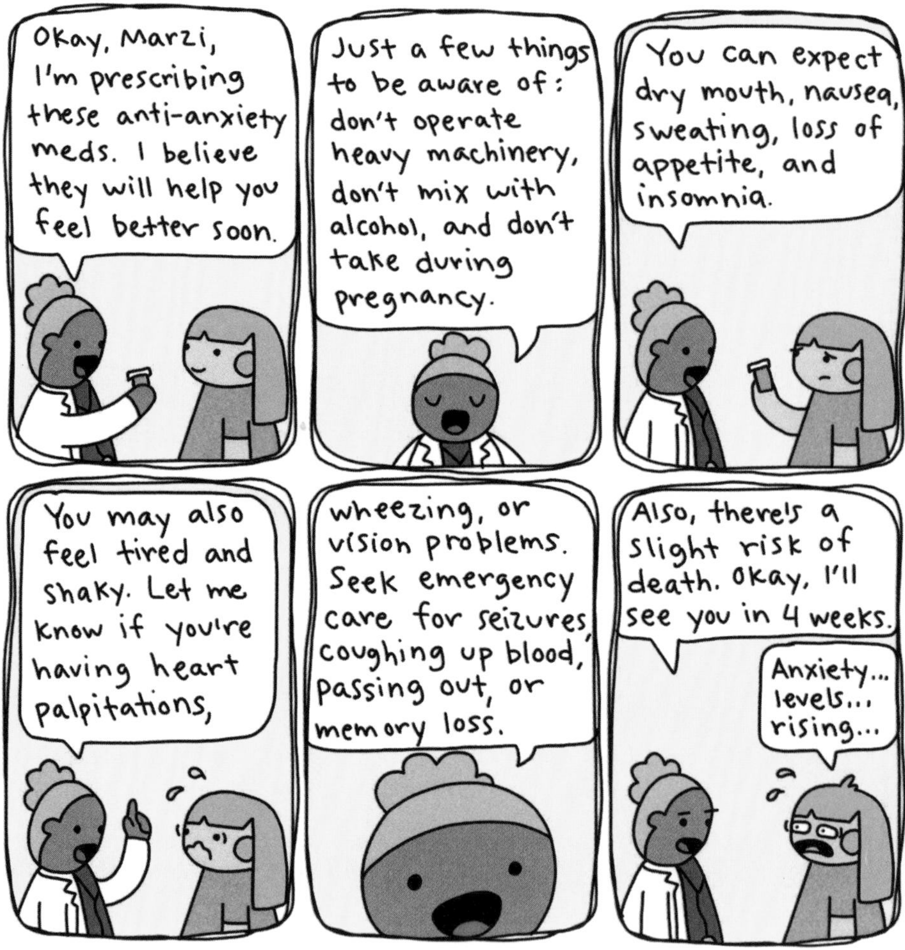
Okay, Marzi, I'm prescribing these anti-anxiety meds. I believe they will help you feel better soon.
Just a few things to be aware of: don't operate heavy machinery, don't mix with alcohol, and don't take during pregnancy.
You can expect dry mouth, nausea, sweating, loss of appetite, and insomnia.
You may also feel tired and shaky. Let me know if you're having heart palpitations,
wheezing, or vision problems. Seek emergency care for seizures, coughing up blood, passing out, or memory loss.
Also, there's a slight risk of death. Okay, I'll see you in 4 weeks.
Anxiety... levels... rising...

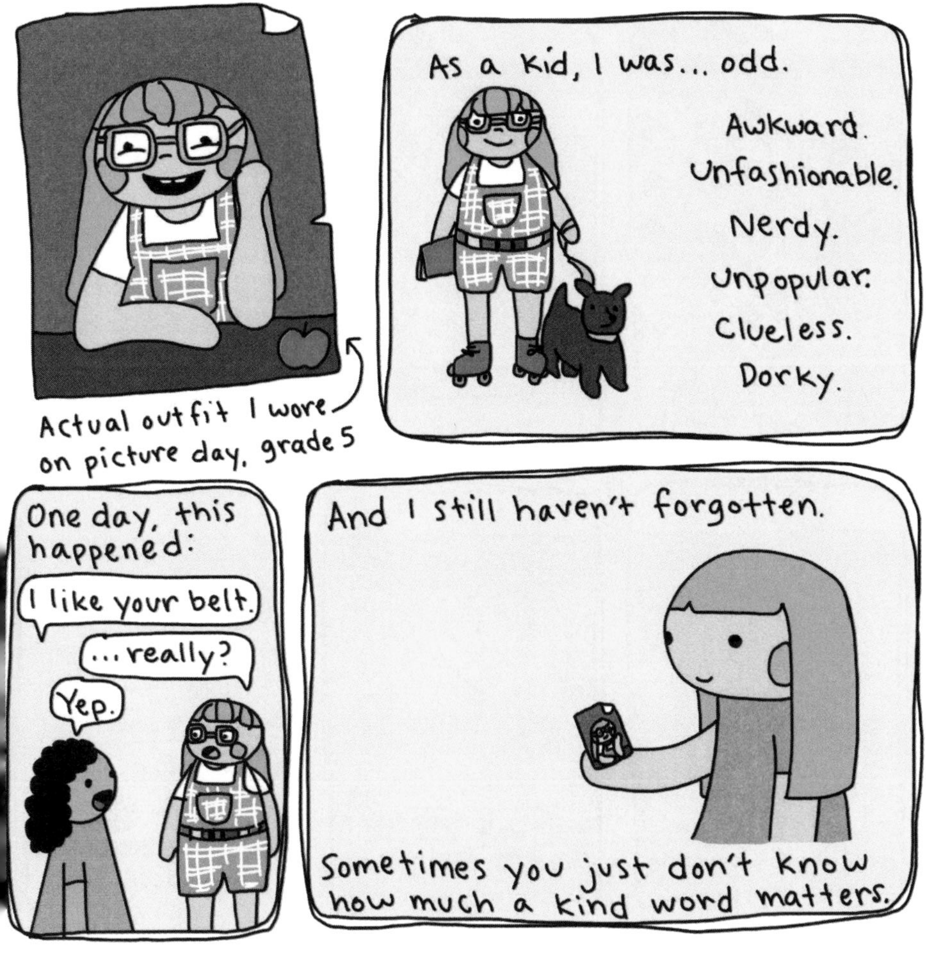
Actual outfit I wore on picture day, grade 5
As a kid, I was... odd.
Awkward.
Unfashionable.
Nerdy.
Unpopular.
Clueless.
Dorky.
One day, this happened:
I like your belt.
...really?
Yep.
And I still haven't forgotten.
Sometimes you just don't know how much a kind word matters.

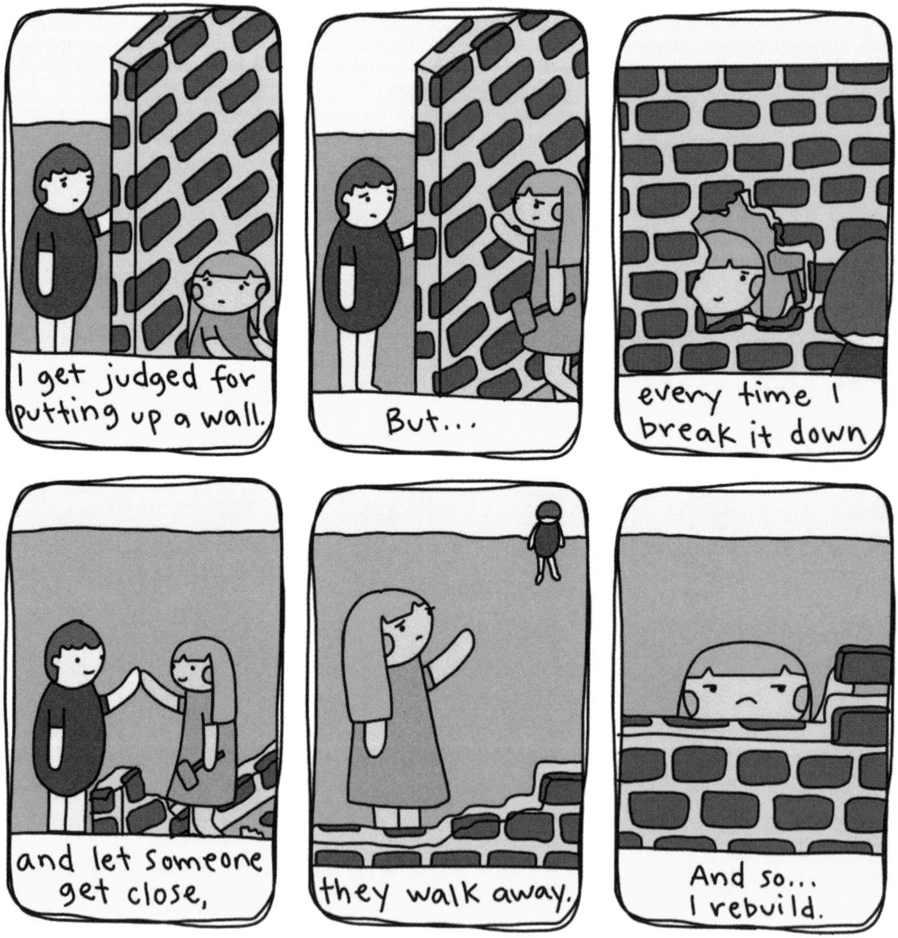
I get judged for putting up a wall.
But...
every time I break it down
and let someone get close,
they walk away.
And so... I rebuild.

THE ONLINE THERAPY OPTION

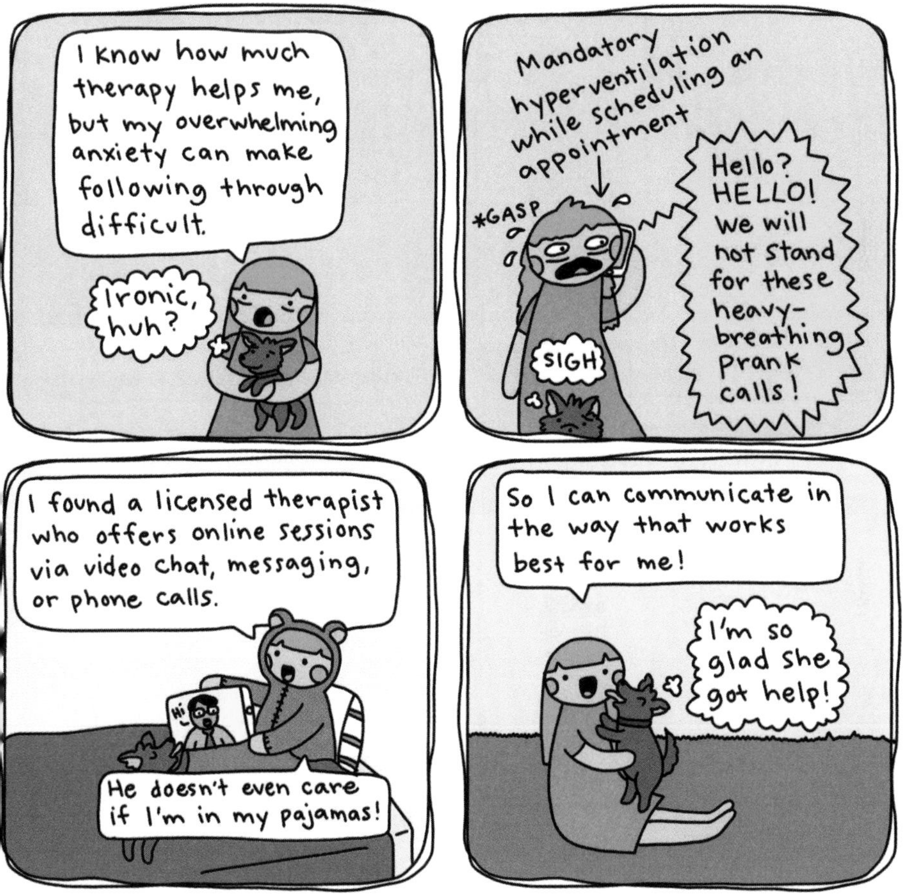
I know how much therapy helps me, but my overwhelming anxiety can make following through difficult.
Ironic, huh?
Mandatory hyperventilation while scheduling an appointment
*GASP
Hello? HELLO! We will not stand for these heavy-breathing prank calls!
SIGH
I found a licensed therapist who offers online sessions via video chat, messaging, or phone calls.
Hi
He doesn't even care if I'm in my pajamas!
So I can communicate in the way that works best for me!
I'm so glad she got help!

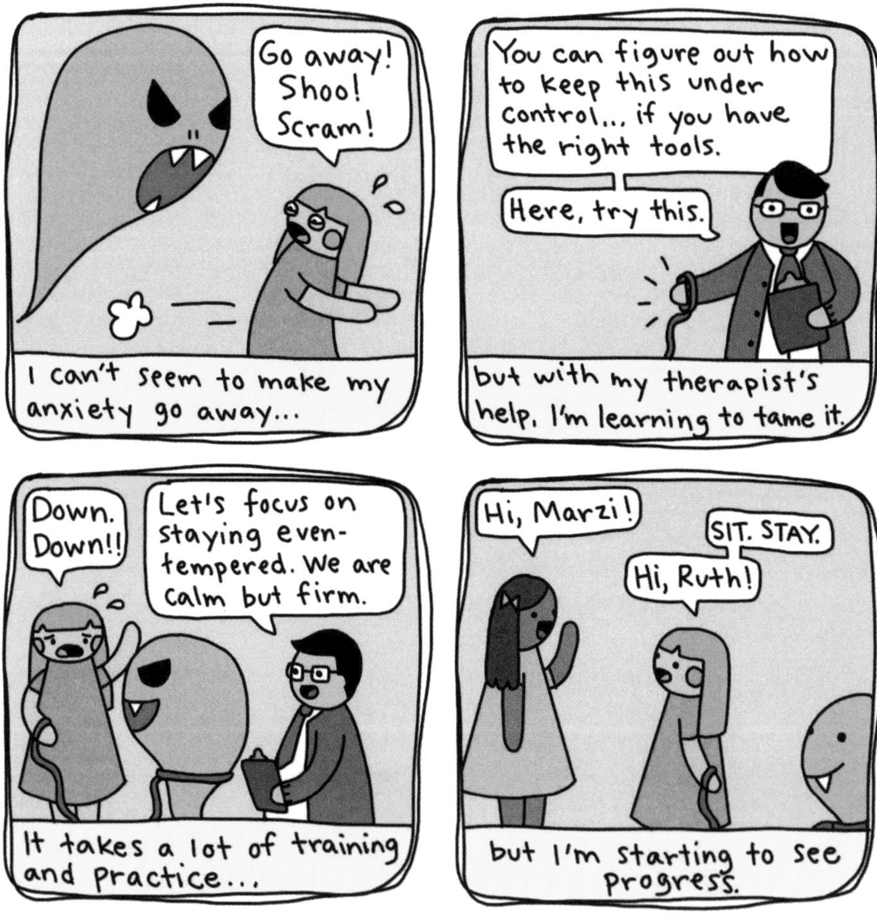
Go away! Shoo! Scram!
I can't seem to make my anxiety go away...
You can figure out how to keep this under control... if you have the right tools.
Here, try this.
but with my therapist's help, I'm learning to tame it.
Down. Down!!
Let's focus on staying even-tempered. We are calm but firm.
It takes a lot of training and practice...
Hi, Marzi!
SIT. STAY.
Hi, Ruth!
but I'm starting to see progress.

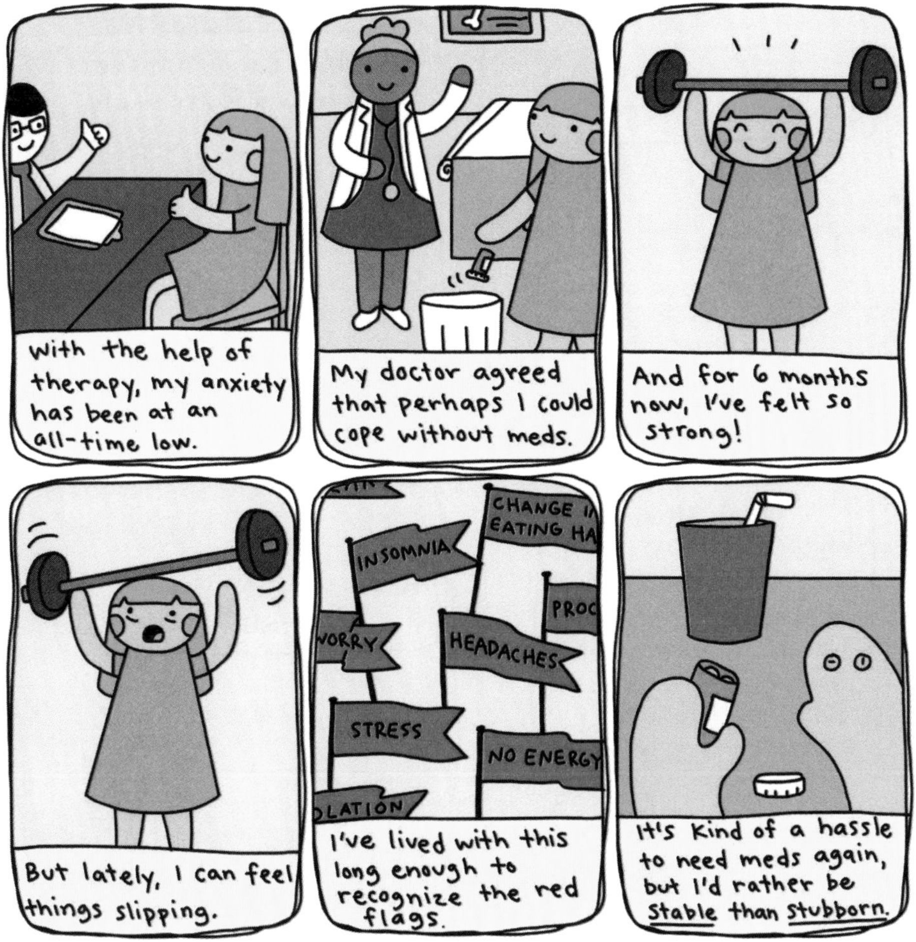
With the help of therapy, my anxiety has been at an all-time low.
My doctor agreed that perhaps I could cope without meds.
And for 6 months now, I've felt so strong!
But lately, I can feel things slipping.
INSOMNIA
HEADACHES
STRESS
NO ENERGY
I've lived with this long enough to recognize the red flags.
It's kind of a hassle to need meds again, but I'd rather be stable than stubborn.

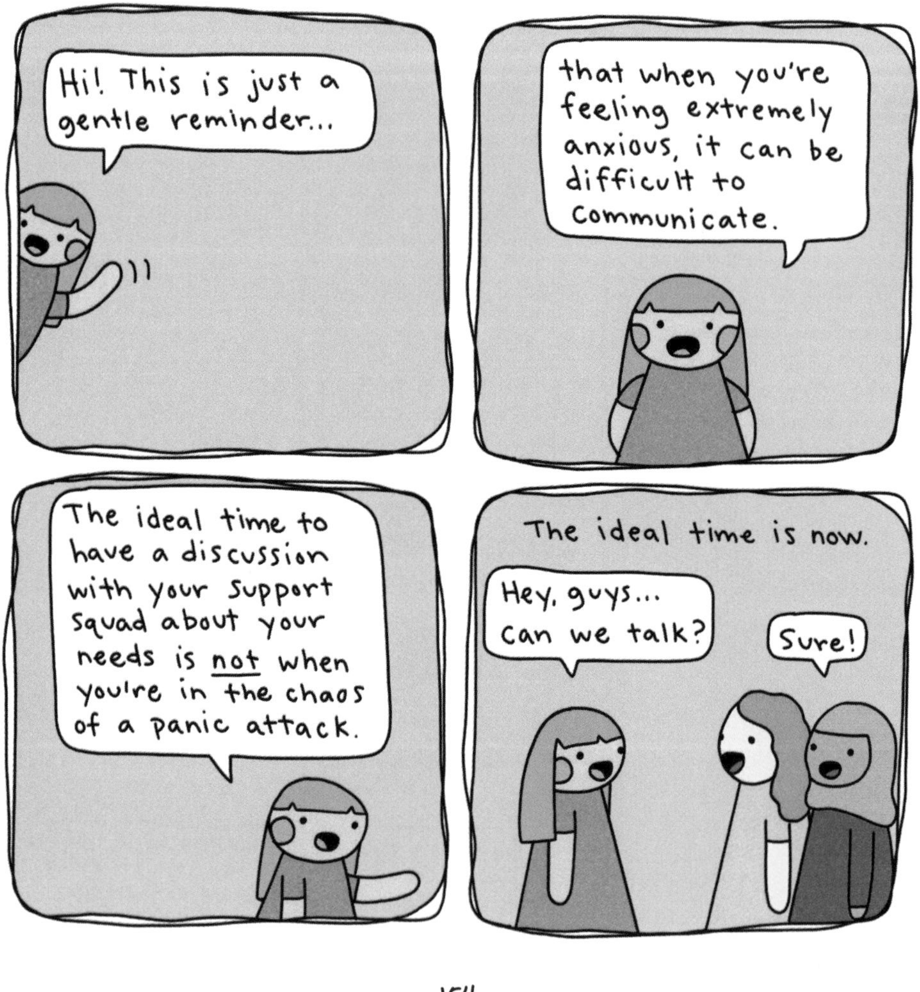
Hi! This is just a gentle reminder...
that when you're feeling extremely anxious, it can be difficult to communicate.
The ideal time to have a discussion with your support squad about your needs is not when you're in the chaos of a panic attack.
The ideal time is now.
Hey, guys... can we talk?
Sure!

I GET BY WITH A LITTLE HELP FROM MY FRIENDS

"They make me tea and play with my hair."

"Simply asking, 'What do you need right now?'"

"They send me funny memes and videos!"

"They give me either space or physical comfort, depending on what I ask for."

"Tacos! When things get really bad, I'll tell my BFF I need a distraction, so we go get tacos."

"They say quietly, 'I know this is hard, are you okay?'"

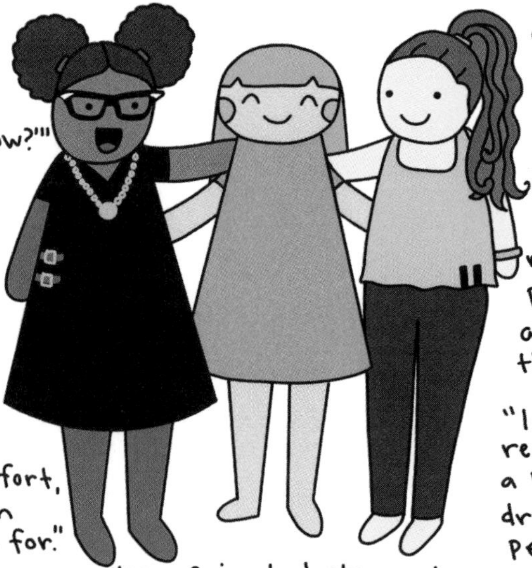

"My friends help me by taking the lead in social situations like parties. I don't have to do much talking that way, and I can add in what I am comfortable saying."

"My friends help by giving me some nonjudgmental alone time when I ask for it."

"They make sure I'm resting when I need to rest, and am not pushing my body and brain more than I should."

"I would definitely recommend having a 'panic-attack drill' with the people you hang out with most."

* this doodle was crowdsourced. Thanks to the contributors!

KIND OF COPING

-figuring out how to $\wedge$ manage-

mostly

I kind of wish this book had a fairy-tale ending. One where I vanquish my anxiety and live happily ever after (preferably in a castle with a pet unicorn).

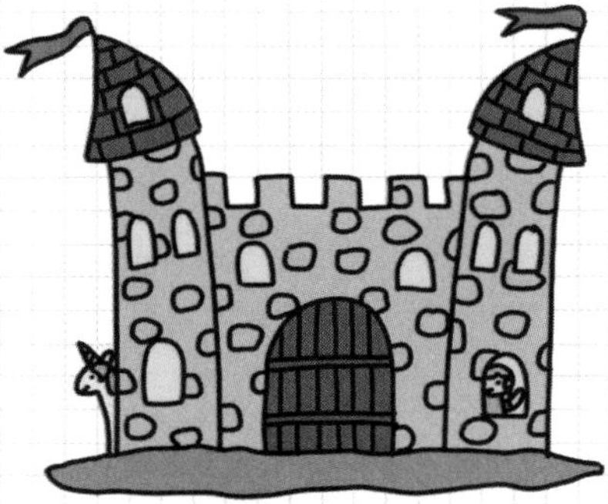

The truth is, I don't have it all figured out yet. I'm not "cured," and I may never be. But I'm kind of coping. I'm learning what my triggers are, and utilizing strategies to deal with them. I'm practicing self-care and showing myself compassion. I'm giving myself pep talks, and cutting myself some slack. I'm doing my best to hold on to hope.

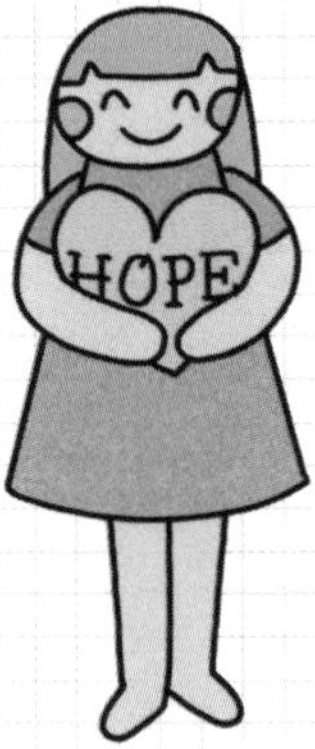
HOPE

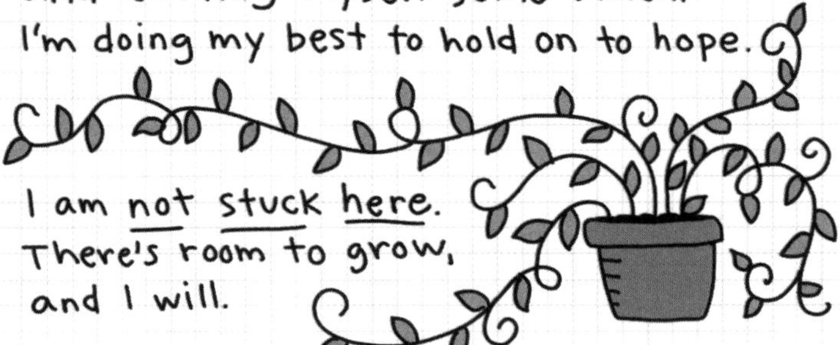

I am not stuck here. There's room to grow, and I will.

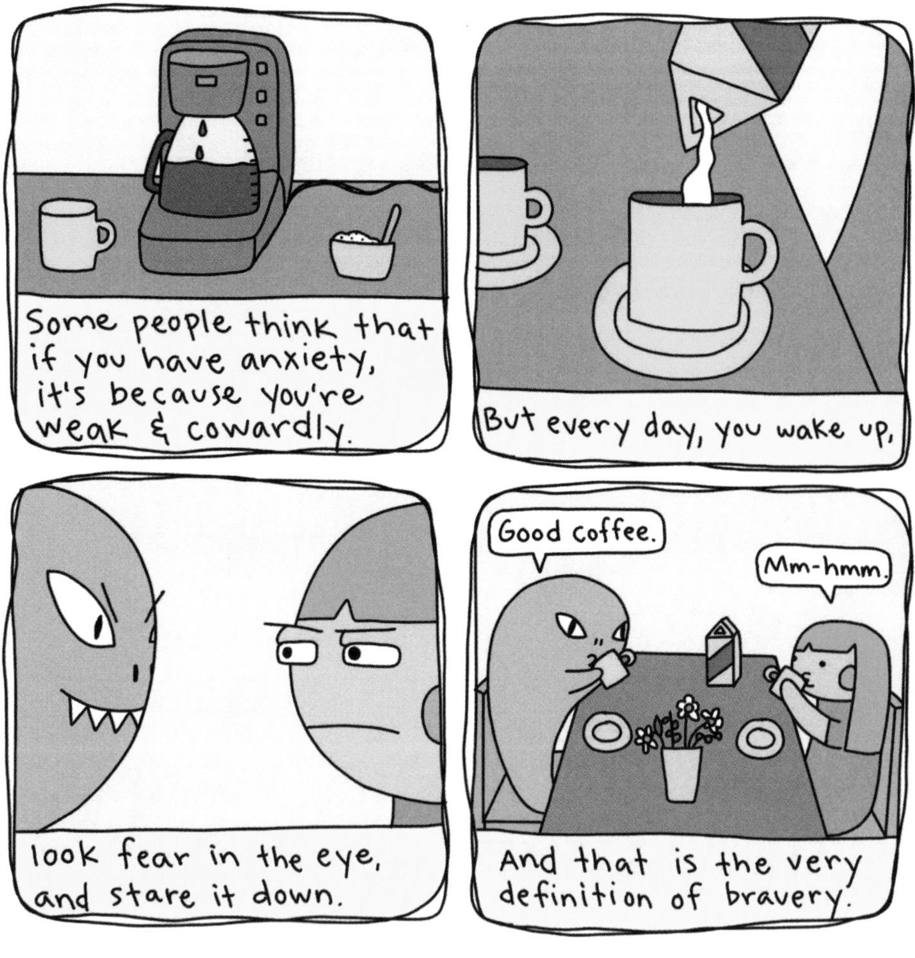
Some people think that if you have anxiety, it's because you're weak & cowardly.
But every day, you wake up,
look fear in the eye, and stare it down.
Good coffee.
Mm-hmm.
And that is the very definition of bravery.

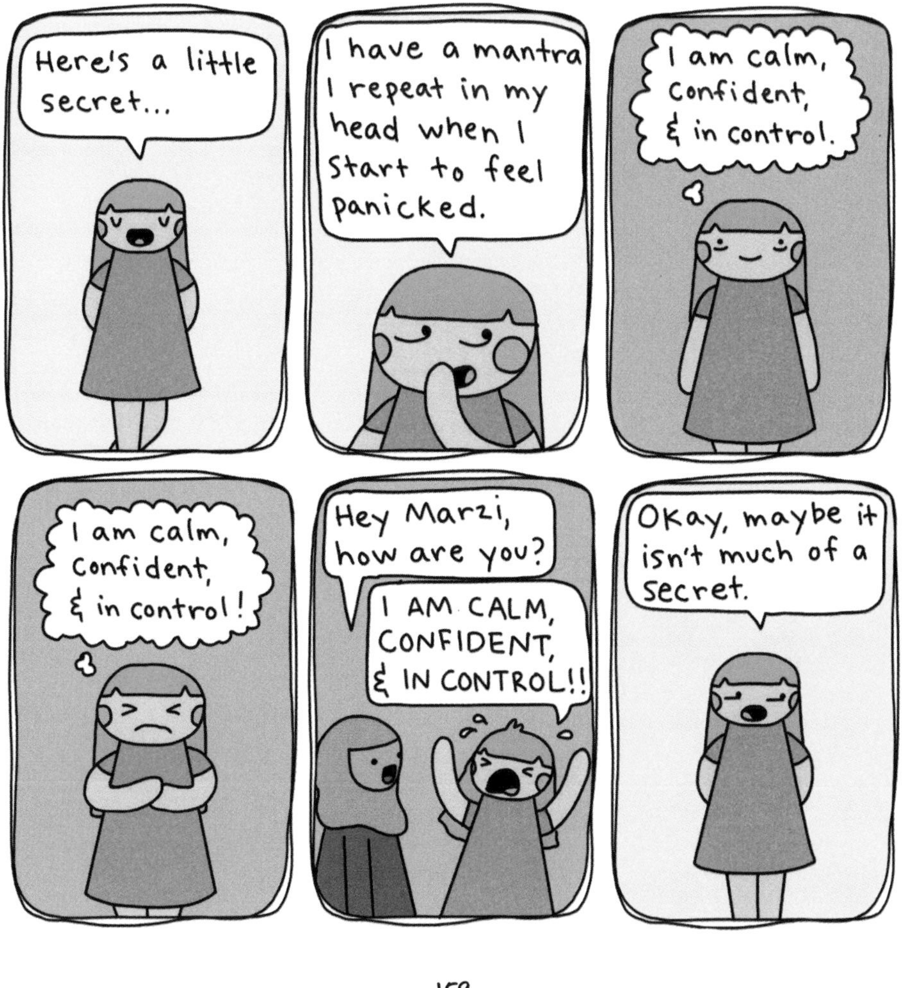
Here's a little secret...
I have a mantra I repeat in my head when I start to feel panicked.
I am calm, confident, & in control.
I am calm, confident, & in control!
Hey Marzi, how are you?
I AM CALM, CONFIDENT, & IN CONTROL!!
Okay, maybe it isn't much of a secret.

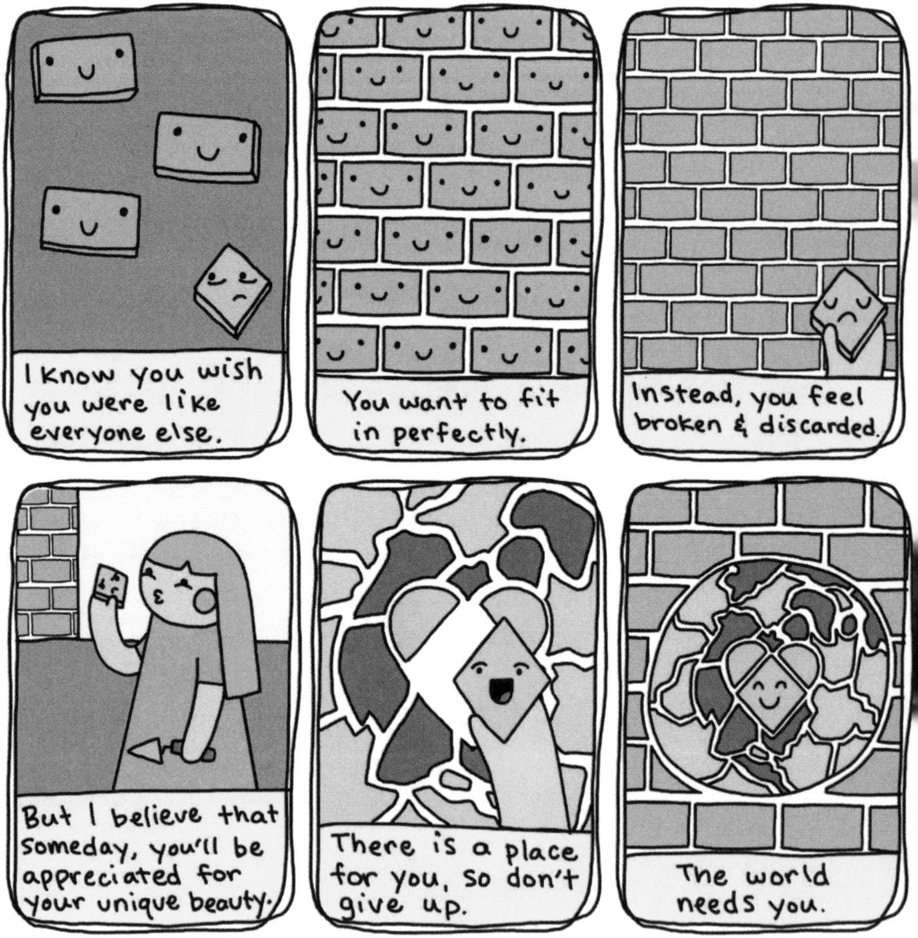
I know you wish you were like everyone else.
You want to fit in perfectly.
Instead, you feel broken & discarded.
But I believe that someday, you'll be appreciated for your unique beauty.
There is a place for you, so don't give up.
The world needs you.

I keep a list of my favorite memories in my purse...

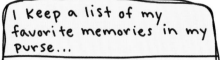

and read it when I'm having a bad day.

When T. demonstrated how a snake farts. 〜

Kissing under a waterfall.

Building with my dad. ♥

When K. laughed so hard, soda came out her nose.

The day I adopted my puppy.

The first time I saw my book in a bookstore.

It's a reminder that my life has been good...

The day I adopted my pu

The first time I saw my book in a book

Winning the hot do

and it helps me believe that it will be again.

WHAT WORKS FOR YOU ON HARD DAYS?

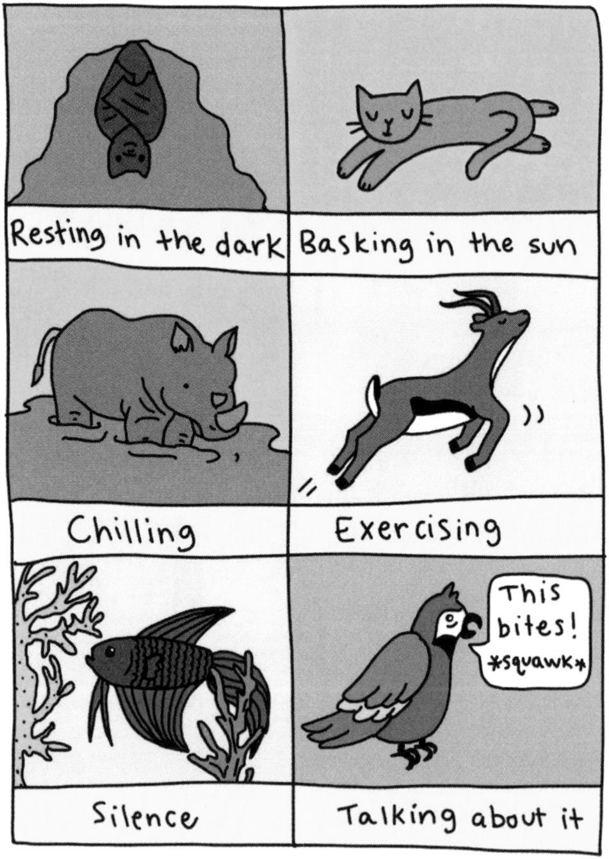
Resting in the dark
Basking in the sun
Chilling
Exercising
Silence
This bites! *squawk*
Talking about it

(we cope in various ways, and that's all right)

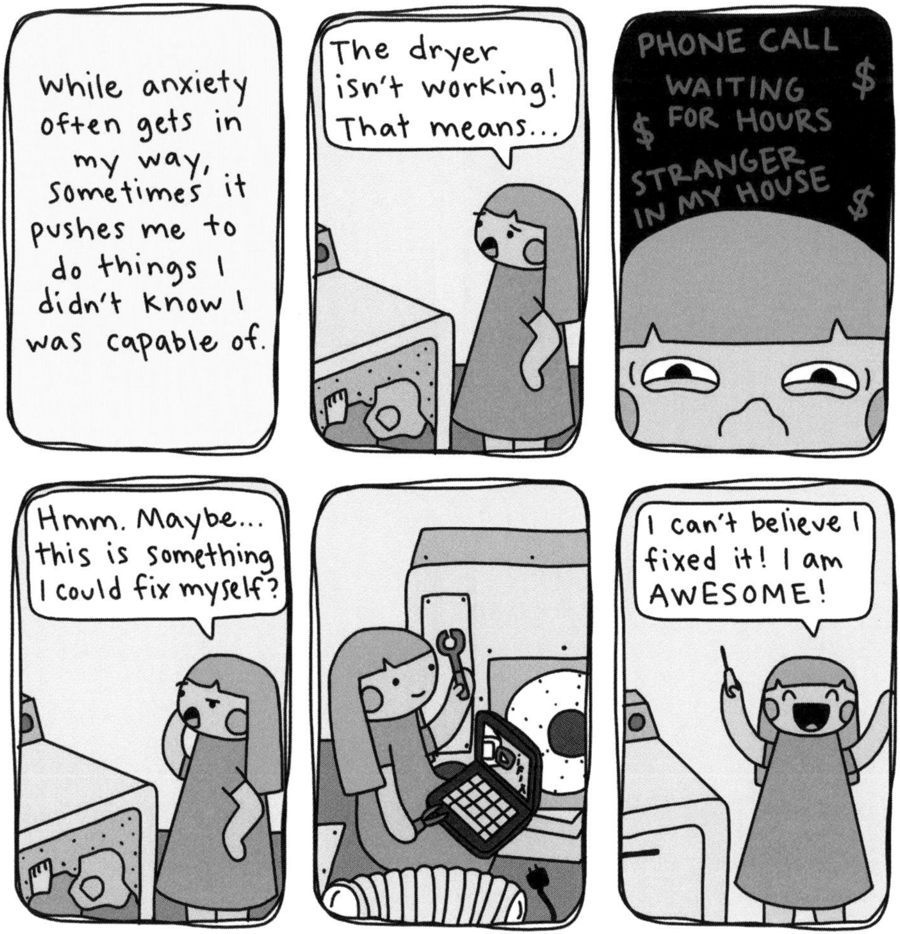
While anxiety often gets in my way, sometimes it pushes me to do things I didn't know I was capable of.
The dryer isn't working! That means...
PHONE CALL
WAITING FOR HOURS
STRANGER IN MY HOUSE
$
$
$
Hmm. Maybe... this is something I could fix myself?
I can't believe I fixed it! I am AWESOME!

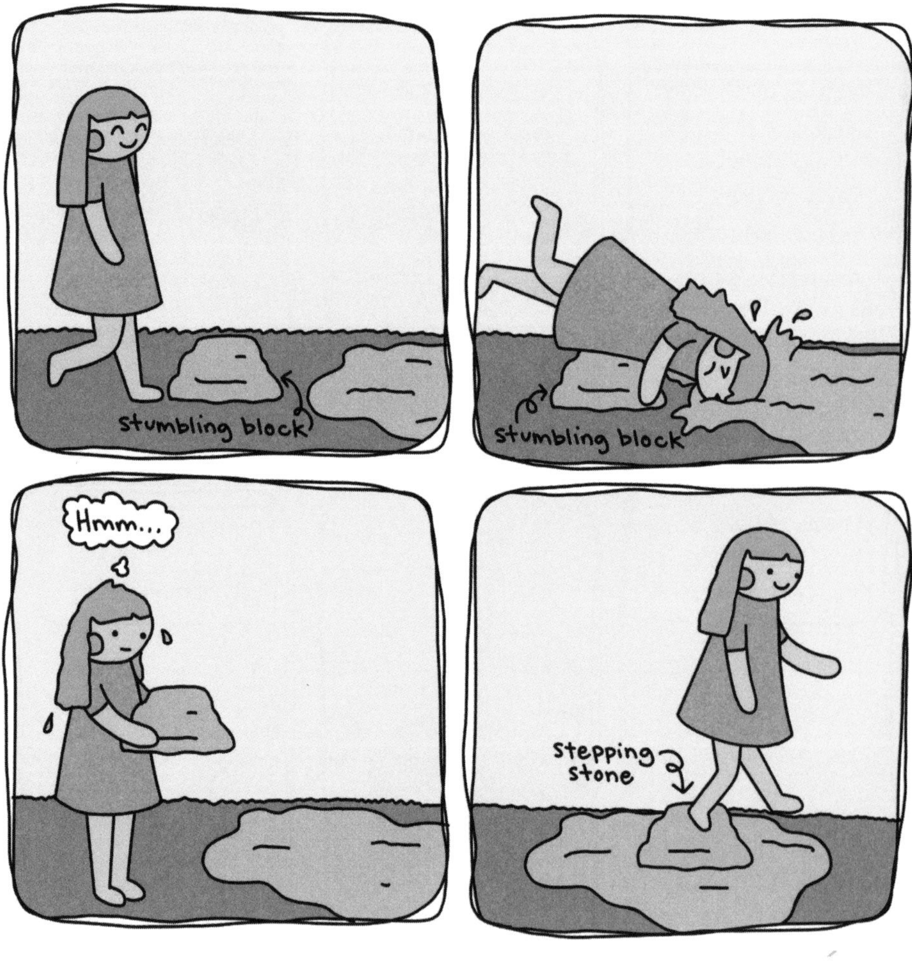
stumbling block
stumbling block
Hmm...
stepping stone

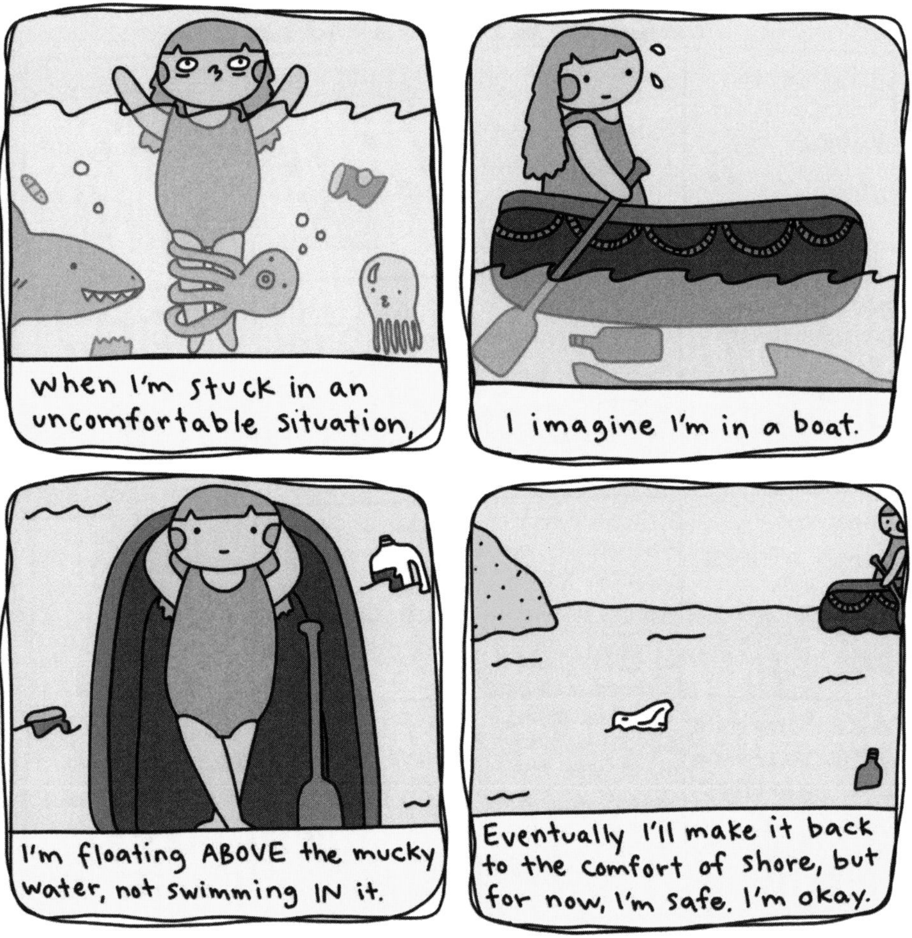
when I'm stuck in an uncomfortable situation,
I imagine I'm in a boat.
I'm floating ABOVE the mucky water, not swimming IN it.
Eventually I'll make it back to the comfort of shore, but for now, I'm safe. I'm okay.

SELF-CARE IDEAS

Listen to that one song. Repeat.	Talk to a friend. Or pet. (Wait, those are synonyms.)	Comfort food.	Fold laundry. (Repetition + Productivity = calm.)
Write. Or draw.	Play like a kid. Silly Putty, bubbles, Legos, cartoons, coloring...	Make your bed. Fresh sheets!	Drink cocoa by the fireplace. Don't forget the marshmallows!
Look up funny memes.	Compliment someone and watch their face light up. "Nice hat!"	Take a shower. Better yet, soak in the tub with a magazine.	Read a book. Bonus points if it has pictures.
Make something without caring whether it's "good."	Have a good cry, but keep it short. Use the expensive tissues. PUFFS	Buy yourself a smallish gift, just because. $8	Forgive yourself for what you couldn't do today, and resolve to try again tomorrow.

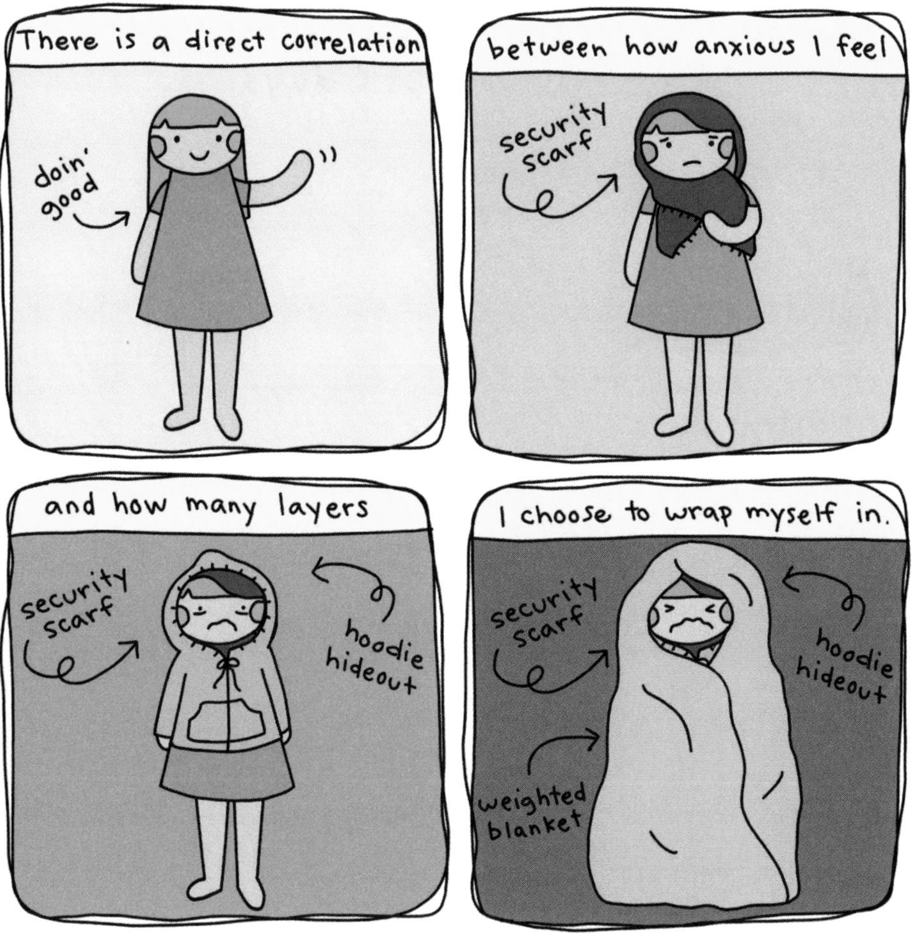
There is a direct correlation
doin' good
between how anxious I feel
security scarf
and how many layers
security scarf
hoodie hideout
I choose to wrap myself in.
security scarf
hoodie hideout
weighted blanket

RECOMMENDED HIDING PLACES

*for high-anxiety days

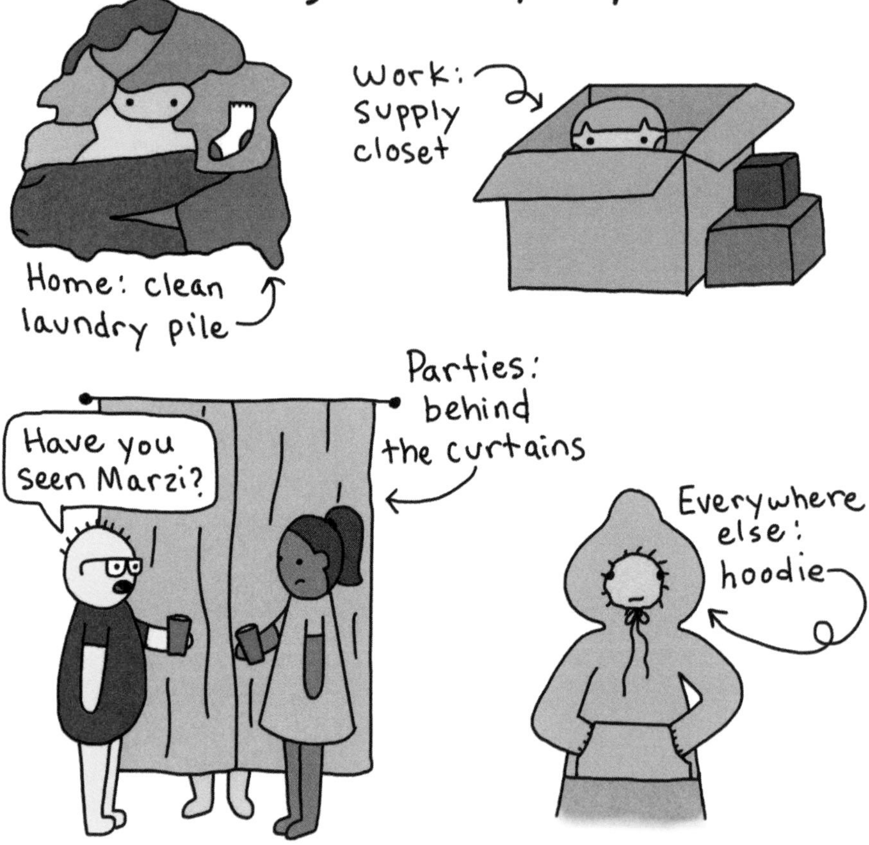
Home: clean laundry pile
Work: supply closet
Parties: behind the curtains
Have you seen Marzi?
Everywhere else: hoodie

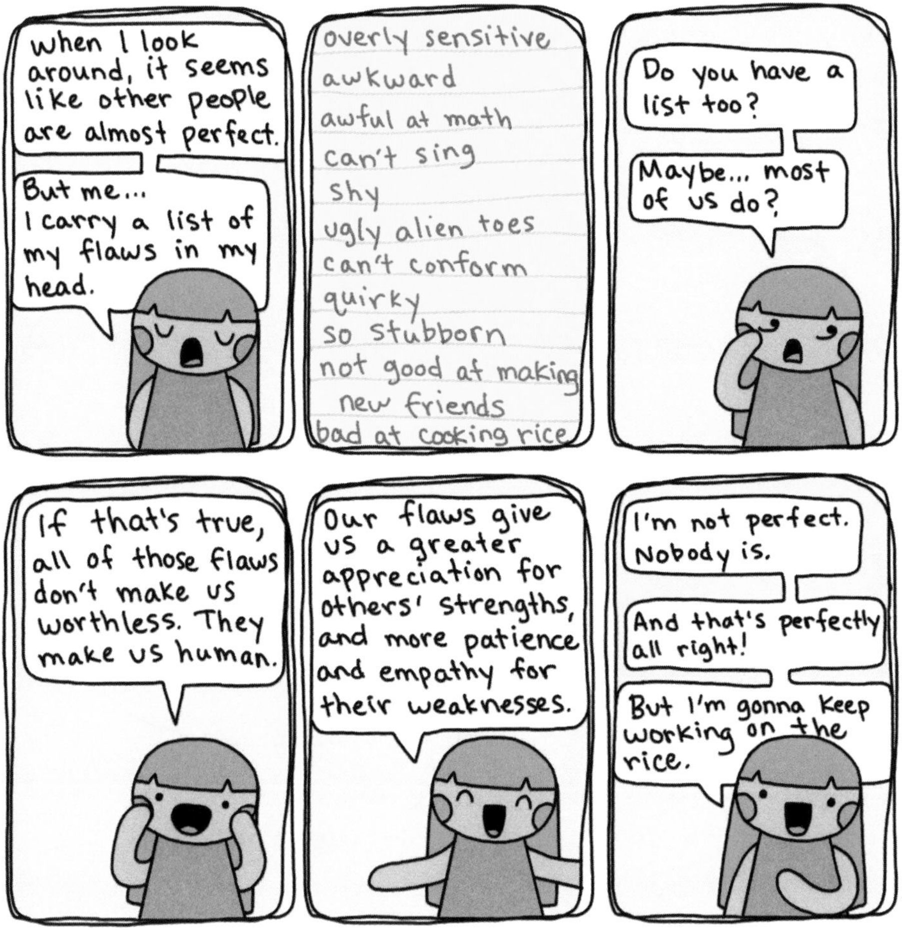
When I look around, it seems like other people are almost perfect.
But me... I carry a list of my flaws in my head.
overly sensitive
awkward
awful at math
can't sing
shy
ugly alien toes
can't conform
quirky
so stubborn
not good at making new friends
bad at cooking rice
Do you have a list too?
Maybe... most of us do?
If that's true, all of those flaws don't make us worthless. They make us human.
Our flaws give us a greater appreciation for others' strengths, and more patience and empathy for their weaknesses.
I'm not perfect. Nobody is.
And that's perfectly all right!
But I'm gonna keep working on the rice.

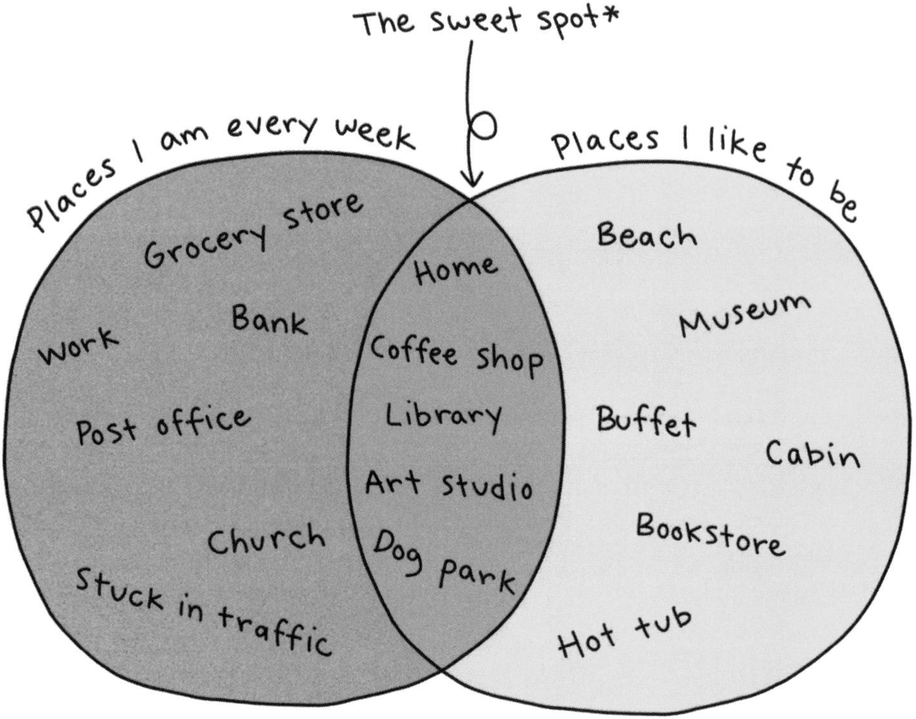

The sweet spot*
Places I am every week
Places I like to be
Grocery store
Work
Bank
Post office
Church
Stuck in traffic
Home
Coffee Shop
Library
Art studio
Dog park
Beach
Museum
Buffet
Cabin
Bookstore
Hot tub

* Focus on this area. Think about what you can add to your weekly routine that will bring you joy.

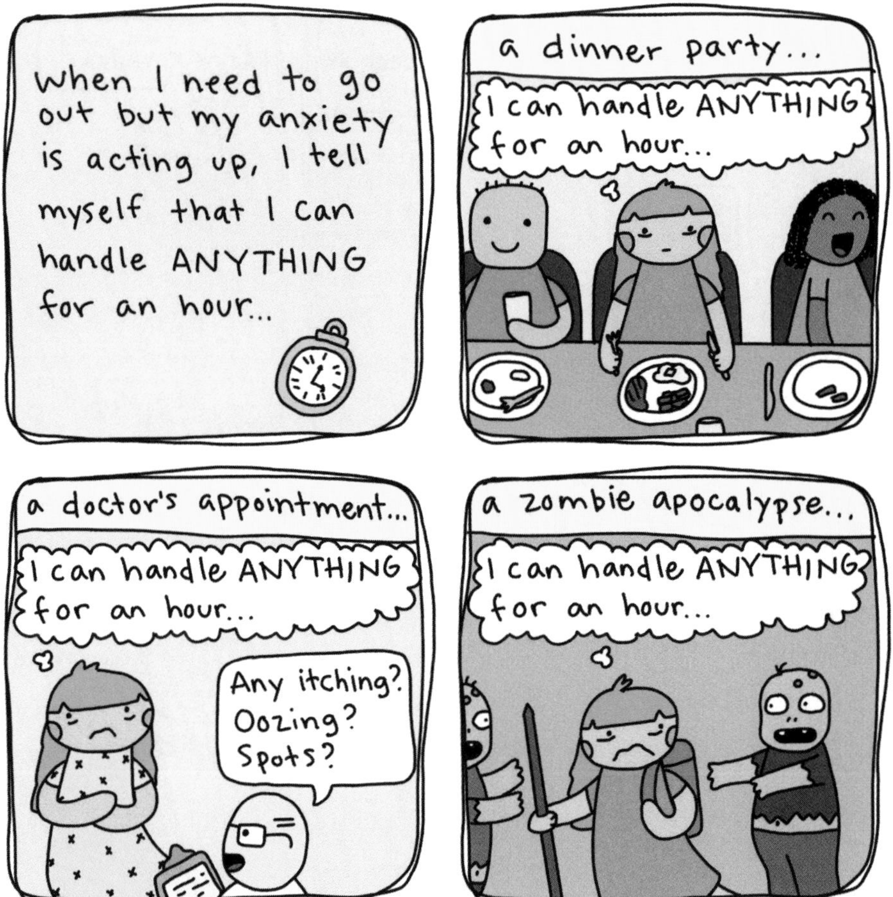
when I need to go out but my anxiety is acting up, I tell myself that I can handle ANYTHING for an hour...
a dinner party...
I can handle ANYTHING for an hour...
a doctor's appointment...
I can handle ANYTHING for an hour...
Any itching? Oozing? Spots?
a zombie apocalypse...
I can handle ANYTHING for an hour...

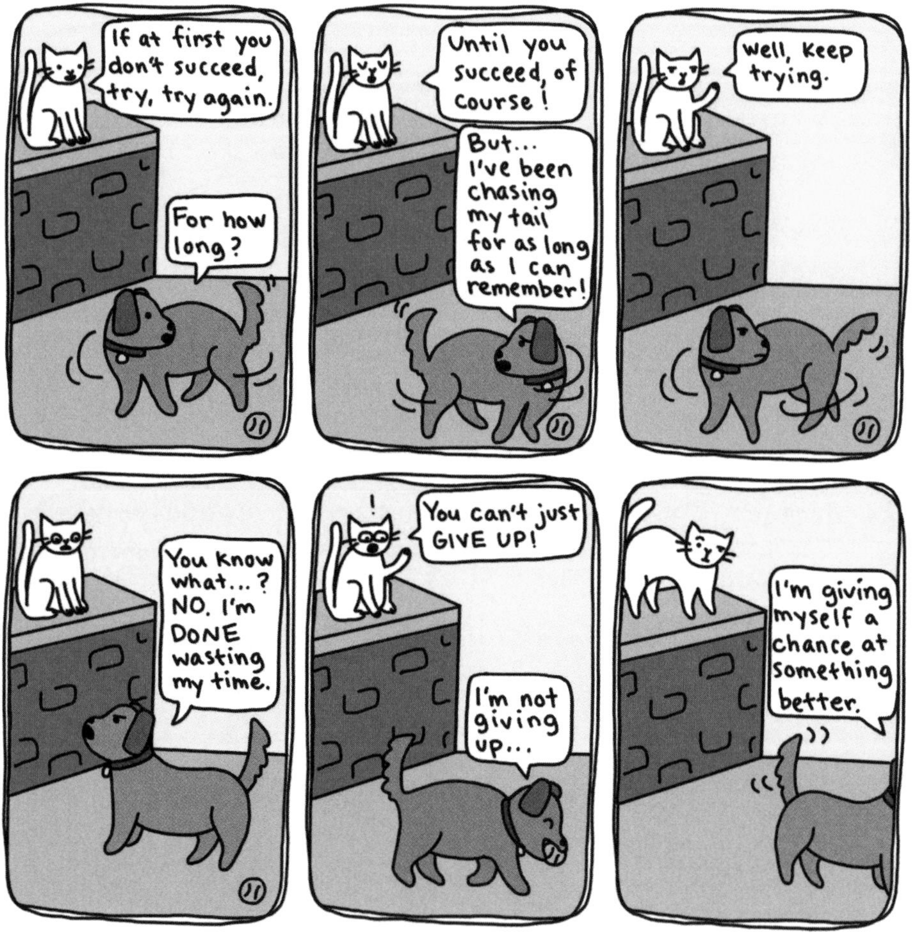
If at first you don't succeed, try, try again.
For how long?
Until you succeed, of course!
But... I've been chasing my tail for as long as I can remember!
well, keep trying.
You know what...? NO. I'm DONE wasting my time.
You can't just GIVE UP!
I'm not giving up...
I'm giving myself a chance at something better.

THINGS I DID AS A KID
(THAT I OUGHT TO START DOING AGAIN)

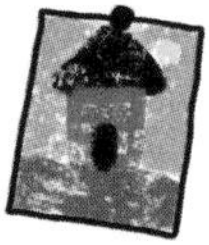

- Write silly notes to my friends.
- Proudly hang my work on the fridge.

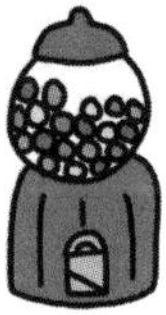

- Take a nap on the clean laundry pile.
- Spend all my change on gumballs and toys from the quarter machines.
- Take a bubble bath with My Little Ponies.

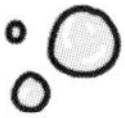

- Wear part of last year's Halloween costume for no reason.

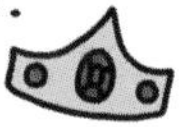

- Climb a tree.
- Make something cool from cardboard boxes.
- Ask for a lollipop at the bank.

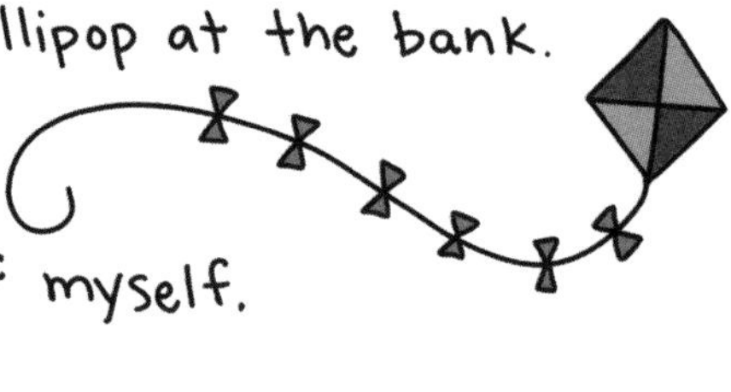

- Fly a kite.
- Feel proud of myself.

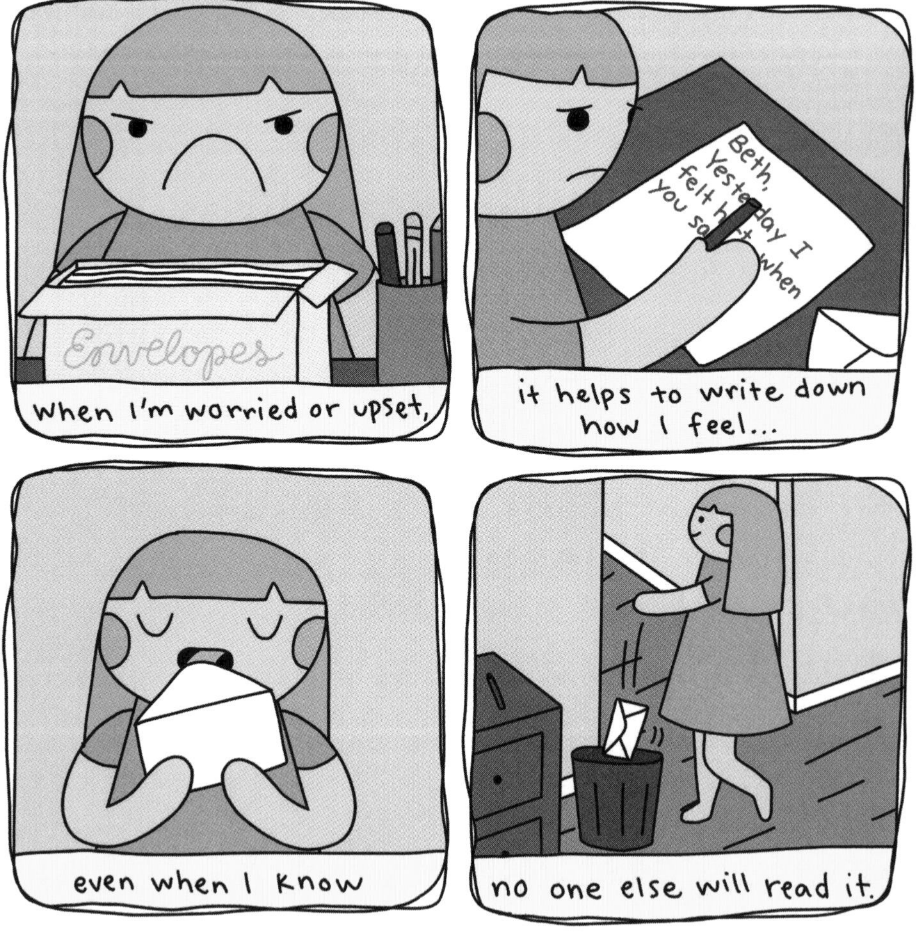
Envelopes
when I'm worried or upset,
Beth,
Yesterday I
felt hurt when
You said
it helps to write down how I feel...
even when I know
no one else will read it.

INNOVATIVE ARCHITECTURE

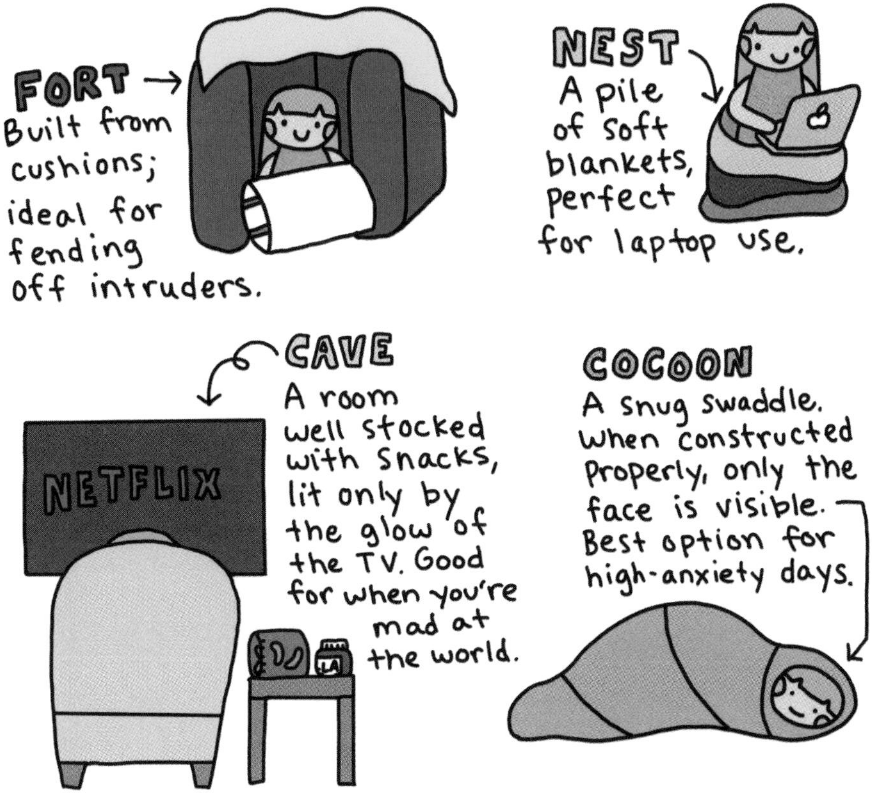

FORT
Built from cushions; ideal for fending off intruders.
NEST
A pile of soft blankets, perfect for laptop use.
CAVE
A room well stocked with snacks, lit only by the glow of the TV. Good for when you're mad at the world.
NETFLIX
COCOON
A snug swaddle. When constructed properly, only the face is visible. Best option for high-anxiety days.

LITTLE REMINDERS

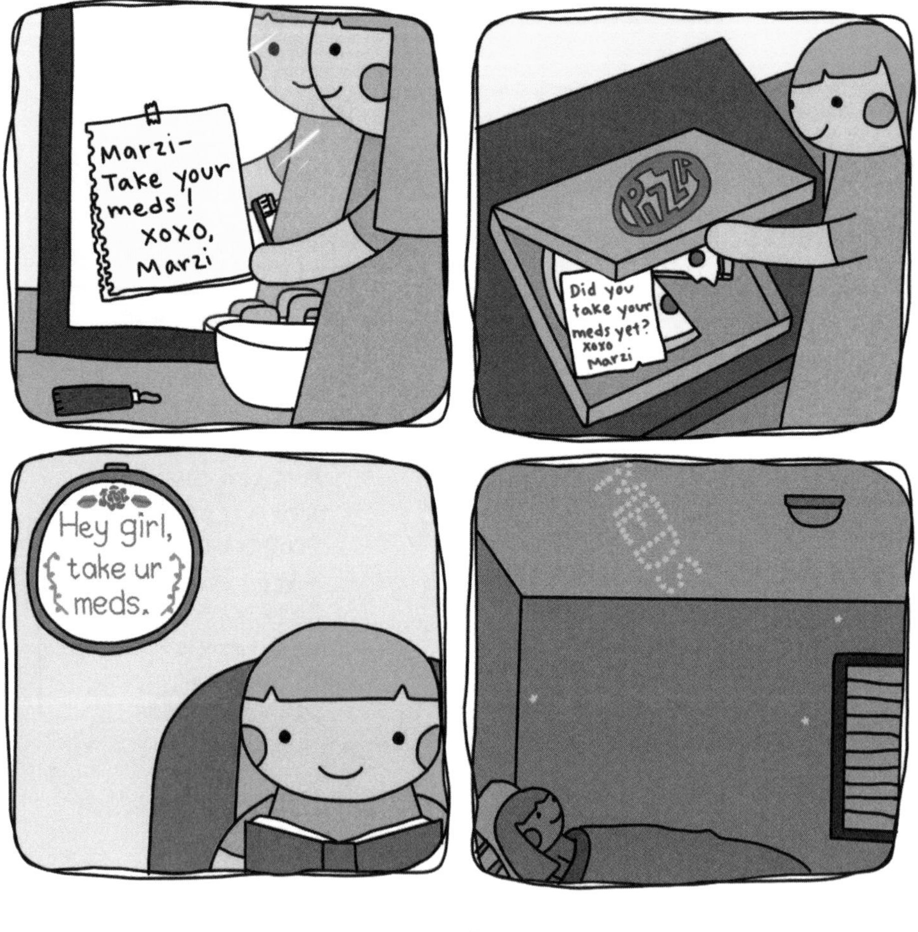
Marzi-
Take your
meds!
XOXO,
Marzi
Did you
take your
meds yet?
XOXO
Marzi
Hey girl,
take ur
meds.
MEDS

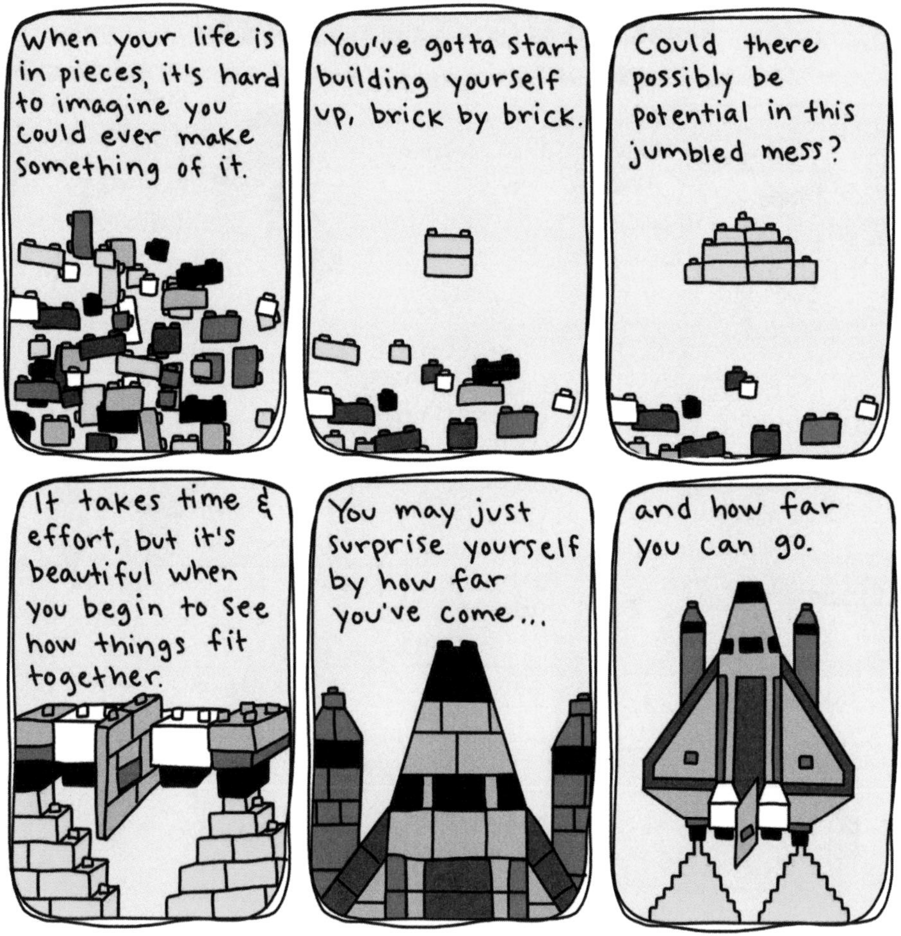
When your life is in pieces, it's hard to imagine you could ever make something of it.
You've gotta start building yourself up, brick by brick.
Could there possibly be potential in this jumbled mess?
It takes time & effort, but it's beautiful when you begin to see how things fit together.
You may just surprise yourself by how far you've come...
and how far you can go.

CALMING THOUGHTS

*use as needed

A seahorse swaying in the current, wearing a tiny bow tie.

Mr. Rogers putting on his shoes.

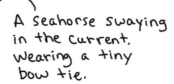
Unicorns roasting marshmallows.

Daddy Penguins.

The fact that sequels exist.

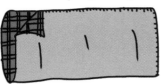
A warm & cozy sleeping bag.

Jell-O.
It's impossible to feel anxious while imagining Jell-O.

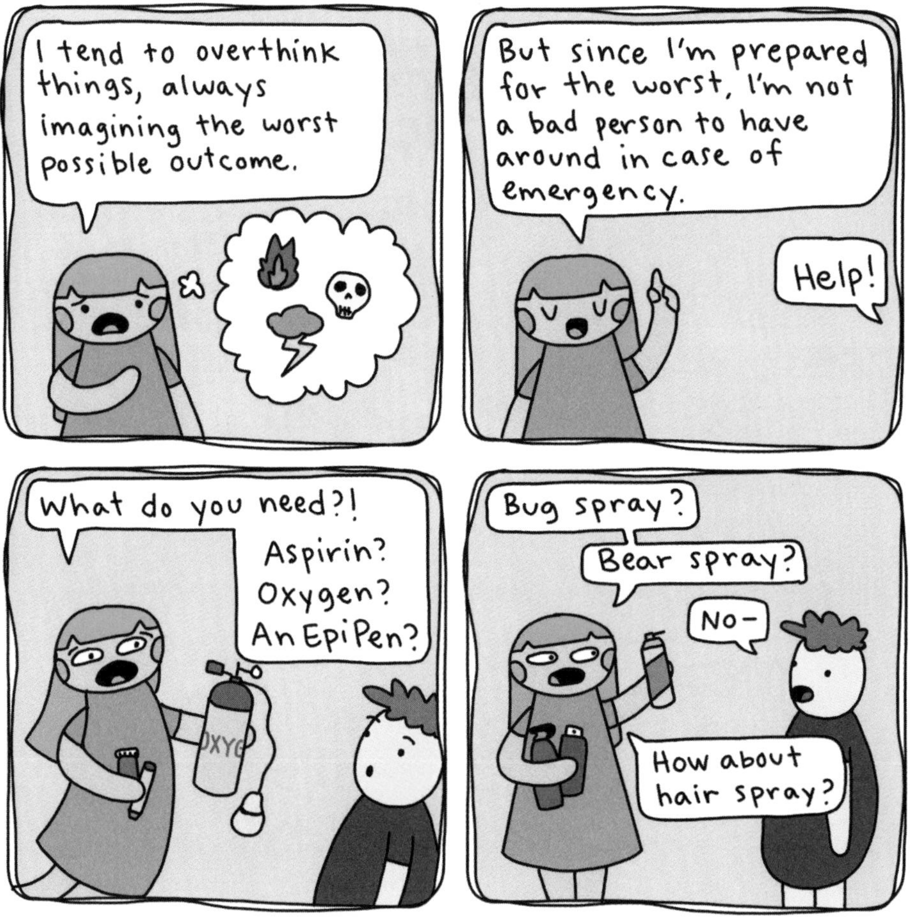

I tend to overthink things, always imagining the worst possible outcome.
But since I'm prepared for the worst, I'm not a bad person to have around in case of emergency.
Help!
What do you need?!
Aspirin? Oxygen? An EpiPen?
OXYG
Bug spray?
Bear spray?
No–
How about hair spray?

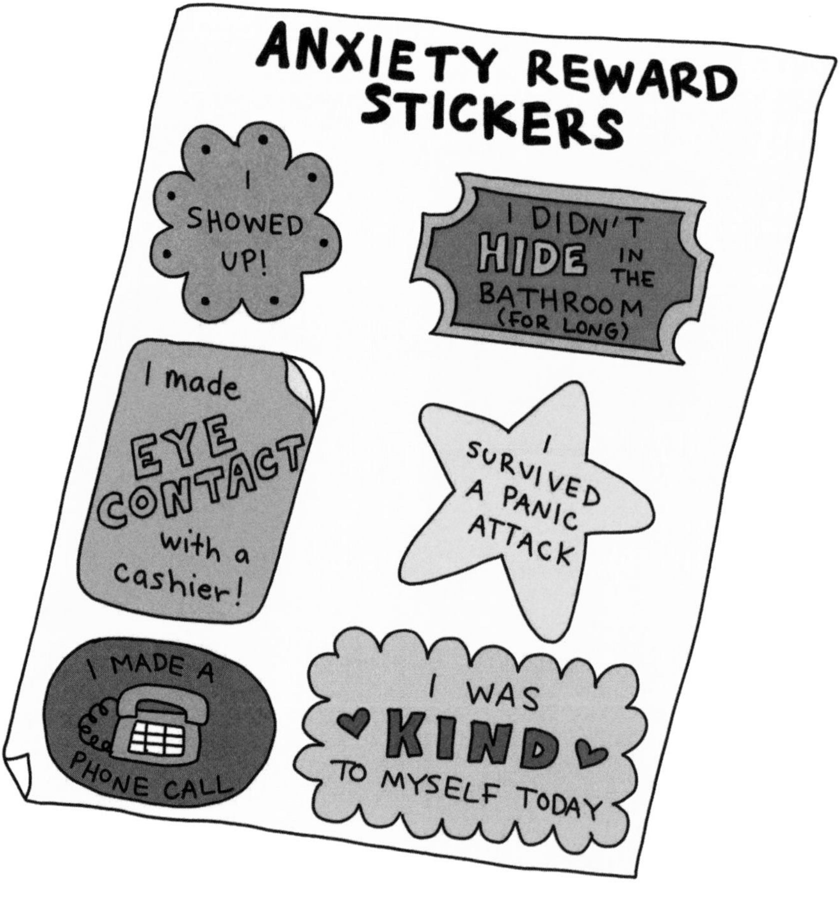
ANXIETY REWARD STICKERS
I SHOWED UP!
I DIDN'T HIDE IN THE BATHROOM (FOR LONG)
I made EYE CONTACT with a cashier!
I SURVIVED A PANIC ATTACK
I MADE A PHONE CALL
I WAS KIND TO MYSELF TODAY

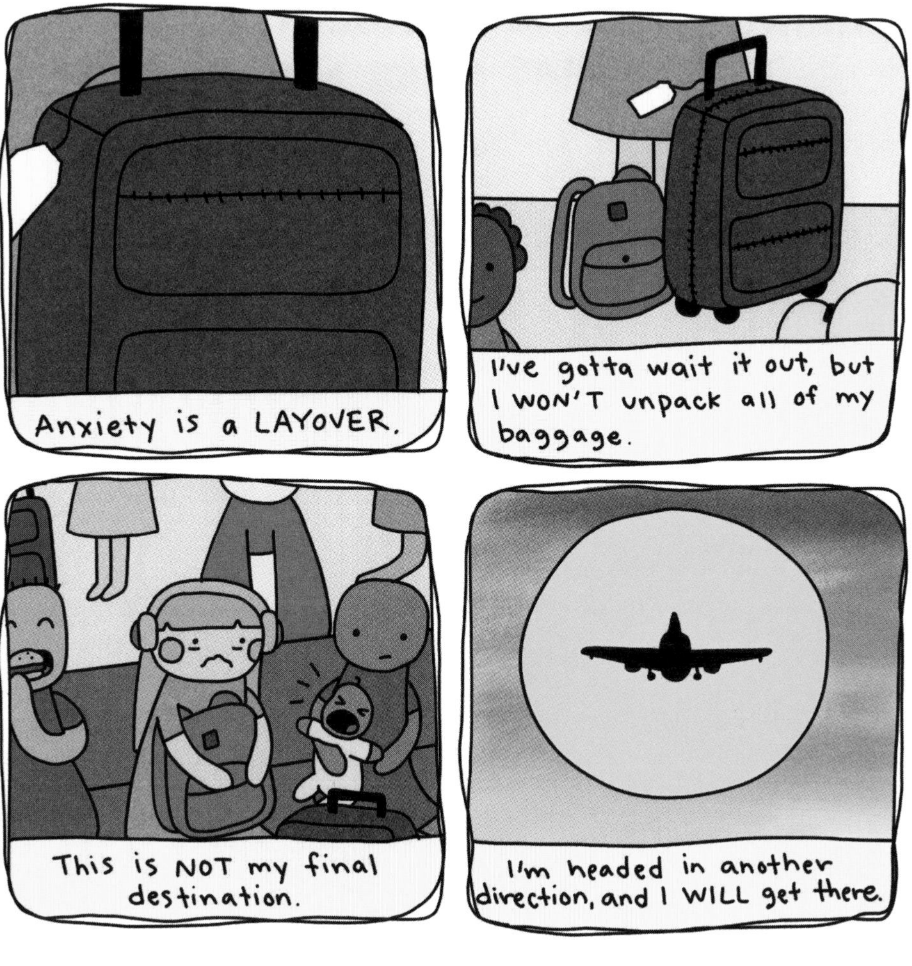
Anxiety is a LAYOVER.
I've gotta wait it out, but I WON'T unpack all of my baggage.
This is NOT my final destination.
I'm headed in another direction, and I WILL get there.

TAKING TIME TO NOTICE THE LITTLE THINGS THAT MAKE ME HAPPY

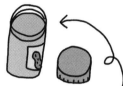

The pristine surface of a new jar of peanut butter

Elderly gentlemen in dapper hats

A tiny flower growing in a sidewalk crack

Finding extra fries in the bottom of the bag

Getting a piece of free candy at the bank

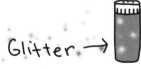

Glitter →

kitten toes

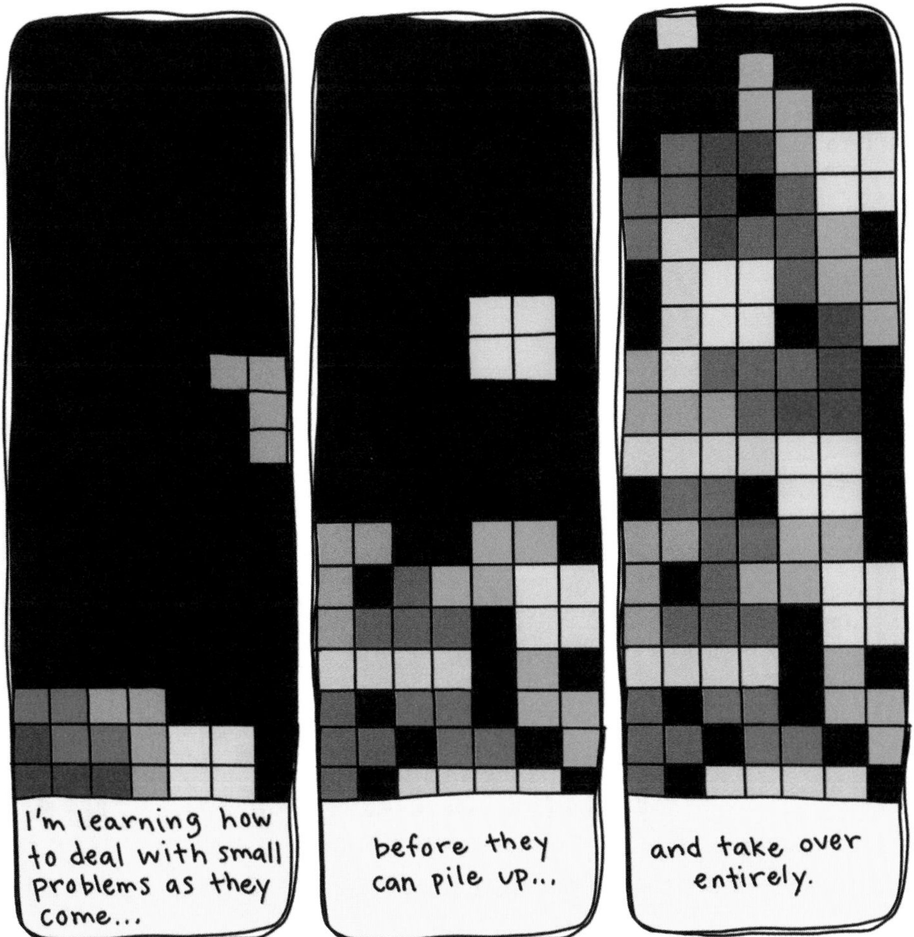
I'm learning how to deal with small problems as they come...
before they can pile up...
and take over entirely.

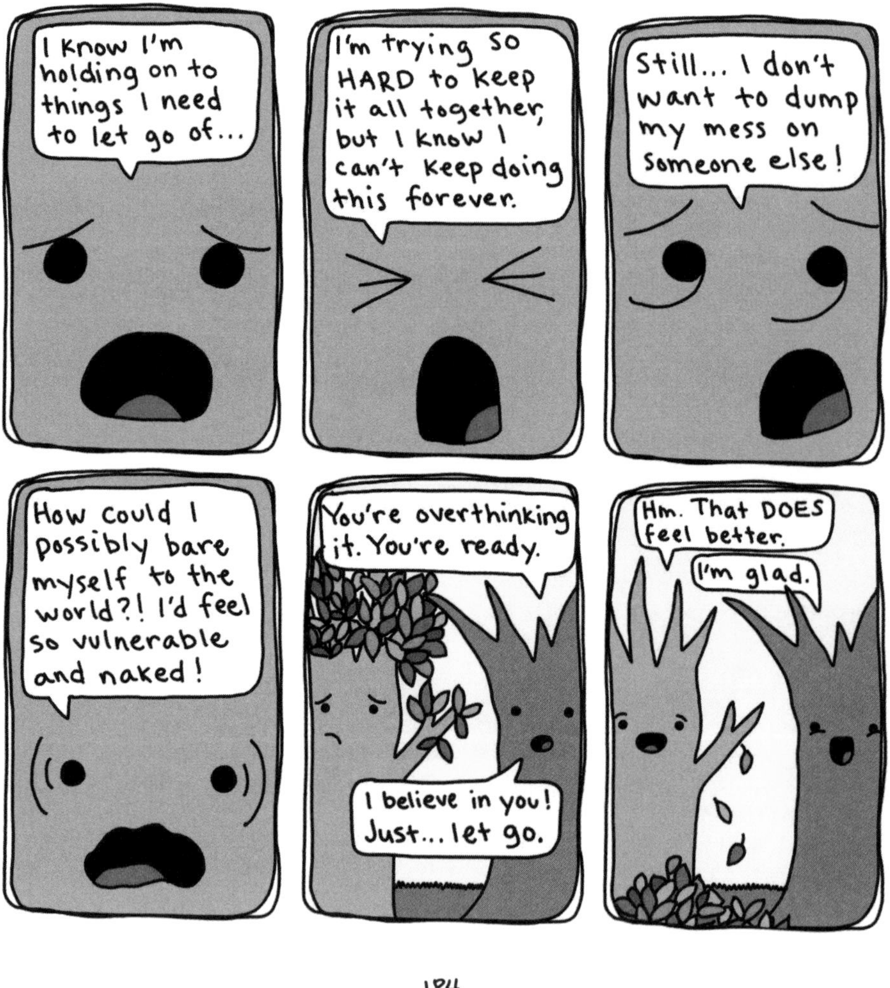
I know I'm holding on to things I need to let go of...
I'm trying SO HARD to keep it all together, but I know I can't keep doing this forever.
Still... I don't want to dump my mess on someone else!
How could I possibly bare myself to the world?! I'd feel so vulnerable and naked!
You're overthinking it. You're ready.
I believe in you! Just... let go.
Hm. That DOES feel better.
I'm glad.

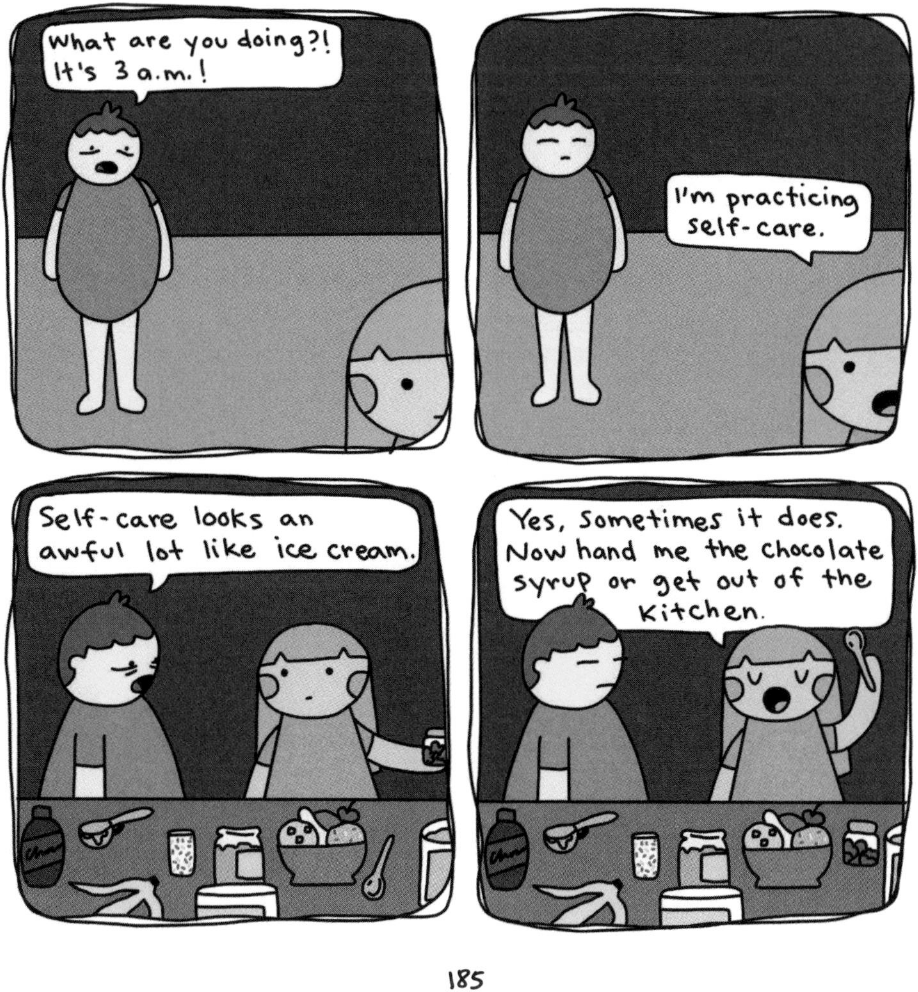
What are you doing?! It's 3 a.m.!
I'm practicing self-care.
Self-care looks an awful lot like ice cream.
Yes, sometimes it does. Now hand me the chocolate syrup or get out of the kitchen.

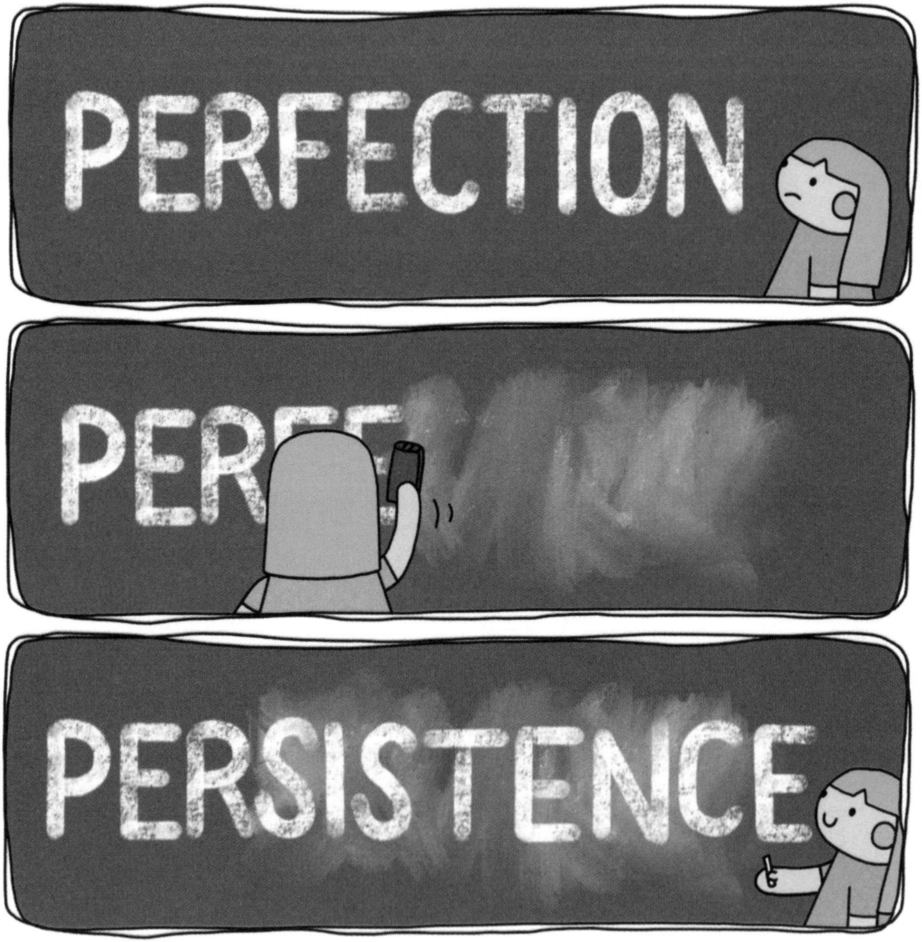
PERFECTION
PERF
PERSISTENCE

IDEAS FOR ESCAPING FROM STRESS

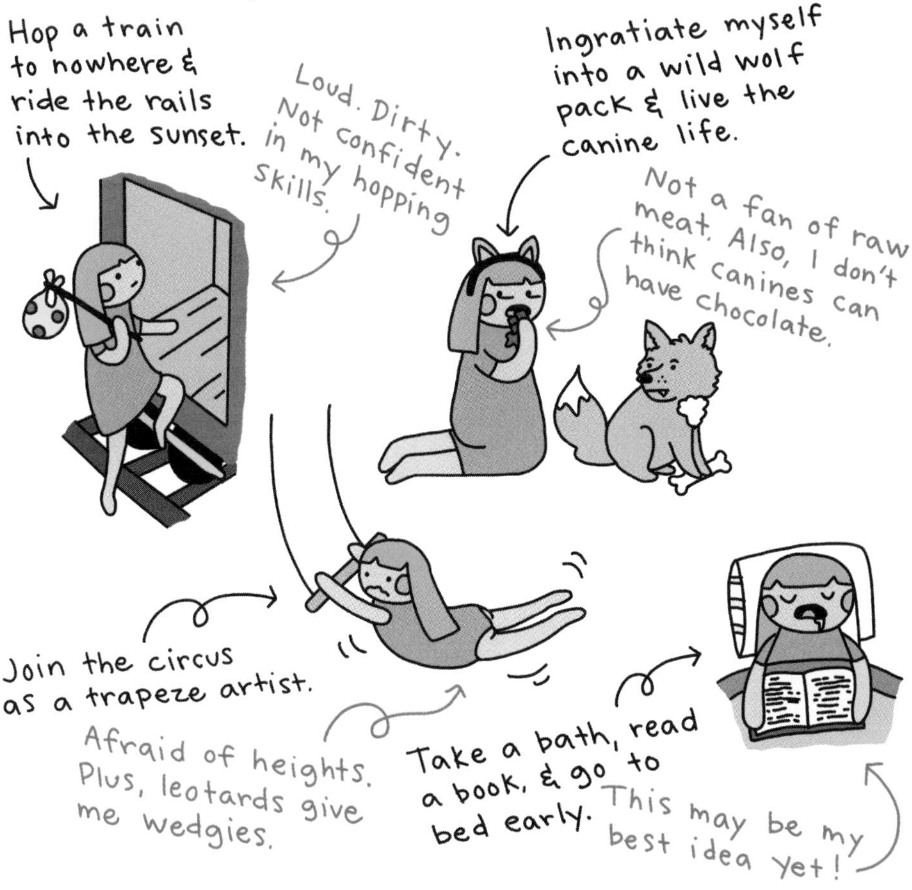

Hop a train to nowhere & ride the rails into the sunset.
Loud. Dirty. Not confident in my hopping skills.
Ingratiate myself into a wild wolf pack & live the canine life.
Not a fan of raw meat. Also, I don't think canines can have chocolate.
Join the circus as a trapeze artist.
Afraid of heights. Plus, leotards give me wedgies.
Take a bath, read a book, & go to bed early.
This may be my best idea yet!

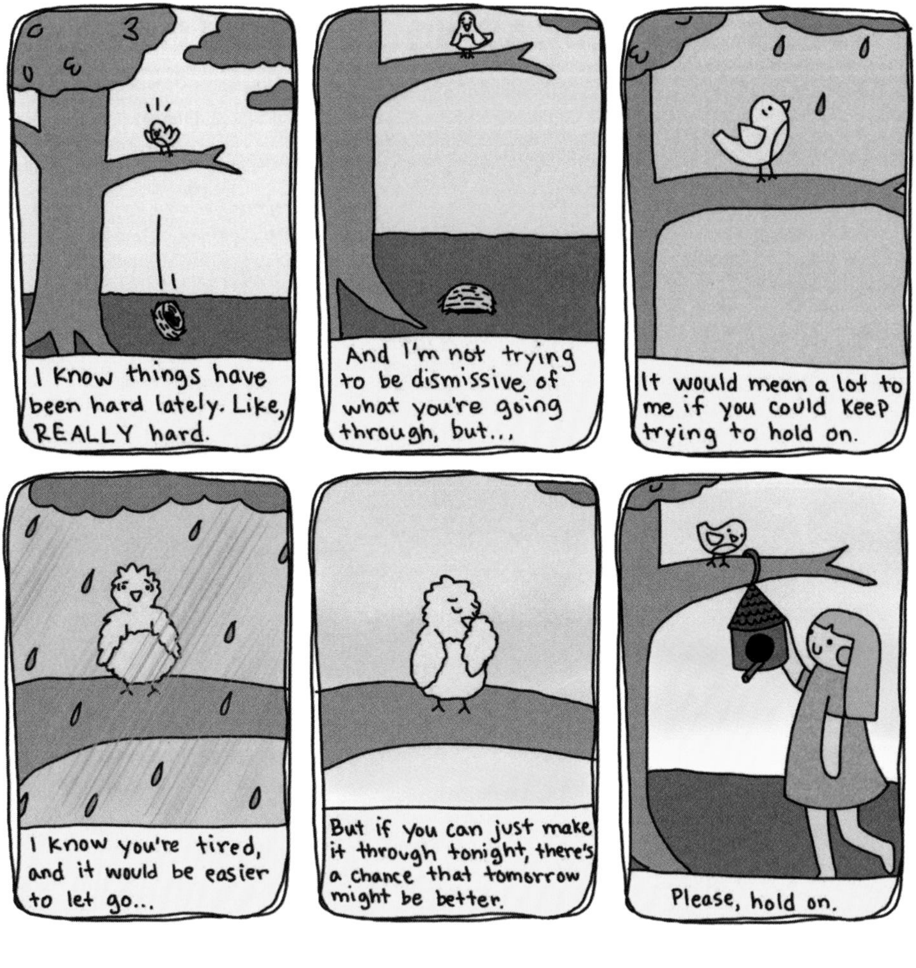
I know things have been hard lately. Like, REALLY hard.
And I'm not trying to be dismissive of what you're going through, but...
It would mean a lot to me if you could keep trying to hold on.
I know you're tired, and it would be easier to let go...
But if you can just make it through tonight, there's a chance that tomorrow might be better.
Please, hold on.

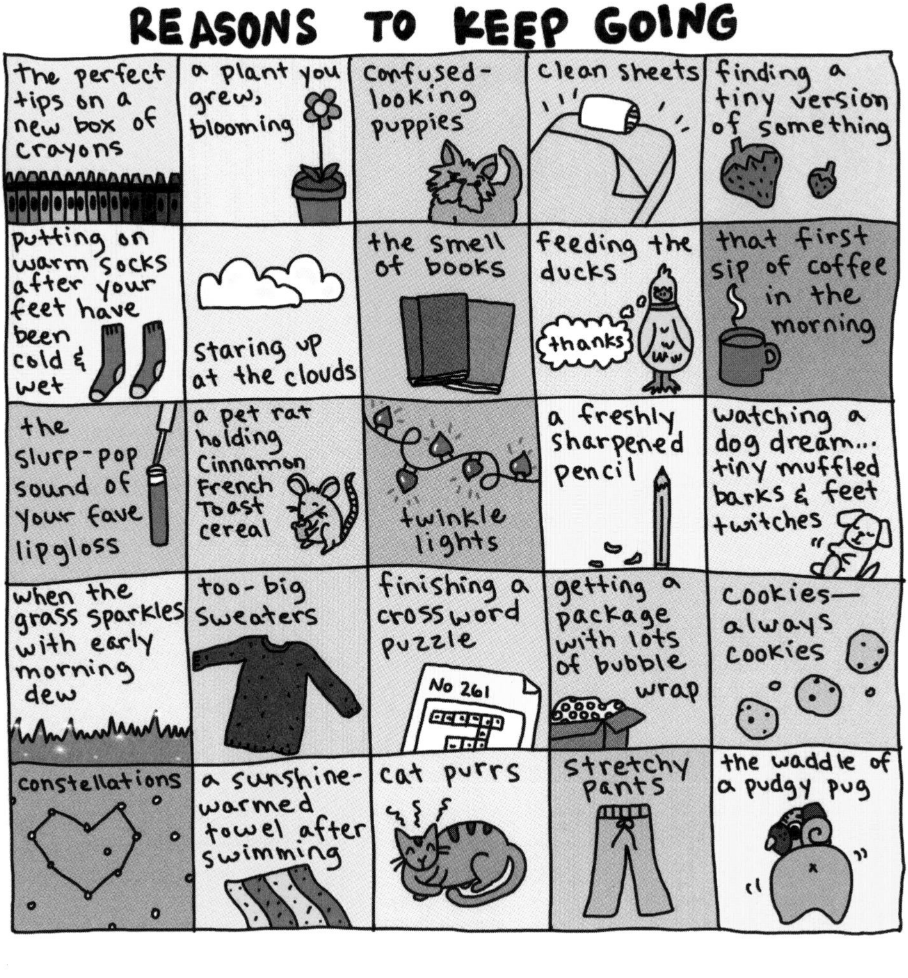
REASONS TO KEEP GOING
the perfect tips on a new box of crayons
a plant you grew, blooming
confused-looking puppies
clean sheets
finding a tiny version of something
putting on warm socks after your feet have been cold & wet
staring up at the clouds
the smell of books
feeding the ducks
thanks
that first sip of coffee in the morning
the slurp-pop sound of your fave lipgloss
a pet rat holding Cinnamon French Toast cereal
twinkle lights
a freshly sharpened pencil
watching a dog dream... tiny muffled barks & feet twitches
when the grass sparkles with early morning dew
too-big sweaters
finishing a crossword puzzle
No 261
getting a package with lots of bubble wrap
cookies— always cookies
constellations
a sunshine-warmed towel after swimming
cat purrs
stretchy pants
the waddle of a pudgy pug

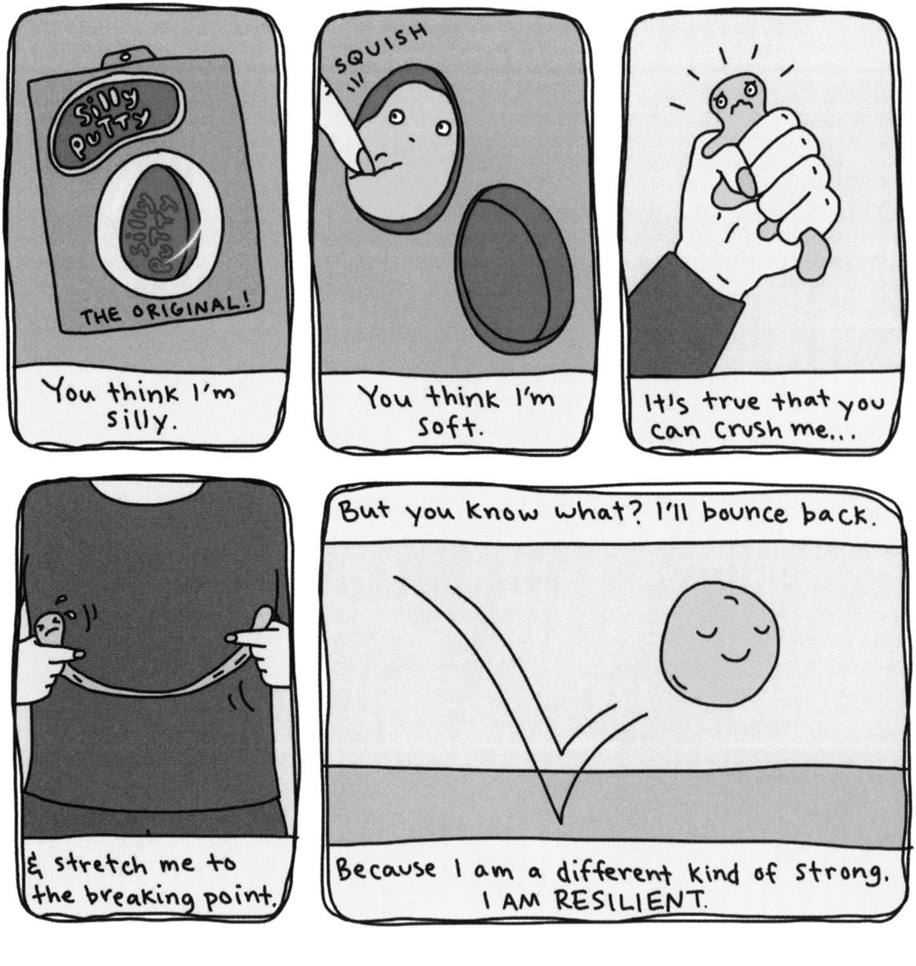
Silly Putty
THE ORIGINAL!
You think I'm silly.
SQUISH
You think I'm soft.
It's true that you can crush me...
& stretch me to the breaking point.
But you know what? I'll bounce back.
Because I am a different kind of strong.
I AM RESILIENT.

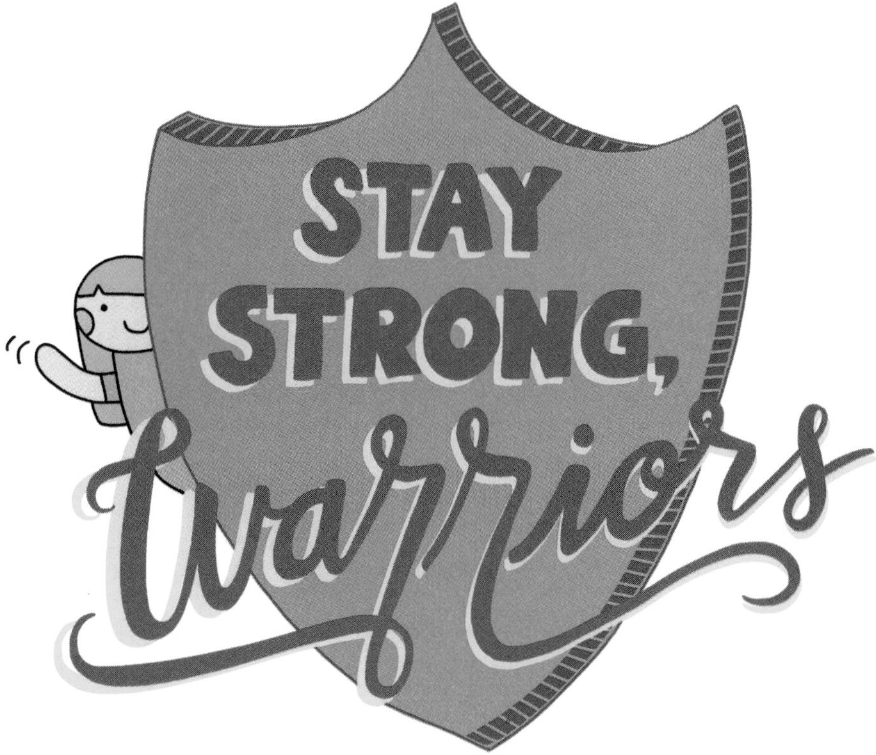
STAY STRONG,
warriors

ABOUT THE AUTHOR

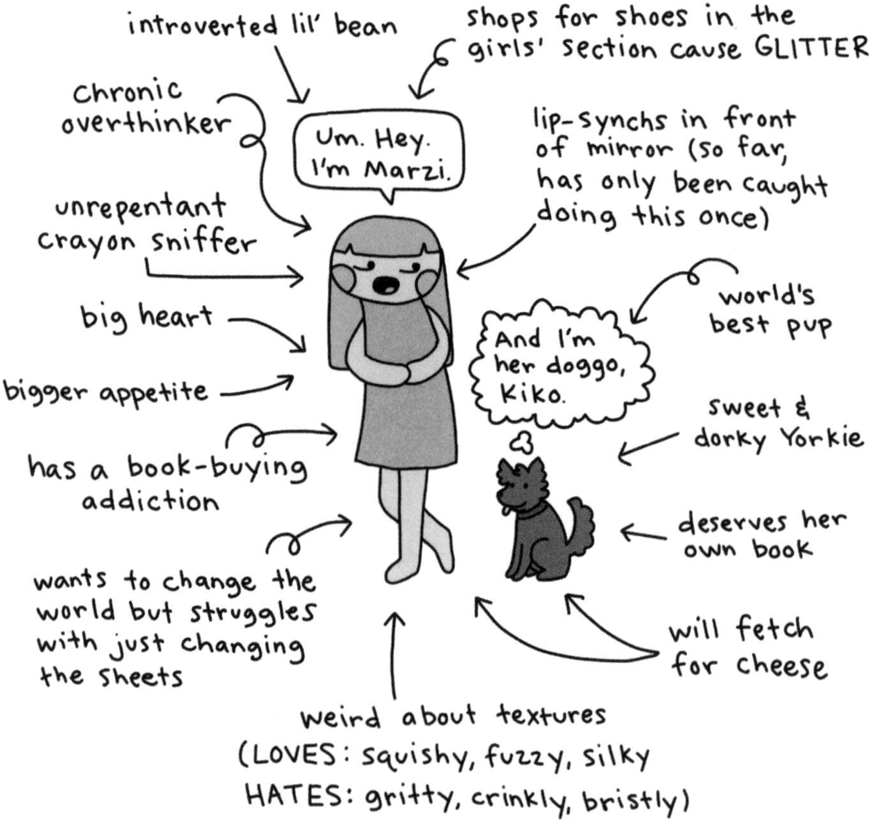

introverted lil' bean
shops for shoes in the girls' section cause GLITTER
chronic overthinker
Um. Hey. I'm Marzi.
lip-synchs in front of mirror (so far, has only been caught doing this once)
unrepentant crayon sniffer
big heart
world's best pup
And I'm her doggo, Kiko.
bigger appetite
sweet & dorky Yorkie
has a book-buying addiction
deserves her own book
wants to change the world but struggles with just changing the sheets
will fetch for cheese
weird about textures (LOVES: squishy, fuzzy, silky HATES: gritty, crinkly, bristly)